Lightning Strikes Twice

ALSO BY LEW FREEDMAN
AND FROM MCFARLAND

*Cy Young: The Baseball Life and Career* (2020)

*Buffalo Bill Cody: The Man Who Shaped the Wild West Legend* (2020)

*Ernie Banks: The Life and Career of "Mr. Cub"* (2019)

*Connie Mack's First Dynasty: The Philadelphia Athletics, 1910–1914* (2017)

*Baseball's Funnymen: Twenty-Four Jokers, Screwballs, Pranksters and Storytellers* (2017)

*The Boyer Brothers of Baseball* (2015)

*Joe Louis: The Life of a Heavyweight* (2013)

*DiMaggio's Yankees: A History of the 1936–1944 Dynasty* (2011)

*The Day All the Stars Came Out: Major League Baseball's First All-Star Game, 1933* (2010)

*Hard-Luck Harvey Haddix and the Greatest Game Ever Lost* (2009)

*Early Wynn, the Go-Go White Sox and the 1959 World Series* (2009)

BY GEORGE ALTMAN WITH LEW FREEDMAN
AND FROM MCFARLAND

*George Altman: My Baseball Journey from the Negro Leagues to the Majors and Beyond* (2013)

# Lightning Strikes Twice
## *Johnny Vander Meer and the Cincinnati Reds*

LEW FREEDMAN

McFarland & Company, Inc., Publishers
*Jefferson, North Carolina*

All photographs from the National Baseball Hall of Fame and Museum, Cooperstown, N.Y.

Library of Congress Cataloguing-in-Publication Data

Names: Freedman, Lew, author.
Title: Lightning strikes twice : Johnny Vander Meer and the Cincinnati Reds / Lew Freedman.
Description: Jefferson, North Carolina : McFarland & Company, Inc., Publishers, 2021 | Includes bibliographical references and index.
Identifiers: LCCN 2021013325 | ISBN 9781476681573 (paperback : acid free paper) ♾
ISBN 9781476641089 (ebook)
Subjects: LCSH: Vander Meer, Johnny, 1914-1997. | Pitchers (Baseball)—United States—Biography. | Baseball players—United States—Biography. | Cincinnati Reds (Baseball team)—History—20th century. | No-hitters (Baseball)—History—20th century. | World Series (Baseball) (1939) | World Series (Baseball) (1940) | BISAC: SPORTS & RECREATION / Baseball / History | BIOGRAPHY & AUTOBIOGRAPHY / Sports
Classification: LCC GV865.V36 F74 2021 | DDC 796.357092 [B]—dc23
LC record available at https://lccn.loc.gov/2021013325

British Library cataloguing data are available
ISBN (print) 978-1-4766-8157-3
ISBN (ebook) 978-1-4766-4108-9

© 2021 Lew Freedman. All rights reserved

*No part of this book may be reproduced or transmitted in any form or by any means, electronic or mechanical, including photocopying or recording, or by any information storage and retrieval system, without permission in writing from the publisher.*

Front cover: Cincinnati Reds pitcher Johnny Vander Meer
(National Baseball Hall of Fame and Museum, Cooperstown, New York)

Printed in the United States of America

*McFarland & Company, Inc., Publishers
Box 611, Jefferson, North Carolina 28640
www.mcfarlandpub.com*

# Table of Contents

*Introduction*   1

1. 1937: The New Look Reds   5
2. Bill McKechnie   12
3. Vander Meer Makes the Cut   18
4. Frank McCormick Long Time Coming   24
5. Ernie Lombardi   29
6. Vander Meer Pitches a No-Hitter   35
7. Vander Meer Pitches a No-Hitter—Another One   43
8. Aftermath   55
9. The Reds of 1938   62
10. Paul Derringer and Bucky Walters   68
11. Johnny and the Players of 1939   76
12. Johnny and the 1939 Pitching   87
13. The 1939 World Series   94
14. The 1940 Regular Season   107
15. The 1940 World Series   121
16. The Year 1941   137
17. War Changes Everything   145
18. The Reds During World War II   152
19. When Johnny—and the Reds—Came Marching Home   163
20. Double No-Hit for the Rest of His Life   173

*Chapter Notes*   181
*Bibliography*   189
*Index*   191

# Introduction

Johnny Vander Meer's main Major League Baseball achievement is the type of accomplishment that gets mentioned in the first line of obituaries. It is the type of thing done only once and remembered forever, and paramountly, no matter what else a person does during his lifetime.

For one week in 1938, Vander Meer was the king of the baseball world. He did something unique. From the beginning of the National League in 1876, through the decades that have followed, no one has been able to match, never mind exceed, Vander Meer's record of throwing two straight no-hitters.

It is the dream of every big-league hurler to someday toss a no-hitter during his career. No one ever talks about the possibility of throwing two in a row. The odds are extremely high that Vander Meer's record will last forever. After all, the idea of a pitcher's hurling three no-hitters in a row is inconceivable. Some day, someone may come along and tie Vander Meer, someone who is as lucky and skilled as he was for two consecutive nine-inning games. More than 90 years have passed without such an occurrence, but it is not impossible that some day baseball fans will awake to the news that for a second time lightning has struck twice.

At his very best, Johnny Vander Meer was very good. During a Major League career spent mostly with the Cincinnati Reds, he was selected for four All-Star teams. He played in the big leagues between 1937 and 1951 and was a member of the Reds' 1939 National League pennant-winning club and the 1940 World Series championship club. But others were more responsible for bringing the Reds that success.

Vander Meer did something special in the majors, but he encountered several difficulties during his career and when he retired he did not even own a winning record. His was a major-league stay marked by extraordinary highs and many lows, grand successes wrapped around disappointments.

For those reasons Vander Meer is not a member of the Baseball Hall of

Fame. He did not sustain long-term, high-level performance. Or not such performances frequently enough to measure up to the best in the game for the necessary decade or more. Many excellent ball players turned in first-rate careers marked by singular achievements. Either for a game (or two, like Vander Meer), or for a season, they did magical things with a baseball, or to a baseball. Slugger Roger Maris broke Babe Ruth's single-season home-run record with 61 in 1961 while playing for the New York Yankees, but is not in the Hall of Fame. Maris' situation is somewhat analogous to Vander Meer's.

Several pitchers have thrown as many as two, and more than two, no-hitters. Hall of Famer Nolan Ryan authored a record seven no-hitters during his 27-season, 324-victory career. The Dodgers' Sandy Koufax threw four no-hitters. Cy Young, the winningest pitcher of all-time with 511 victories, fireballing Bob Feller, and pre–20th-century twirler Larry Corcoran all threw three no-hitters. Still-active Justin Verlander recently joined that small club.

Through the 2019 baseball season, some 303 no-hitters had been registered. Included are 36 pitchers who have thrown at least two. Besides Vander Meer, only Ryan, Virgil Trucks, Allie Reynolds, and still-pitching Max Scherzer, have pitched two no-hitters within one season under the current Major League rules defining a no-hitter. Jim Maloney, another Reds pitcher, seemingly pitched two in 1965, but one was removed from official consideration after later evaluation. During the 2010 season, Hall of Famer Roy Halladay pitched one no-hitter (a perfect game) during the regular season and another during the playoffs.

In addition to his 1938 week of glory, Vander Meer's stay in Cincinnati aligned with the Reds' greatest, least-remembered World Series championship in 1940. The franchise was founded in 1890 and won world championships in 1919, 1940, 1975, 1976 and 1990. Cincinnati won its first pennant in 20 years in 1939 and Vander Meer was also part of that club that lost to the New York Yankees in the World Series.

The victory in 1919 was completely overshadowed by the Black Sox Scandal. More fans recall the White Sox losing the Series that year than Cincinnati winning it because of the post–Series repercussions. Those included lifetime bans handed out by Judge Kenesaw Mountain Landis in the newly created position of commissioner, to eight White Sox players for tampering with the results. The mid–1970s group, called the Big Red Machine, is regarded as being among the greatest teams ever. The 1990 victory symbolized a short-term return to glory.

The 1939–40 Reds featured a cast of characters who presented the city with a grand prize a generation after the 1919 controversy. Vander Meer was a cog in all of that and the years surrounding the satisfying result. Due to the no-hitters, he is better remembered than many other stars of that team. Others are quite worthy of having the spotlight, from Hall of Fame manager Bill McKechnie, to players Ernie Lombardi, Frank McCormick, Bucky Walters and Paul Derringer, all of whom out-shone a physically troubled Vander Meer during the seasons immediately after he became the no-hit phenom. Cincinnati won 197 games over those two seasons, 100 of them in 1940.

Vander Meer is linked with the 1939 and 1940 teams' achievements, but his most outstanding moments came at the front end of his career. He won as many as 18 games in a season and led the National League in strikeouts three times. He also missed two years of his prime during World War II serving in the Navy. He served, but didn't fight, representing the Navy baseball team stateside.

It is inevitable that despite his presence on the Cincinnati Reds roster those two seasons of 1939 and 1940, whenever talk turns to Johnny Vander Meer's baseball career, the attention is always paid to Mr. Double No-Hitter. The guy pitched the best ball of his life in two straight games, and for that he will always be remembered.

# 1

# 1937: The New Look Reds

The 1937 Cincinnati Reds needed pitching, but in spring training all of the talk was about a prospect well-known to the organization after his original signing by former vice president–general manager Larry MacPhail in 1934. He had been through some short stays with the team, flashing teases of big-league stuff, but was always sent back to the minors.

This was the year, the team was sure, when the southpaw would stick with the big club and become a difference-maker. The Reds of 1936 finished 74-80, fifth in the National League under manager Chuck Dressen, drawing just 466,345 fans to Crosley Field. The team's top pitcher was the reliable Paul Derringer, though his record was just 19-19 that year.

Reds officials were aching to supplement the rotation and the hot fella in Tampa seemed to be the remedy. Spring training is like spring planting. The cultivators begin the season with optimism, nurturing with care and watering a dream that might flower. Only when the crop is harvested can they be certain of success.

The flavor of the month in February for the Reds had been singled out as a minor leaguer worth watching by *The Sporting News*, seriously at least since 1936. In 1937, the Reds were indeed scrutinizing Lee Grissom, who for three seasons had tantalized the front office with glimpses of potential in a handful of appearances. Working out beside Grissom in camp, receiving comparatively little attention, was another left-handed pitcher, named Johnny Vander Meer.

The eyes were all focused in the wrong direction. That would change in the near future. Grissom, who was born in 1907 in Sherman, Texas, stood 6-foot-3 and weighed 200 pounds. When he dropped out of school in junior high, with the family living in California, he went to work on his father's farm. By the standards of the times he was a big man and scouts were fascinated with his power pitching, only, as the *Brooklyn Eagle* pointed out from spring training in 1937, they were torn about his potential, as well. A headline and subhead in that New York paper read, "See in Grissom, Reds' Pitcher, Another Dizzy: He Has Great Speed, Is Fearless, But At Present Pretty Wild."[1]

Every team in baseball sought to unearth another Dizzy Dean, who could throw a fastball through a cement wall. Grisson seemed to possess that type of arm strength, but also Dean's offbeat sense of humor. The Brooklyn newspaper called Grissom "a dark horse" to make the team, per Dressen's word, and "eccentric," per Grissom's behavior.

In 1934, when he was already 26, Grissom appeared in four games and went 0-1 with a 15.43 earned average. In 1935, he was used in three games and went 1-1. In 1936, he also went 1-1. This was actually pretty good because Grissom never played baseball until he was 19. He was very raw, both in experience and development, and got into fights within the team periodically, which did not work in his favor. He also suffered from a couple of ill-timed illnesses. Finally, he was healthy in 1937 and it was time to perform.

Before the season began, though, Grissom was in Cincinnati and available when the team staged a startling picture to illustrate the Great Ohio River Flood. Grissom, teammate Gene Schott, and groundskeeper Matty Schwab, were rounded up, placed in a boat and with flood stage at 21 feet in Crosley Field, they rowed over the outfield fence and onto the submerged field for a photograph.[2]

At last, as the 1937 season approached, Grissom was healthy, and as the beneficiary of much tutoring from Dressen and pitching coach Tom Sheehan, seemed prepared for a full year of pitching. Only then he held out for more money, refusing to sign a Reds contract. This attracted the attention of critical sportswriters, one of whom was the well-known New York columnist Joe Williams who wrote, "Mr. Grissom won exactly one ball game for the Reds last season and on the strength of this tremendous achievement he is a holdout. This is said to constitute an all-time record in baseball. Not even such perennial holdouts as Babe Ruth, Bill Terry, or Edd Roush (all in the Hall of Fame) came close to it." It was noted if Grissom "wins but two games, he will be twice the pitcher he was last year."[3]

When the season began, Grissom was not only in the rotation, but the best starter Cincinnati had going. He did well enough during the season's first half to be selected for the National League All-Star team. He faltered later in the season, finishing 12-17, the most wins he ever recorded, although he also went 9-7 for Cincinnati in 1939.

In 1938, when he had a game well under control and was on first base, Grissom got the urge to steal second. He took off and on his slide he broke an ankle. Next thing you knew, he was with the New York Yankees for the 1940 season. When he showed up in spring training with that team, Grissom denied being a screwball, and got mad when challenged about having that reputation. Lefty Gomez, perhaps the funniest man to ever play baseball, intervened, and blessed Grissom's arrival. "I have turned over the nut

## 1. 1937: The New Look Reds

title of the Yankees to Grissom," Gomez said. "He looks as if he might have great possibilities. He insists he isn't screwy. But he can't fool me because I am left-handed, too."[4]

Grissom spent parts of eight seasons in the majors and his lifetime mark was 29-48. His much younger brother Marv was better known during a career in which he compiled a 47-45 pitching record with 57 saves. Lee Grissom lived to be 90, passing away in 1998.

Meanwhile, Vander Meer, while somewhat overshadowed by Grissom, thought he was also ready for the majors in 1937. Born in Prospect Park, New Jersey, on November 2, 1914, he was 22 when the season began and felt he was seasoned enough to move up.

Of Dutch origin, Vander Meer's family history was very much linked to many of the stereotypes that transferred to the New World when forebears established New York. Vander Meers worked on canal boats in Holland and even wore wooden shoes, it was said. And yes, there was a background of speed skating on the frozen canals in winter, racing against the neighbors. His parents moved to Midland Park, New Jersey, when Johnny was four and old trophies were stored in the house from those skating days. Johnny's father Jacob, a stone mason by trade, came to the United States when he was 17.

The younger Vander Meer took up baseball when he was 12 and played for the same youth team until he was 15, one called Bill's Dairy. He became a solid first baseman, but eventually, on emergency call, he filled in as a pitcher. It didn't go well. Vander Meer could not locate home plate with radar and was pulled after two innings. "I don't blame them for yanking me," Vander Meer said much later. "I was as wild as a hawk. I don't know how many players I hit, but I think I walked at least 10 in less than three innings. I did not give up many hits. I walked too many to let them hit me."[5]

When Vander Meer was young, baseball scouting was not very sophisticated. There was no organized draft of players. It helped to know someone to obtain a tryout. Vander Meer was discovered in a unique way. Vander Meer stumbled into a film role that publicized his name and led to the upgrade in his baseball status from playing semi-pro ball. The National League was working on a short movie to play in theaters around the country as an accompaniment to full-length feature presentations. The idea was to show people around the land that anyone could become a big-league ball player. At the time, Vander Meer was playing baseball for his local church.

"That was publicity of the National League and I was picked like an All-American boy," Vander Meer said decades later. It was more or less a good fortune random selection. "Any boy in America could have the opportunity to play in the big leagues."[6] The film was advertising the chance every kid wanted to think was available to him. It was much like mothers telling their children that anyone could grow up to become president of the United States.

"Of course, it was a one-in-10,000 shot if you broke into the game and played 10 years," Vander Meer said. "That's what the odds were at that time. But it was put out by Columbia Pictures and it was just a short shot to prove that every American kid had a chance in this country, and I think we still have. It was something done 60 years ago that still holds true in our country."[7]

Pumped up on screens across the nation, big-league clubs decided to take a look at what Vander Meer had to offer. He stood 6'1" and weighed 190 pounds. They saw a sturdy frame and a strong left arm. No scout could measure speed in the 1930s, but they trusted their eyes and believed Vander Meer had the fastball necessary to make it as a professional. He did not have the necessary control, but that was what the minors were all about, honing the natural talent.

Vander Meer was 18 when the Reds signed him and sent him to Class C Dayton for the 1933 season where he went 11-10. He was promoted to Class A Scranton the next season and finished 11-8. However, he stayed in Scranton for the 1935 season and did not thrive, going 7-10. Things may have stalled out there, but in 1936 Vander Meer made a brief stop in Nashville, going 0-1, then settled in for the summer with the later-famous Durham Bulls in North Carolina where he pulled things together. At 21, Vander Meer posted a 19-6 season. Vander Meer credited catcher-manager Johnny Gooch for helping him limit the kind of wildness that had plagued him periodically since his first stint on a mound as a kid.

While the Reds were preoccupied with Grissom, their other southpaw in training camp, they found room for Vander Meer on the early-season roster, too. Vander Meer made his Major League debut on April 22, 1937—as a pinch-runner. It was the second game of the season, a 14-11 loss to the St. Louis Cardinals.

Vander Meer got his first career decision as a pitcher on May 19 when the Reds lost to the Boston Bees, 3-1. For a stretch of time the Boston Braves, for some inexplicable reason, chose to be called the Bees. They subsequently returned to the Braves name before moving to Milwaukee and then on to Atlanta. Vander Meer started the game and went all nine innings. He deserved better than the loss, allowing just five hits and three runs, none of them earned, while striking out 11 batters. He even went one-for-two at the plate. He also picked future Hall of Famer Al Lopez off first base. However, Vander Meer did walk five, showing that hint of wildness.

Ten days later, Vander Meer took his second loss, dropping a 4-2 contest to the Chicago Cubs. He again went the distance. He also went one-for-two at the plate again. This meant he was batting .500, but his

## 1. 1937: The New Look Reds

Johnny Vander Meer had a lot to smile about during the 1938 baseball season after becoming the first—and thus far only—Major League pitcher to throw no-hitters in two consecutive starts, against the Boston Bees and the Brooklyn Dodgers.

pitching winning percentage was .000. Finally, on June 2, Vander Meer walked off the mound with a victory. He may not have felt worthy of this triumph, though. Walking eight men, Vander Meer was relieved after five innings, though the Reds defeated the Philadelphia Phillies, 8-4. Once more Vander Meer got a hit at the plate, though, leaving him at .429.

As the season wore on, it was apparent Vander Meer was not going to be a regular member of the starting rotation, but only a fill-in. Eventually, after starting 3-4 he was sent back to the minors, this time to Syracuse. There his record was only 5-11 in 17 games, but he did not permit a lot of runs and was recalled at the end of the season, losing one more game to finish his abbreviated rookie campaign 3-5. Still, Vander Meer was only 22 at season's end and 1937 was a good time to be a young Cincinnati Reds prospect. The franchise was undergoing changes.

MacPhail took over the Reds in 1933 after making the minor-league Columbus, Ohio, team a major success at the gate for the St. Louis Cardinals. He had run the Reds from 1933 through the 1936 season and seemed to have them on the move in the standings. The team's last winning record was 1928 and they finished either last or next-to-last in the National League every season between 1929 and 1934. The 1937 season did not indicate so much progress as promise when after a two-year upgrade the club finished last again. But things were happening.

On MacPhail's watch, the Reds had been part of the first night game in Major League Baseball history. Cincinnati was hosting the Philadelphia Phillies at Crosley Field on May 24, 1935, when by pre-arrangement President Franklin D. Roosevelt was able to push a button alerting MacPhail to flip on the lights at the ballpark. The Reds won a rather average 2-1 game, but history was recorded. Minor league teams had dabbled with lights at their parks since 1930 when the Des Moines, Iowa, team met Wichita in a Western League game. Once the lights were installed, the Reds regularly played night games and the habit expanded from there across baseball.

MacPhail was an innovator, but had a drinking problem that led him to lose his temper often and engage in inappropriate fights. He departed Cincinnati with some ill feelings from management, though MacPhail and owner Powel Crosley, Jr., denied it publicly. Upon his departure, he said, he "may go fishing for a while."[8] Such sojourns did not last very long. He soon surfaced as an executive with the Brooklyn Dodgers, bringing night baseball there and adding talent that brought the borough its first pennant in 1941. MacPhail then bought the New York Yankees and presided over some of their World Series victories. MacPhail was inducted into the Baseball Hall of Fame in 1978.

When MacPhail and Crosley parted, the Reds owner needed a new personnel man. It was Branch Rickey, then in charge of the Cardinals, who enthusiastically endorsed Warren Giles. Giles' way to the top position in St. Louis was blocked by Rickey himself. Rickey thought it would be good for Giles' career to move on, even though he believed the Reds were a lousy team. "Hell, I've got a better ball club than he's got," Rickey said of his own top minor-league team, the Rochester Red Wings.[9]

Initially, when Crosley reached out to Giles he turned down the overture, partially because he was under a long-term contract with the Cardinals. But this was an opportunity to go to the majors. Rickey, Giles said, had previously told him he would not "stand in my way if I had a chance to better myself."[10] Rickey voided Giles' five-year deal and he signed with Cincinnati for $25,000-a-season.

Giles, born in 1896 in a tiny town called Tiskilwa in Illinois, was a career baseball executive. By age 23 he was running a Moline, Illinois, Class B team called the Plowboys. When the Reds needed help, Giles was an emerging star within the Cardinals organization, ready for a move to the majors. He became the Reds' general manager in 1937 and supervised the daily operations of the franchise through 1951, also adding the title of president, before becoming the president of the National League from 1952 to 1969. It was under Giles' leadership that the Reds matured into two-time pennant-winners and a World Series champion within a few years of his taking over.

When Crosley hired Giles, the Reds were $700,000 in debt and had been a flop on the field for years, with the exception of their flirtation with a few higher notches in the standings under MacPhail. Charley, or Chuck, Dressen, was the Reds manager when Giles took over. Dressen had a fascinating sports life. He was born in 1894 in Decatur, Illinois. Beginning what was about a seven-year big-league playing career, Dressen made his Major League debut for the Reds in 1925. Before that he had spent a few years as a quarterback with some unheralded teams during the National Football League's fledgling days.

Dressen was tight with MacPhail and the former Reds executive is the one who brought him back to manage the club in 1934. He presided over the brief rise of the Reds in the mid–1930s, but when they dropped back to last place in 1937, Giles fired him. Much later, Dressen led the early 1950s Brooklyn Dodgers "Boys of Summer" great teams to considerable success.

Giles felt he had given Dressen a chance, but was not tolerant of another backwards-stepping, eighth-place finish. He was diplomatic in letting Dressen go. "Dressen is a fine leader and a fine man," Giles said. "But I felt the situation needed somebody with wider experience in handling tough problems."[11] He knew who he wanted as the next manager of the team, but wasn't sure he could get him. Giles told Crosley he was after Bill McKechnie, his former partner in Rochester. The dismissal of Dressen and the availability of McKechnie dovetailed for the 1938 season.

"I had Bill with me in Rochester," Giles said of watching McKechnie work up close, "and knew exactly what he could do and how he worked. He was my idea of the greatest manager in baseball."[12] McKechnie, nicknamed "Deacon" because he sang in the choir of his church, did not smoke, drink or use profanity. His nickname could have just as easily been "Choirboy." After his uneven showing with the 1937 Cincinnati Reds, this was the man Johnny Vander Meer would have to please to earn a 1938 roster spot, and a full-time place in the pitching rotation. A new face at the helm promised a fresh start.

# 2

# Bill McKechnie

Warren Giles' version of how he hired Bill McKechnie to manage the Reds for the 1937 season was sometimes simplified. Yes, he wanted McKechnie because he knew the man well and respected his work. But McKechnie had a good job and was reluctant to leave it. And others with Powel in Crosley, Jr.'s ear lobbied for other choices.

McKechnie had been manager of the National League Boston team since 1930. When he was hired, they were still the Braves. They switched to Bees for the 1936 season and kept the name for a while. Same franchise, though. Boston was one of the weak links in the NL, although coming off the 1937 season with a 79-73 season Boston was on an upswing. With the new nickname of Bees, some jokingly referred to McKechnie as "the beekeeper." He was concluding a five-year contract with Boston when Giles came after him for Cincinnati.

The other contenders for the Cincinnati job in the background were Gabby Hartnett, the Chicago Cubs star catcher who later made the Hall of Fame, and Jimmie Wilson, another veteran catcher who was a two-time All-Star with the Philadelphia Phillies, as well as being a star soccer player at one time. Part of the appeal of hiring one of those guys was their willingness to come cheaper than McKechnie.

Negotiating with McKechnie meant a payout of between $55,000 and $65,000 a year for two years, it was reported by one source, a high price to pay for a team that was accumulating debt, which thought those dollars more likely represented a combined two-year deal. It was reported elsewhere the deal was for at least $25,000-a-year for each of two years, but it was speculated the arrangement was probably for more than that. Giles believed McKechnie, who had won a World Series title leading the Pittsburgh Pirates and took the St. Louis Cardinals to a pennant, was worth the cash.

Although he had sailed through some tough times with Boston, including a bottoming-out 35-115 record in 1935, McKechnie was content enough with the Braves/Bees. Nothing was driving him away from Boston, he said. It was Giles' perseverance that made him jump teams. "He did it," McKechnie said. "He wanted me, and the way he put it to me, I practically had to go." Giles once again confirmed he had decided from the get-go McKechnie was the man he had to have to run his team on the bench. "I had been watching him a long time," Giles said. "I was so impressed with the way he ran the Rochester team I made up my mind that if I ever had a big-league ball club he would be the fellow I would want to manage it. This was the first opportunity I had to grab him."[1]

McKechnie was born August 7, 1886, in Wilkinsburg, Pennsylvania, and before he was 18 got his first chance to play for pay in the minors. By then his father had passed away and his mother, Mary, approved his pursuit of making a living in this manner, as long as he did not play games on Sundays. He made his Major League debut as a player in 1907 with the Pittsburgh Pirates, which made sense since his hometown was close to Pittsburgh, though the franchise had only been in business for a few years before it signed him.

He also spent varying periods in the majors with the Boston Braves, New York Yankees, New York Giants, the Reds in 1916 and 1917 and the Pirates again, concluding his playing career in 1920. In 1914 and 1915, McKechnie played for the Indianapolis and then Newark teams in the Federal League. His best season at the plate was recorded in Indiana, where he batted .304, once had a five-hit game, scored 107 runs and stole 47 bases. It was a good opportunity for players like McKechnie, who had insecure status in the NL. Only the Federal League's challenge to gain staying power as a third Major League expired after a few years. McKechnie returned to the National League, though it was difficult to find a job.

It was the Giants and John J. McGraw who rescued him. McGraw understood McKechnie's pluses and minuses and analyzed how he would fit in with the New York club. "I knew Bill was not much of a hitter," McGraw said, "that aberration in Indianapolis notwithstanding, but he was always a good fielder and what we needed most was steadiness at third."[2]

McKechnie played part of the 1916 season and all of his 1917 season with the Reds, although he was used only irregularly on the field that year. In 37 games after coming over from the Giants in '16, McKechnie batted .277. He got into only 48 games the next year, hitting .254. That 1917 Reds team, which finished fourth in the league, had a huge amount of star power in terms of historical perspective. The manager was the great hurler Christy Mathewson, before he went off to World War I service. Jim Thorpe, the greatest all-around athlete of all time, played 77 games for the Reds that year at age 30, hitting .247. Future Hall of Fame outfielder Edd Roush batted .341 and won the batting crown. Greasy Neale, like Thorpe, a future Pro Football Hall of Famer, was another outfielder who batted .294. Fred Toney, an excellent pitcher of the time period, went 24-16. It really was a stunning group of big-name versatile athletes.

At 31, McKechnie sensed the end of his playing days were on the horizon. The Pirates gave him the final chances of his 11-year Major League career, though, when they purchased him from the Reds for $20,000. Always an infielder, and mostly a third baseman, the 5-foot-10, 160-pound McKechnie was overall a middling hitter with a lifetime .251 average, but the Pirates needed help at his favorite position and he appeared in 126 games in 1918. True to general form he batted .255 during a season cut short by baseball authorities due to the United States' decision to enter World War I.

Displaying a keen mind for the game and its strategy during some of his end-of-career playing stops, McKechnie received encouragement to become a manager from Frank Chance, the Cubs star, and John J. McGraw, the legendary Giants manager, along the way. Immediately after retiring as a player, McKechnie spent a year managing in the minors before the Pirates hired him for the 1922 season.

Pirates owner Barney Dreyfuss, who made a habit of wearing black bowler hats, was the man who brought the Pirates to Pittsburgh in 1900 after running the franchise as the Louisville Colonels from 1890 to 1899. He was the one who had Forbes Field built in 1909. Having Dreyfuss (a future Hall of Famer himself) in your corner insured a future with Pittsburgh and he was a fan of McKechnie's, convinced he would be a winning manager.

From 1918 through 1920, the Pirates showed promise, finishing a handful of games over .500. The big breakthrough came in 1921 when Pittsburgh won 90 games, finished second, and drew more than 700,000 fans, second in the league. The team was managed by George Gibson, who had been a well-respected catcher as a player and guided the Pirates to those improvements in records beginning in 1918. However, Gibson was known as a harsh disciplinarian, prone to blowing up at players who made mental mistakes. A couple of players behaved wildly, one being Hall of Fame shortstop Rabbit Maranville, and the other being Moses Y. "Chief" Yellow Horse, who went 5-3 with a 2.98 earned run average in 1921. Yellow Horse was from the Pawnee Tribe and was credited with being the first full-blooded Native American to play Major League ball. When the Pirates slumped to a 32-33 start in 1922, Dreyfuss canned Gibson.

Maranville and Yellow Horse felt no responsibility to follow any team rules apparently, and Dreyfuss worried they would take advantage of rookie manager McKechnie. Dreyfuss approached McKechnie and asked, "Well, have you figured out how to make your players behave?" McKechnie told him not to sweat it, replying, "Everything is hunky-dory, Mr. Dreyfuss. I'm going to room with that pair."[3]

## 2. Bill McKechnie

They called Bill McKechnie "Deacon" because he was a churchgoer who did not drink or swear. He piloted the 1940 Reds to a World Series championship and was elected to the Hall of Fame.

He rented a suite for the three of them. One night, returning to the room, McKechnie was surprised by his two mates being in bed snoring. That alone should have made him suspicious. When he opened a closet door, a flock of pigeons enticed into the room by the miscreants, nearly knocked him over as they flew out. That was one prank he fell for, for sure.

The Pirates finished out the 1922 season 53-36 (with one tie) under McKechnie. The next year Pittsburgh went 87-67 in McKechnie's first full year in charge, and in 1924, the Pirates finished 90-63. Pittsburgh was third behind the Giants, 93-60, and Brooklyn, 92-62, in a wild pennant race. At last, in 1925, it was Pittsburgh's turn. The Pirates won the flag with a 95-58 record, some eight-and-a-half games ahead of New York. They faced off in the World Series against the Washington Senators, representing the American League. Washington great Walter Johnson had finally won a Series crown in 1924, and he was back for another shot.

Plagued by rain and delays, the Series went seven games. Before Game 3 commenced in Washington, D.C., a contingent of Pittsburgh team officials, including owner Dreyfuss, manager McKechnie, and his son Bill, Jr., were able to visit the White House and President Calvin Coolidge. The Series games themselves did not play out well for Pittsburgh at first, but after trailing 3-1, the Pirates rallied and captured the crown, 4-3. Max Carey, Kiki Cuyler and Pie Traynor were three future Hall of Famers McKechnie could put in his lineup. "What can I say?" McKechnie did say when the bounceback was complete. "We're overjoyed at the victory after coming back from Washington one behind. But after we started hitting Monday, didn't I predict that we would take 'em? Well, we did and there's not much to say."[4]

McKechnie never was considered a quote machine, but he got the job done and brought a championship to Pittsburgh. It was the first one since 1909 and the last one until 1960. Of course, no one could foretell the future. But there was optimism for a repeat. There were uncomfortable rumblings inside the team and when Pittsburgh fell off by 11 games in the win column in 1926, McKechnie was ousted. That led him to the St. Louis Cardinals, who won 95 games and the 1928 pennant with him as boss. The next season was a bit of mess and the team blew through three managers.

By 1930, McKechnie was in Boston, and that's where Warren Giles plucked him from to lead the Reds. Boston did want to keep McKechnie, but after Giles' sweet-talking, the Braves agreed to let him depart because they couldn't match the money being offered. Boston team president Bob Quinn was the one who made the call, with reluctance, because he felt it would be unfair to McKechnie to pressure him to stick around at a financial loss. "I knew that four or five clubs were after McKechnie," Quinn said of the potential bidding war when he was paying only $18,000. "But I was in hopes that we could keep him in Boston where we looked upon him as the best manager in baseball."[5]

People kept saying that. The supporting evidence was McKechnie leading the Pirates to a World Series title and then leading the Cardinals to a National League pennant in his first season. McKechnie did not go around boasting. He let his work and others speak for him. His track record in Boston hadn't been all that great because he never felt he had the type of players he could win with. Now he was starting over with Cincinnati, another seemingly moribund club, at least on paper. The Reds were a last-place team in 1937, finishing 24 games behind his own Boston Bees in the standings. What would it take to make them winners? And how long would it take?

# 3

# Vander Meer Makes the Cut

Johnny Vander Meer spent a decent chunk of the 1937 season with the last-place Cincinnati Reds, but it was obvious manager Chuck Dressen had only limited faith in him. Vander Meer was an irregular starter and very much a regular bench-sitter. The lefty had managed a 3-5 record in his 19 appearances, 10 as a starter, nine in relief. His earned average was an acceptable 3.84, but he was by no means secure in his roster spot. Being shipped to AAA Syracuse for a portion of the summer told him more than his end-of-season call-up did.

However, the firing of Dressen, and the ascension of Bill McKechnie as the new manager, who was hailed as an expert for his ability to handle pitchers and get the most out of them, gave Vander Meer the fresh chance he sought. Although still just 23, Vander Meer had bounced around the minors for five years and seemed to be only on the fringe of the Reds' plans. Vander Meer loved baseball and believed in his talent, but had pretty much made up his mind that if he did not have a breakthrough in 1938, he was going to retire and take up another profession.

"If I don't make good in '38," Vander Meer said, "it's goodbye baseball for me."[1] It is possible the Reds would also view him as expendable, too, if he didn't cut it that spring. What Vander Meer heard when he showed up for spring training at the Reds' camp that year was the buzz about McKechnie, as in, "If you can't pitch for McKechnie, you can't pitch for anyone."[2]

Vander Meer's Achilles heel had always been his inability to maintain control over his best pitches long enough to repress hitters for several innings. McKechnie appreciated Vander Meer's raw skill and thought he could help him. Everything was new to McKechnie with the Cincinnati club that year and he had much to absorb, as well as evaluating talent and picking a roster.

In what turned out to be a perfect pairing of teacher and pupil, McKechnie asked Lefty Grove to work with Vander Meer and to harness those pitches who produced too many walks for enemy batters. It was a bold request. Robert Moses "Lefty" Grove, on his way to the Hall of Fame with a lifetime 300-141 pitching mark compiled for the Philadelphia Athletics and Boston Red Sox, was still active. He was 38 years old that season and still had enough left in his arm to win the final 43 games of his career and to lead the American League in earned run average twice more.

McKechnie, coach Hank Gowdy, and Grove all tag-teamed Vander Meer. Gowdy was a savvy baseball man who played catcher and first base before turning to coaching. He was known as the first Major League player to enlist in the United States Army to fight in World War I. Gowdy also rejoined the service at 53 during World War II and became a major. In between, he coached, overlapping with McKechnie, and later became the Reds manager himself.

Beginning during Vander Meer's days with the Durham Bulls, and continuing with tutelage from McKechnie and Gowdy, there always had been coaches urging him to alter his delivery to the plate. One day that spring in Sarasota, Gowdy recounted this history to the hurler and changed tactics. "Well, today I'm not going to talk. I'm going to let you LOOK." Across the field, Grove was warming up and Gowdy pointed out that other left-hander. "Watch Lefty closely. See how he keeps the ball in front of him all the time. That's what I've been trying to tell you."[3]

This was home schooling. Vander Meer studied Grove's methods from afar for some time. When Grove concluded his workout, Vander Meer walked over and introduced himself, asking for assistance, one southpaw to another. Grove was sympathetic and invested an hour talking to Vander Meer about his own technique. Although no two pitchers are exactly alike, what Vander Meer absorbed that day was life-altering.

The combination of Grove's advice, Gowdy's tutoring, and McKechnie's interest and the patience he was known for working with pitchers, conspired to boost Vander Meer's confidence when he most needed the help. Vander Meer changed his delivery, shifting the position of his throwing arm from partially side-arm to more overhand. "I was able to concentrate exactly on what he told me," Vander Meer said of Professor McKechnie. "I knew I didn't have to rush or be afraid if I took my time."[4]

Coming out of spring training, Vander Meer made the big-league club. It was a very different club than represented Cincinnati the year before. In 1937, the Reds finished eighth and last in the National League with a 56-98 record. In fact, new general manager Warren Giles did not even keep Dressen around till the final buzzer. Bobby Wallace managed most of the last month, contributing a mark of 5-20 to that final overall record.

Giles was hired by Powel Crosley, Jr., to turn the Reds into a winner. If McKechnie was the man he was going to utilize to run the field operation,

Giles also knew he had to provide better players if the Reds were going to start winning right away. For the time being, without really knowing what players were going to represent the Reds, Giles pumped up the generally reserved McKechnie to the public. The Reds Official Score Book for the 1938 season—costing 10 cents—featured a cartoon-like visage of McKechnie. If only the bargain prices for spending a day at Crosley Field were still available. The admission tickets listed for that season included $2 for promenade and upper boxes for Sunday and night games, $1.75 for lower boxes and the first four rows of the grandstands. These days the decimal point would have to move a couple of places to the right for the best seats. The cheapest seats in 1938 were 60 cents for the bleachers, though children under 12 could be admitted for 55 cents.

The Reds home park at Findlay Street and Dalton Avenue opened in 1912 and was known as Redland Field through 1933. On April 11, opening day, the Reds beat the Chicago Cubs, 10-6. Capacity from its beginnings through 1926 was listed as 20,696. Expanded seating brought the limit to 29,401 just in time for McKechnie's inaugural season in 1938. Feeling that this was just the beginning of something special, Giles presided over another expansion almost right away, with the addition of second decks above the right-field and left-field grandstands, lifting capacity to 30,210. Some might call that a gesture of optimism.

Crosley dated to Deadball Era days that, prior to some of the distances being lessened, was quite spacious: 360 feet to left field, 360 feet to right and 420 feet to dead center. With those dimensions, good pitchers were needed and power hitters had to work doubly hard for home runs.

In 1937, the Reds really had an abundance of neither and Giles went shopping for talent of any kind to improve on the dismal record of that season. In 1930, McKechnie's first year managing the Boston Braves, a rookie outfielder named Wally Berger appeared on the scene. Berger smacked 38 home runs that season, setting a rookie record for home runs that stood for years, although since eclipsed more than once. Berger was traded by Boston to the New York Giants in 1937 and Giles made a swap for him, sending light-hitting infielder Alex Kampouris to New York in June of 1938. Berger was in his early 30s and nearing the end of his career, but stepped in as a regular in the outfield.

At about the same time that month, Giles, certain that right-handed pitcher Bucky Walters was better than his record to date with the Philadelphia Phillies, spent big to obtain him. Giles gave up two players and $50,000. Walters had suffered through some tough times with Philadelphia, but also had achieved some solid marks with a terrible team. He even made his first All-Star team with a 14-15 record in 1937. From 1933 through 1945, the Phillies never finished better than seventh in the National League and most of the time were last. Giles bringing Walters to the Reds was pretty much a mercy rescue that paid dividend after dividend for Cincinnati.

Cincinnati did not miss lefty Al Hollingsworth, surrendered in the deal, but Hollingsworth had to miss Cincinnati. Most of his worst seasons in the bigs followed with Philadelphia. The other party to the trade was back-up catcher Spud Davis, who had to know what he was in for since he had already played for the Phillies.

Even before the start of the season Giles made some decisive moves, exiling big names. In 1937, Kiki Cuyler, one of McKechnie's stars with the 1925 Pirates, played 117 games in the outfield. Then at 38 he batted an OK .271, but hit zero home runs with just 32 runs batted in. Cuyler was a future Hall of Famer, but Giles felt he did not have enough sting left in his bat to be helpful. Cuyler played one more season with the Brooklyn Dodgers, hitting a still-respectable .273, but with just two home runs and 23 RBIs in 82 games before retiring.

Chick Hafey, another outfielder bound for the Hall of Fame, who played 89 games for the Reds at 34 in 1937, met the same fate. Hafey retired prior to the 1938 season. Age was the main reason Giles made the moves. No general manager can stand still with a last-place team and he knew that. These once-great players were expendable.

During spring training, McKechnie was cagey and reserved in divulging much about his view of the talent displayed before him on the diamond. There was quite the crowd vying for a spot on the roster, nearly five dozen players trying to impress him. "Yes, sir, 57," McKechnie told a sportswriter who nicknamed him "Mild Will." "But don't ask me who they all are and what they play. I'm still a stranger around here myself."[5] When that article appeared in print opening day was exactly one month away. It wasn't as if McKechnie didn't know who the veterans were because he had been managing in the National League for years. But that was not the same as knowing all their strengths and weaknesses and what made them tick. "Looking at them from the Cincinnati dugout gives you a different view of them," he said.[6]

There were several good reasons for McKechnie's reticence. Only a year before patrolling the same training camp, Chuck Dressen made the mistake of suggesting the Reds might win the 1937 pennant. When McKechnie was reminded of what turned out to be a serious error in judgment, he furiously backpedaled from any such lapse. A pennant? "Land o' living, no!" he said. "This club finished in last place, 25 games away from the first division and ended the season by losing 14 games in a row. That doesn't make it look like the start of a big bid for the pennant this year."[7]

Of course, that dose of reality was not what everyone wanted to hear. McKechnie was a heralded get for the Reds and inheriting a bottom-of-the-league team was serving as a symbol for fan true believers to latch onto their favorite team for a fresh season without hopelessness. McKechnie was never the kind of rah-rah guy who would jazz things up for sportswriters and he knew he had to lead the team to improvement to justify his high salary. But before the season began he did not have either Berger or Walters and with the departure of men like Cuyler and Hafey his team was even more anonymous than previously.

He was not going to gush or make foolish promises. He was not about to make the mistake of overrating a team that not only statistically, but up-close and personal, had not shown him enough in spring training for a bold statement. McKechnie announced to the masses of fans and sportswriters that he believed this one thing about the 1938 Cincinnati Reds: They would not finish in last place again. That was as far as he would go. "Well, we hope to get out of the cellar and climb by easy stages," McKechnie said. "But the drastic changes will have to wait until I find out what these fellows can do and what else we need."[8]

At that point in spring training, as proof McKechnie was still undergoing an immersion education, he was using the same starting infield that Dressen was writing on the lineup card up till his firing. Lew Riggs was playing third base, Bill Myers shortstop, Kampouris second base and Frank McCormick first. Soon enough, Kampouris would be traded away and McCormick would emerge as a star, but no one foresaw that in March. Listening to McKechnie at that stage, he was very much a manager with an open mind, and a closed mouth, restraining himself from making too many comments about the prospects. What did he know and when did he know it? It was not clear yet.

He danced around several questions like a politician avoiding commitment to a side on a public issue, which this was. When he was asked if Ernie Lombardi, the team's outstanding slugger would surely be the starting catcher, he even sidestepped that one. Asked about his pitching, McKechnie basically only listed the right-handers and the left-handers, without saying what they might bring to the table. At least Vander Meer was in the forefront of his mind. Good old flamboyant Lee Grissom wasn't even mentioned without a prod.

Perhaps the most unusual walk-on at the Reds camp was an aspirant named John Doehring. From 1932 through 1937, the Milwaukee native played football for the Chicago Bears and the Pittsburgh Steelers, mostly as a running back. But by 1938, he was making some money in professional wrestling. Big and strong, he showed up at Reds spring training requesting a tryout. McKechnie wondered if he could pitch, hit or field. "Well, he was down here in Tampa wrestling five nights a week," McKechnie said. "The boys told me about his football reputation, so when he walked in and asked could he work out with us, I thought he just wanted to keep in condition. But he wanted to play ball."[9]

Admiring Doehring's muscular build, McKechnie said he thought the 26-year-old might be able to throw. A little bit, it turned out, but not big-league enough. Doehring was signed by the Reds and sent to Class B Columbia in the Sally League, where he went 2-1 in four games. This half-analytical, half-secretive preview of the Reds offered by McKechnie was terminated when he told his questioner politely that he had to be going to study up. "Excuse me, now," he said, "while I try to find out about this ball club myself."[10]

Given all of the attention lavished on him by McKechnie, Gowdy and special advisor Lefty Grove, Vander Meer could discern that the Reds cared about him—to a degree. At least he seemed to have a chance to fit in with this evolving team.

# 4

# Frank McCormick
# Long Time Coming

No one had more faith in Frank McCormick's ability to play baseball than Frank McCormick. It just took him a little while to prove to others how good he was. He did not lack confidence, or perseverance, or otherwise he might have been discouraged into following his father's line of work for a railroad company.

Growing up in New York City, McCormick, born in 1911, played ball in the streets and in church leagues, primarily as an outfielder. By age 17 he decided if someone just paid attention to him he could make it to the major leagues. He harbored that thought along with tens of thousands of other teenaged American boys, that is. McCormick wasn't just sitting around idly wishing and hoping, however. However he managed his research, he began showing up at tryout camps.

In an era before there was much serious scouting of young players, no way to see them play unless they appeared in games nearby, and no video or television, never mind the internet, young talent was discovered by word-of-mouth or through cattle-call tryout sessions. A player not only had to be good, he had to be lucky to be noticed at a given camp when a hundred, or even hundreds of boys, showed up, got a couple of swings, fielded a few ground balls, and were supposed to make an instant impression before being sent home by dark.

McCormick made whatever rounds he could, performing for the Philadelphia Athletics, Washington Senators and New York Giants and being dismissed almost as swiftly as most hopefuls seeking a singing gig at a bar. He was 23, poor, and still dreaming when he learned of a Cincinnati Reds tryout about to be conducted in Beckley, West Virginia, in 1934. He borrowed $50 from a supportive uncle to make the journey, and heeding the advice of a local coach, changed his focus to first base. The theory behind the position switch was that fewer young men would try out for that job than as an outfielder.

Whether McCormick had discovered a magic formula, or really was a better ball player by then, seeking the tryout with the Reds meant he had explored his options with 25 percent of the existing 16 Major League teams. The man presiding over the session was a wizened baseball man. Bobby Wallace, born in 1873, spent 25 seasons in the majors, from pre–1900, through the Deadball Era, and then took turns managing, coaching and scouting. Briefly, in 1937, after Warren Giles canned Chuck Dressen, Wallace managed the final 25 games of the disastrous season. However, he was on the road in West Virginia for the team when McCormick showed up. His 50 bucks did not provide enough cash for McCormick to do more than drive to his destination and eat a little bit. He could not afford a hotel room, so slept in the automobile. Whenever he emerged from it, though, he made an impression. The fourth time being the charm, Wallace signed McCormick to a Reds contract.

McCormick told the story of the cash loan from a relative financing the 525-mile drive from the Bronx. A few years later a Cincinnati sportswriter reported a different tale to readers. The story said a fan of McCormick's wrote several letters to Larry MacPhail urging him to sign the young player and that McCormick took a bus to West Virginia, the trip paid for by the Reds. The first account seemed more believable.

The Reds probably kept first baseman Frank McCormick in the minors too long. He did not play his first full season until he was 27, but then won a Most Valuable Player award and was an eight-time All-Star.

McCormick had grown to stand 6-foot-4 and he weighed about 205 pounds. The Reds broke him into the pros right where he signed, with a Class C minor-league team called the Beckley Black Knights. In 120 games, McCormick batted .347. It was the low minors, but the Reds were enamored enough with this sample of his work to rush McCormick to the big club for the last couple of weeks of the same 1934 season. In 12 games he hit .313 off National League pitching.

McCormick made his debut against the St. Louis Cardinals as a pinch-hitter on September 11. On the mound was a right-hander named Emil Leonard, who was one of two big-league hurlers nicknamed "Dutch." This Dutch was a five-time All-Star and won 191 games over a 20-year career. The story told of that day by a Cincinnati sportswriter has Burt Shotton, later much better known as a manager, but acting as a coach, conferring with McCormick before he was inserted into the game. Shotton said, "Think you can hit that fellow?" McCormick replied, "I can hit any pitcher." While that was probably the right thing to say in such a circumstance, McCormick later admitted his emotions were quite different than his outward cockiness. "I was so scared when I faced Leonard my knees knocked together."[1]

The article said McCormick hit the ball so hard it zoomed through the infield, making it sound like a hit. It may well have been a hard shot, but the box score indicates McCormick reached on an error by Brooklyn second baseman Jimmy Jordan. It might be surmised that with a mediocre team that little season-closing run of hitting would gain McCormick the opportunity to show more for the Reds in 1935. Instead, the front office never let McCormick get closer to Cincinnati than Dayton, one of his handful of minor league stopovers that year. McCormick was lucky if he could remember his managers' names, never mind those of teammates in five cities. He hit .277 during his Greyhound Bus tour of the region.

Nor did McCormick get a wink or a nod in 1936. The Reds played on without him as McCormick batted .381 to capture the Piedmont League batting title for the Durham Bulls. And not even that showing allowed McCormick more than a cameo stay with the Reds in 1937. Despite that horrible team's performance, McCormick was only used in 24 games, and sure enough hit .325 for the Reds. "I think I'm here to stay this time," McCormick said at that time.[2]

McCormick's youth was wasting away in the minors, the property of a Reds team desperate for good hitting help, but seemingly determined to ignore what it had. The difference in 1938 was a fresh management outlook. Giles and new manager Bill McKechnie scrutinized everyone in the organization. McKechnie was reviewing 57 roster candidates and no one stood out among those he knew little about more than McCormick.

## 4. Frank McCormick Long Time Coming

Finally, at age 27, someone else believed as much in Frank McCormick as Frank McCormick. Handed the first-base job, McCormick exploded on the National League scene in 1938. He batted .327, drove in 106 runs, and led the league with 209 hits while being chosen for the first of his nine All-Star games. As McCormick might have said, but was not quoted as saying, "Duh."

McCormick was the NL's freshest sensation. By mid-season, McCormick, who played every inning of the Reds' schedule, was garnering attention from sportswriters around the league wondering about his sudden impact on the game. It wasn't only those who covered the game commenting on his play, but some who missed the chance to sign him. When the Reds visited the Giants at the Polo Grounds, New York great Bill Terry, the Hall of Fame first-baseman then managing the team, either recognized McCormick or was informed about his pass-through with the club. "Is that the kid who worked out with us that time four or five years ago?" Terry said. "Why, he's grown up."³

McCormick reflected on his wearying road to big-league success and how long it took to fight his way to a full-time spot with the Reds. He admitted it was sometimes frustrating to experience the return trips to the minors spread over several years. "I feel like I'm doing a man's work," McCormick said. "It was fun playing in the minors, but somehow never wholly satisfying. Maybe I was too impatient, but I did feel like an apprentice kid learning a trade. The big league is where the men play, and now, to find myself a part of it, well, the only comparable thrill I can recall is the first time I stepped into a pair of long pants. You know in my neighborhood (Yorkville), you had to be pretty well grown, 15 or 16, before they allowed you that privilege."⁴

Anyone who followed his odyssey, or in this case was determined to catch up, understood that McCormick never wanted to be a doctor, a lawyer or fire chief, only a baseball player. He set his mind to that task early, but was not recognized as a prodigy, so had to invest time and effort away from the spotlight before he could make it big. "I guess I was cut out to be a ball player," McCormick said. "There never was a time I can remember when I wasn't crazy to play. Lou Gehrig came from Yorkville, too, and his success was an incentive to all us kids. He's still my idea of what a ball player should be."⁵

McCormick could not know it at the time he was speaking during the summer of 1938, but Gehrig was in the midst of his last full season. He was about to learn he was coping with a life-threatening disease that would kill him by 1941. Gehrig completed the 1938 campaign and appeared in just eight games the next year before retiring. Whether really accurate or not, manager McKechnie thought McCormick facially resembled Gehring. It was in 1938 that he began hitting like him in most ways except for home runs. McCormick didn't have Gehrig-like power, hitting just five home runs that first full season.

What surprised even McCormick somewhat was shining in the field. He had come late to the position after a youth spent as an outfielder, though he adapted quickly in the minors. The difference between minor-league ball and the majors, though, was substantial. Yet, just as he drew praise for his very solid hitting, McCormick found he was being evaluated quite favorably for his work with the glove, too. Many baseball men were saying he was the best-fielding first sacker in the league as a rookie. Compliments came at him faster than grounders or pitched balls, as if the entire world couldn't wait to make up for the slights of his being sent home by big-league clubs at their tryout camps, or for the neglect of the Reds keeping him down on the farm so long.

McCormick was no plodder around the bag when it came to gloving hard shots, or taking pickoff throws from his pitchers, but he said he did have a learning curve. "That was the hardest thing to learn, to shift my feet," he said. "Once I got my feet under control, I was on my way."[6]

Although the rookie-of-the-year award commonly referred to during the modern era of baseball was not presented officially through voting by the Baseball Writers Association of America until 1947, and was named for Jackie Robinson in 1987, over the preceding decades various players were deemed to have been the top rookie in the NL and the American League. From 1940 to 1947, the Chicago chapter of baseball writers gave a rookie award called the J. Louis Comiskey Memorial Award. Other times, less officially, sportswriters proclaimed top rookies. That recognition came to McCormick after the 1938 season.

Normally, when a homegrown player plays in a city near the smaller town where he grew up, he is greeted as local-boy-makes-good. McCormick was from the big city, though, a New Yorker, where the community was flooded with daily newspapers. But he was such a hot commodity when the Reds showed up to play the Giants, he did receive some of that same type of attention. Indeed, many tickets were set aside for the McCormick family in 1938 to see a favorite son play.

"Every time I come to the Polo Grounds with the Reds, the folks come down to see me play," McCormick said, "and so far I've always disappointed them. I don't think I've gotten more than one hit in any game."[7] It was a good thing McCormick collected about 200 hits elsewhere then, or he never would have been acknowledged as the finest National League rookie of 1938. By any definition, he was the league's find of the year in the field.

# 5

# Ernie Lombardi

The big man behind the plate for the Cincinnati Reds was a man of conspicuous distinctions. Ernie Lombardi, who stood 6-foot-3 and weighed 230 pounds, may have been the slowest runner in baseball history, with a nose to match Jimmy Durante's, but the wielder of a bat so potent every National League pitcher who had common sense feared him. By 1938, when Bill McKechnie arrived on the Cincy scene, Lombardi was the one rock-solid piece of the lineup, an established star who perhaps even more than the originator of the phrase Willie Keeler, did "hit 'em where they ain't" because he had to or he would not reach base. He certainly wasn't going to beat out infield hits.

Lombardi was born in Oakland, California, in 1908 and everyone who knew him as a kid recognized his special skill as a baseball player, figuring from the start he would make a splash in that endeavor. He and his friends would play for hours on end at the local fields, taking turns hitting and pitching. The hard work paid off and by the late 1920s he was mashing Pacific Coast League pitching for the hometown Oaks. He hit .377, .366 and .370. Those eye-popping averages did not go unnoticed and Lombardi was in demand.

Brooklyn, temporarily using the team name of Robins rather than Dodgers, bid for Lombardi, sending Oakland two players and $50,000 for him. One thing noted upon Lombardi's acquisition in Brooklyn was his Italian-American heritage. The point was made that the Robins were "a melting pot, a team of all nations" because of the composition of the roster. Lombardi merely added to the mixed nature of backgrounds for a team that already had a Spanish-American, Cuban-American and a player of Czech descent.[1]

Lombardi made his Major League debut for Brooklyn in 1931. He promptly showed he could hit big-league pitching about as well as minor league pitching, batting .297 in 73 games. However, despite the investment and the Lombardi positive sneak preview, before the next season, in a Brooklyn error in judgment, Lombardi was sent to the Reds as part of a six-man deal. Babe Herman, like Lombardi another future Hall of Famer, accompanied him to Cincinnati. The Robins-Dodgers did not get equivalent value back. Manager Wilbert Robinson, for whom the Robins' nickname was used, never liked Lombardi much and made the bad trade.

For most of the next decade, Lombardi caught about three-fourths of all Reds games and batted more than .300 almost every season, some years significantly higher. He definitely owned a sharp hitting eye. Somewhat surprisingly given his size, Lombardi was not much of a home-run hitter, generally swatting 10 or 12 per season. The extra-large size of Lombardi's nose provided him with the nickname of "Schnozz." He was such a good-natured man, though, Lombardi did not let that bother him. "They first began kidding me about the nose and calling me 'Schnozz,' back in the Coast League," Lombardi said. "But the funny thing was, I didn't get too much razzing from the bench jockeys. Mostly, it came from the fans."[2] Still, there was publicity about the size of his proboscis and once Durante met Lombardi at a ballpark and a faceoff. They posed for pictures together. Durante analyzed the situation this way: "Lom's is bigger, but mine is more educated."[3]

Between 1932 and 1934, Lombardi hit .303, .283, and .305 for the Reds. Stardom beckoned and he became an eight-time National League All-Star. One story goes that in 1934, while posing for a picture with the Chicago Cubs' renowned catcher Gabby Hartnett, the photographer told Lombardi he was going to be the league's next great catcher. Hartnett snapped, "I'm not ready to relinquish it yet."[4] Maybe not, but Lombardi did force him to slide over and make room for him in the penthouse of best catchers. Still, when McKechnie showed up and was ordered to reshape the Cincinnati roster he even gave consideration to parting with Lombardi, the franchise's most valuable property. He backed off from that idea to the mutual benefit of the team and Lombardi.

Lombardi liked playing for McKechnie more than he had Wilbert Robinson in Brooklyn, and echoed others' viewpoints about the placid demeanor McKechnie projected. He was not a yeller, but could be stern when he thought it necessary. He came off more like a forceful teacher than a loud disciplinarian, but got his point across. "I liked to play for Bill," Lombardi said. "He was quieter than other managers. But all he had to do was look out at you over the top of his glasses and you'd know you'd done something wrong."[5]

There was no question Lombardi was a stuck-in-the-mud runner, whether it was trying to beat the ball to first base on a grounder, or when he was on the base paths after a safety. He did not ever pretend he was going to qualify for the Olympic trials 100-meter dash. Lombardi spent 17 years in the majors and played in 1,853 regular-season games, but stole just eight bases. To say opponents did not consider him to be a Ty Cobb–like threat was an understatement.

Ernie Lombardi was the Reds' stalwart catcher who won two National League batting titles and eventually was enshrined in the Baseball Hall of Fame in Cooperstown, New York.

One of Lombardi's rare stolen bases was recorded against Brooklyn. Since it was Lombardi on first base the Dodgers never gave a thought to a sneak attack. When catcher Mickey Owen received the pitch and saw Lombardi was going, he was poised to throw him out at second base. Only neither shortstop Pee Wee Reese, nor second baseman Billy Herman were covering the bag. "They couldn't move when I stole," Lombardi joked. "I was just too fast for them."[6]

Lombardi also told another story on himself, reminding a listener that once he smacked a ball so hard off the left-field wall that when it ricocheted to a fielder he was thrown out at first base. There was a time when an aging Lombardi, nearing the end of his career, and of course not getting any faster, was the punch-line of a joke that once again he did not seem to mind. A sportswriter recalled that, "It went something like 'Lombardi doubled to left and beat out a single.'"[7]

Once Lombardi became the regular catcher for the Reds in 1932, he swiftly became the top hitter on the team. After his first-rate, three-year start he got even better. In 1935, Lombardi batted .343, then .333, and in 1937, when Cincinnati slumped back into last place, it most assuredly wasn't his fault. He hit .334. Along the way, Lombardi posted a six-for-six batting day. By the time the new regime was shaking things up in 1938, Lombardi was a two-time All-Star. During that horror of a 1937 season, Lombardi was the only one other than part-timers who made a limited number of appearances to bat .300. Yes, maybe the Reds could have received multiple players in a deal for Lombardi leading up to the 1938 season, but finding reliable stars can be difficult and also be hard to replace. The stand-pat decision by general manager Warren Giles and McKechnie was the prudent choice.

Given his size and his ingrained reputation as a slow-moving bus on the bases, it was remarkable how often Lombardi was referred to as "lumbering" in print. The word showed up so often next to his name that it almost seemed as if it had been on his birth certificate. He was described as lumbering coming out of his crouch behind the plate, as lumbering his way down to first base after stroking the ball, and sometimes even as lumbering as he rose from his dugout seat to take an at-bat. A writer might have written that as Lombardi lumbered to the plate to take his turn swinging he was carrying a hefty chunk of lumber to swing with, but such humorous phrasing was not easily found.

In retrospect, it is humorous in this modern age of the computer to be able to surf the internet and view many stories ranking the slowest men ever to play big-league ball. Lombardi is always there, as if decades after his retirement and death he is still being timed running to first with a sundial. A 2011 article rated the 25 slowest snails of all time. The list included many great players, including Jim Thome, David Ortiz, Willie McCovey and Edgar Martinez. Many in the group were tall and thick of body, most of whom would be considered heavyweights. No. 1 in the rating? Ernie Lombardi. The man's reputation endured.[8]

The ranking system relied heavily on how few stolen bases and triples a player recorded while coming to the plate thousands of times. In Lombardi's case it was noted that he also hit into 261 double plays, the number so high because he could not beat the relay to first. In fact, many opponents' managers ordered their infielders to play deep, back on the grass, giving them more range for balls with the knowledge they could still throw Lombardi out on grounders. He did steal only those eight bases and he did crack only 27 triples in 6,352 plate appearances. So it was not just an impression formed by his contemporaries; all the empirical evidence points to Lombardi being slow afoot.

For all of that, the righty swinging Lombardi still was a perennial .300 hitter, somewhat astonishing for a guy who was only going to get an infield hit about as often as Haley's Comet came around. In fact, the same rating of Lombardi as the slowest of the slow also described him this way: "He was so slow that the infielders would play in the outfield grass, yet he still hit for such a high average, as he really is one of the most underrated hitters of all time, but also the slowest player in MLB history."[9]

Another thing that made Lombardi stand out was his grip on the bat. His hold was described as more of a golf grip than a standard baseball use of the hands. One sportswriter said, "Ernie Lombardi is the only player in the big leagues to use an interlocking golf grip at the bat, and strangely, he has never swung a golf club in his life. When the bulky Cincinnati catcher grips the stick, he clamps the left index finger over the little finger of the right hand."[10]

If Lombardi was one big out, some coach or manager would have ordered him to make some changes. But since he was almost always the best hitter on his team, no one suggested he tamper with success. There are generally accepted right ways of taking stances, but the exception is always granted to the truly talented. St. Louis Cardinals outfielder Stan Musial had his crouch. Boston Red Sox outfielder Carl Yastrzemski had his own style. Others did not emulate their uniqueness because what they did came naturally to them.

Lombardi adopted his personal grip while playing with the Oakland Oaks. Lombardi said circumstances demanded an adjustment because he had a blister on his little finger. "It was impossible for me to get any power into my swing with a regular grip because I could not press the little finger to the bat," he said. "So I locked it under the index finger of the other hand, and I've hit that way since."[11] The only times Lombardi doubted himself was when he went into a slump. Even the most confident of hitters sometimes have their beliefs challenged when they go oh-for-10 or something like that. Lombardi admitted when those bad stretches arose he occasionally dabbled in a purer bat grip in batting practice, but never wavered when it counted in a real game. "But always I feel sort of funny," Lombardi said when he went through such phases, "and I go back to the golf grip. No one ever told me to take a regular grip on a bat."[12]

Since Lombardi reached the majors during the Depression, when most teams, if not all, not only the Reds, were losing money, and his other main prime years directly followed, he did not get rich playing baseball. Cincinnati paid Lombardi $16,000 for the 1938 season (and he never made much more than that). But the Reds were certainly not paying him to steal bases. His role was to wield that lumber in menacing fashion and he did so quite determinedly and successfully.

As the 1938 Reds season began, Lombardi was the team's starting catcher. Neither he nor his bosses knew he was about to turn in the finest season of his career, and some of his biggest thrills were about to take place in the field, not at bat.

# 6

# Vander Meer Pitches a No-Hitter

He made the team. That was Johnny Vander Meer's first objective for the 1938 season. He wanted to be on the Cincinnati Reds' roster when the team broke camp to start the new campaign. First mission achieved. Vander Meer impressed new manager Bill McKechnie sufficiently that the boss wanted to keep him around. McKechnie and some of his lieutenants had already devoted enough time to Vander Meer to demonstrate they read potential in his throws. Now he was going to get the chance to produce, to contribute more than he had in his brief fling with the big club in 1937 when he finished 3-5.

Coming off the last-place finish of 1937, there was a sense of optimism that things would be more exciting at Crosley Field this time around. It was very much cautious optimism, however. General manager Warren Giles was trying to lay a foundation. McKechnie was a fresh face as a decision-maker. But he really did not know what he had, if he had enough material at his disposal to catch some of the other National League teams in the standings. Vander Meer had to come through for the sake of his own career, but also for the team. This time around his left arm was going to be important to overall team standing.

As a nod to Cincinnati being the birthplace of professional baseball, dating back to 1869 with the Cincinnati Red Stockings, for decades the Reds, or the Redlegs as they were periodically called, received the honor of opening the new Major League season. For a time it was the Reds on one day and everyone else on the next. No one does opening day better than Cincinnati, even today when the team itself is no longer promised the exclusivity of opening first. Cincinnati throws a parade and missing school for children is an excused absence. No sports fan is happier in Cincinnati than when the Reds are doing well.

In 1938, opening day was April 19 at Crosley and attendance was 34,148, about as many people as could fit inside. The Reds lost, 8-7, to the

Chicago Cubs despite taking an early lead. Three Reds players, Ernie Lombardi, left-fielder Dusty Cooke and shortstop Billy Myers cracked three hits each and Frank McCormick had two. The team had 14 hits, but it still wasn't enough for the win. Gene Schott, who had taken a battering in 1937, started and gave up five runs.

Three days later, Vander Meer got the ball to face the Pittsburgh Pirates. It did not go well. He lasted three innings, allowed five earned runs, and Cincinnati lost, 7-4. On May 2, Vander Meer got another crack at Pittsburgh and gained his first victory of the season, although it would not have stood out in a beauty pageant. He threw eight innings and gave up six runs, four earned, in the 8-6 decision. On May 8, Vander Meer was much sharper, allowing two runs in a complete game versus the Philadelphia Phillies. Only he lost, 2-0. The Phils winner was Bucky Walters hurling the shutout, but soon to become a Reds teammate. Twelve days later, Vander Meer picked up another win, this time with a very fine effort, a five-hit shutout of the New York Giants with nine strikeouts. That win pushed the Reds record to 14-13, over .500.

Vander Meer found a rhythm. He beat the St. Louis Cardinals 2-1 and Brooklyn 4-1, and the Giants again 4-1. Vander Meer was very impressive that day. He allowed just three hits and the one earned run to a good New York team that was 10 games over .500 at the time. National League hitters were flailing at his fastball. After his somewhat wobbly start, when Vander Meer was assigned to take the mound for a June 11 afternoon game at Crosley, he was 5-2.

At this point in his baseball career, Vander Meer was enjoying his first sustained success in the majors, at 23 years old, though he looked younger. His light-colored wavy hair and broad smile stood out in a photograph and almost looked like a Hollywood still photo passed out to movie fans. He definitely felt he belonged in the Reds rotation and the team's faith in his ability was growing by the week. Vander Meer had no way of predicting that when he awoke on that mid–June day, he was about to experience one of the greatest days of his baseball life.

Ironically, general manager Warren Giles did predict it, kind of, sort of. When he came to work that day, he told assistant GM Frank Lane about a dream he had. "I slept restlessly last night," Giles said. "I was dreaming of Vander Meer pitching a no-hitter."[1] Hah, hah. The Reds had not played for three days and brought a 23-20 record into the scheduled 2:30 p.m. start against the Boston Bees, alias the Braves, McKechnie's former team. Boston was 21-19. The most disappointing thing about the day is how many Cincinnati residents stayed home. Attendance was a puny 5,814. That meant in the coming days another 30,000 fans could wistfully say they wished they had been there. It was sunny out, the temperature was neither hot nor cold, nor

## 6. Vander Meer Pitches a No-Hitter

was there a threat of rain in the sky. So meteorologically speaking, they had no excuses.

Righty Danny MacFayden was Boston's starting pitcher. MacFayden was a durable veteran who spent 17 years in the majors and won 132 games, six times winning 10 or more games in a season. But although he won as many as 17 one year, he was never really an ace and lost 159 games in his career. He was about to be a supporting actor in an unfolding drama as Vander Meer accelerated his own status into being the ace of spades, at least temporarily.

Vander Meer showed good stuff from the first inning on. Right-fielder Gene Moore led off for the visitors by grounding out, third-to-first—or from Lew Riggs to Frank McCormick. Johnny Cooney, who played both first base and right for the Bees in this game, popped out to first base. Vander Meer finished off the inning by striking out Vince DiMaggio, Boston's center-fielder, and the oldest, but least-likely-to-hit of the three big-league DiMaggio brothers.

Besides Vander Meer, this was Cincinnati's lineup and batting order for the game: Lonny Frey at second, Wally Berger in left, Ival Goodman playing right, first-baseman McCormick hitting cleanup, Ernie Lombardi,

**Johnny Vander Meer (right) stands with young Bob Feller.**

the esteemed catcher, hitting fifth, Harry Craft in center, Riggs at third, Myers at short and then Vander Meer hitting ninth. Berger had just played against Vander Meer in that three-hit win over the Giants and Giles had traded for him over the few days in-between Vander Meer's starts. So now he was on his side.

Of those nine players, Lombardi would become a Hall of Famer, Berger would be the answer to the rookie-home-run record trivia question for decades, Craft would have a solid career in baseball management, McCormick would forever be a renowned member of the Reds franchise and Vander Meer was destined to become a name always on the lips of baseball historians. The others, Frey, Goodman, and Riggs are not so well-remembered.

MacFayden handled the bottom of the first peacefully. Frey lined out to left, Berger flew out to right and Goodman did the same. MacFayden had not kept the ball in the infield, but there was no real danger of it soaring out of sight, either. The next three hitters for the Bees, second baseman Tony Cuccinello, left-fielder Bobby Reis and third baseman Gil English, all connected with Vander Meer offerings for line-drive outs. English's swat was backed by more power than the others and Craft had to hustle to grab it. Craft spent his entire big-league playing career, 1937-1942, patrolling wide-open spaces for the Reds. He was known for his slick fielding years before he made his mark as a manager, including being the expansion Houston team's first manager in the early 1960s. So that was a quick Boston second inning. In the home half, McCormick led off with a single to right, but Lombardi, his slow-moving feet possibly coming into play here, hit into a double play. Craft made the third out.

The top of the third inning sped by for Vander Meer. Bees catcher Johnny Riddle popped out to short. Shortstop Rabbit Wartsler, a much less famous Rabbit playing the position than Maranville, struck out. Then pitcher MacFayden grounded out, second to first. Vander Meer had rolled through the Bees order without a base runner. Someone once asked Vander Meer if he ever let the thought of throwing a no-hitter intrude on his mind after he got off to a strong start like this one, but he said no, it would be too mentally sapping and distracting. He would never think that way until much later in a game.

While it would have been soothing if the Reds buttressed Vander Meer's sharp pitching with some hitting of their own, MacFayden was keeping Cincinnati bats under control, too. Riggs grounded out to lead off the Reds third. Myers struck out. So there were already two outs by the time Vander Meer came to the plate. He ended up being the one stroking a nice single to left. But since Frey hit a fly out to left, Vander Meer's swing started no rally. The score was 0-0 after three.

## 6. Vander Meer Pitches a No-Hitter

Vander Meer had his first uh-oh moment of the game in the top of the fourth. Moore led off with a walk for Boston, the Bees' first base-runner of the game. In the past, those bases on balls had been a major under-the-skin irritant for Vander Meer. This was not the time for a repeat annoyance, and this was not the old Johnny. Vander Meer promptly induced a double play, though it was not a simple one. Cooney hit a foul ball popup snared by Lombardi, who alertly fired to first to double Moore off the base. Then DiMaggio grounded out. While Berger was always best-recalled for his early-career home runs, in the bottom of the fourth he reached MacFayden for a triple to left. Cincinnati had a man in scoring position with no outs. Time to help Johnny. Goodman was up next.

Goodman did not break into the majors until 1935 when he was 26. It took time for him to accommodate to the level of professional pitching. His breakthrough came in Rochester in 1934, but before that he seemed more baffled than effective with the bat. "Couldn't hit the size of my hat," he said. "But base hits were not so elusive when I did get going."[2] He would have been a more likely candidate to triple than Berger since Goodman twice led the National League in those hits. In a 10-year career despite his late start, Goodman batted .281. He also made two All-Star teams for the Reds and in 1938 while batting .292 he collected single-season highs in home runs and runs batted in. Goodman sent a MacFayden pitch deep to left, scoring Berger with a sacrifice fly. After that, with the bases empty again, McCormick grounded out, Lombardi singled, but Craft grounded out. Still, Cincinnati had a 1-0 lead.

Vander Meer himself made things nerve-wracking for everyone in the top of the fifth by walking Cuccinello and English, but wrapped around Reis flying out, Riddle grounding out, was Cuccinello being careless. Once again Lombardi's fielding prowess contributed. Cuccinello took a large lead off first and Lombardi's gun of an arm picked him off. Riggs shook up MacFayden by leading off the bottom of the fifth with a triple. Originally from North Carolina, Riggs spent one year with the Cardinals at the beginning of his Major League career and was in the middle of a six-year stint with the Reds in 1938. He had made something of a reputation for himself being chosen for the 1936 All-Star game. Generally, he was more of a reliable fielder than a sterling hitter.

After that, though, MacFayden pitched as if he was insulted by Riggs' hit, striking out Myers, getting Vander Meer on a ground ball, and striking out Frey. The Reds were not giving McFayden much of a hassle this day, either. Nor did Vander Meer seem to be weakening in the Bees' sixth. It was a 1-2-3 showing, Vander Meer easily setting down Warstler, MacFayden, and Elbie Fletcher at first base. Six innings into the contest, it was officially a pitcher's duel.

Berger led off Cincinnati's sixth with a walk. In a game when every base runner seemed precious this charged up the Reds dugout. Goodman frustratingly went down on a foul pop to first base. McCormick lined out to right. Would Berger's walk be wasted? No. It was Lombardi with the star turn once again. He ripped a MacFayden pitch out of the park and Berger scored ahead of him. That made the score 3-0 Cincinnati and gave Vander Meer some exhaling room.

Once again Vander Meer quickly retired the side in the top of the seventh inning, culminating in a caught-looking strikeout of Cuccinello after he had coaxed Cooney and DiMaggio into back-to-back fly outs. Vander Meer was now reaching the point in the game by which pitchers, players, and fans would start to legitimately think they might witness a no-hitter. The Reds made no dent in expanding the lead in the bottom of the seventh, MacFayden handcuffing Myers, Vander Meer and Frey at the plate without a significant challenge. While the Reds seemed in command, the 3-0 lead was by no means insurmountable, and the Bees took their batting turn in the eighth with every thought of catching up and winning, not just breaking up Vander Meer's no-hitter. Nothing doing. Three straight hitters easily retired.

In the bottom of the eighth, the Reds would have loved to provide a larger cushion for Vander Meer, but the still-in-there pitching MacFayden discouraged such a suggestion by making just one mistake, hitting Goodman with a pitch. Otherwise, he got easy outs. That set up the top of the ninth inning, Vander Meer poised for a win, a shutout, and a no-hitter, though Boston was going to try and make it as difficult as possible to achieve.

The Bees' manager was Casey Stengel, who had succeeded McKechnie. Stengel was a solid player in his day, and in the early stages of what would be a Hall of Fame managing career with Brooklyn, Boston, and famously with the New York Yankees (where he won 10 pennants in 12 years) and infamously with the New York Mets, where he presided over one of the worst teams in baseball history. Even Vander Meer said Stengel repeatedly shouted at him during the late innings attempting to distract him, but then afterwards told the pitcher Boston wasn't trying to beat him, but only put a hit on the board. For that matter, Vander Meer said he didn't realize he had a no-hitter underway until the seventh inning when Stengel and his coaches, George Kelly and Mike Kelley, began trash talking.

In any case, Stengel certainly played out the ninth inning in a manner suggesting the Bees were still after victory. Rabbit Warstler was due to lead off for Boston. Stengel sent in Bob Kahle as a pinch-hitter. The right-handed hitting Kahle was 22 and in his only brief, big-league season. He appeared in eight games—only as a pinch-hitter or pinch-runner—and collected three hits in eight tries for a .333 average. This was not one of those times he produced a hit, grounding out to first with Vander Meer covering.

Next due up was MacFayden. Stengel called for another pinch-hitter, Harl Maggert. Maggert was the son of a former big-leaguer of the same name, but like Kahle, his own Major League appearances were all confined to 1938 with the Bees. He played more than Kahle, showing up in 66 games, and batting .281 with three homers. None of those homers were recorded this day, either. Vander Meer struck him out.

With two outs, Boston was down to Elbie Fletcher. Stengel decided to let it come down to somebody else and inserted a third straight pinch-hitter, a more experienced Ray Mueller. Mueller had a 14-year Major League career and one season, several years later, made an All-Star team for the Reds. He was Vander Meer's last obstacle of this day. Mueller hit a ground ball at Riggs on third. Riggs fielded the ball cleanly, threw the ball across the diamond to McCormick, and it was over. Johnny Vander Meer had pitched a no-hitter. As an illustration of the rarity of a no-hitter being hurled by any pitcher on a team, it was the first since 1919 when Hod Eller completed the task.

"Gee, I had no idea of pitching a no-hitter," Vander Meer said after the game. "My arm felt better as I went along. I just kept pouring 'em in. My arm seemed to become stronger as the game went along. I had excellent control of my curve in the final four rounds, which made my fastball doubly effective. I put everything I had on every pitch in the ninth against pinch-hitters Kahle, Maggert and Mueller."[3]

Vander Meer said for good reason he did not expect to throw a no-hitter. No pitcher does. There are too many quirks to the sport, too many times off-beat little things affect the outcome. A ground ball that looks like a sure thing to be fielded can hit a pebble and bounce over a fielder's head, or hit him in the head. The wind can carry a seemingly easy-to-grab fly ball out of the reach of fielders. An exceptionally fast hitter, the anti–Ernie Lombardi, can drop down a bunt and beat it out. Not only must the pitcher be on with his throws, he must have a little bit of good luck, that on his day fate will not deny him, and neither will the skill of big-leaguers coming to bat.

Jim Bunning, a Hall of Fame pitcher who later became a United States Senator from Kentucky, tossed a no-hitter for the Detroit Tigers and a perfect game for the Philadelphia Phillies. He once said, "A no-hitter is a freaky thing. You can't plan it. It's not something you try to do. It just happens. Everything has to come together all on the same day, good control, outstanding plays from your teammates, a whole lot of good fortune on your side, and a lot of bad things for the other guys."[4]

Of course, the pitcher can influence the bad things happening for the other guys. On the day he no-hit the Bees, Vander Meer walked three batters and struck out four. It was his fifth win in a row, so he was already in a good groove, and Boston just could not get good wood on his throws. "I was lucky," Vander Meer said of his achievement in keeping with Bunning's opinion not uttered until many years later. He classified Stengel's and the coaches' comments as "kidding" and added, "I didn't think anything about it then. All I was interested in was a winner, and I was quite certain of that, especially after Lombardi hit that two-run homer in the sixth."[5]

Throwing a no-hitter was a great moment for Johnny Vander Meer, raising his record to 6-2, yes, but also giving him more confidence that he had won himself a job with the Reds and that his arm could best others' bats. His next scheduled start was June 15. Vander Meer had four days to enjoy his big game, but then he had to put it in the rearview mirror as the season ground on. Maybe he could revisit the Boston victory after the season and savor it a little bit more. But his next assignment was to beat Brooklyn at Ebbets Field.

Before the game, Vander Meer bumped into Babe Ruth. The great slugger was three years into retirement with his seemingly unbreakable mark of 714 home runs. Since Ruth always had trouble matching names and faces, the fact that he recognized Vander Meer as being the guy who just pitched the no-hitter, was praise in itself. Vander Meer said Ruth told him, "Nice going, kid" and he was pleased the most famous man in baseball provided the comment.[6]

It was going to be a special night at the ballpark with Brooklyn, not because anyone thought they were going to observe a second straight no-hitter from Vander Meer, but because the game marked the introduction of lights for the team's first home night game. That's why Ruth was there, as a featured attraction as part of the festivities. The whole thing was Larry MacPhail's idea, the same person who presided over the first Major League night game ever when he was running the Reds. In the Bible's book of Genesis, the phrase "Let there be light" is part of the creation message right after the part about God establishing the heaven and the earth. Larry MacPhail got to say it twice.

# 7

# Vander Meer Pitches a No-Hitter—Another One

Johnny Vander Meer's first no-hitter was a memorable occasion, a cool accomplishment for him, a nice milestone for the Cincinnati Reds. Vander Meer's second no-hitter in a row rearranged the universe. Two straight no-hitters? Unprecedented and unbelievable. Astonishing and astounding. Someone could have gone on a camping trip or hunting excursion into the wilds and not heard any news for a week, only to return home and be asked by a friend if he had heard about that Reds no-hitter. The individual might say, sure, by that young left-handed kid, right? Wrong. The OTHER one. What do you mean? What other one?

In less than a week's time, Vander Meer transformed from a slightly known Major League ball player to the sensation of the moment, from a rookie scrapping for job security to a nationally publicized figure. In 1938, there were more limits on celebrityhood than there are in 2020. Newspapers were the primary source of information. Radio did its thing and television was just starting but not yet much of an impact. This was far before the start-up of the internet where anyone from Timbuktu to Bosnia can access scores with a few clicks.

If anyone who accompanied Vander Meer to the park that night suggested he was going to pitch another no-hitter he never spoke up. Presumably, Warren Giles did not have another dream, either. Even the ether zone of his subconscious probably had its limits. However, a sportswriter at Vander Meer's hometown New Jersey newspaper, the *Paterson Morning Call*, seemingly acting as a salesman for the Brooklyn game, did enter the realm of the crystal ball with his own quasi-reckless take: "Watch Johnny Vander Meer repeat his no-hit, no-run game. And don't be surprised if he does it tomorrow night at Brooklyn to reward his Midland Park and local fans, who will give him a 'day,' along with a number of gifts."[1] The main question after that spiel was whether or not the writer played the lottery.

Vander Meer, being young, foolish and on a roll, however, did in giddy moments secretly imagine another nine innings of hitless pitching going up in a succession of zeroes on the scoreboard. Only afterwards, when the mini-miracle was in the books, when Vander Meer had raised his stature to a baseball god level, did he admit publicly what his silly mind and determination embraced when manager Bill McKechnie sent him to the mound. "I was trying for it all the way," Vander Meer said. "From the first batter on, I bore down. I tried to whip that ball past every one of 'em. No flies, no grounders, I wanted strikeouts."[2]

Aside from what might occur on the field, this was a lollapalooza of an event for baseball fans. Heralded as special for being the first night game in Ebbets Field history, the Brooklyn–Cincinnati showdown was scheduled to be more than just another game. Fans got caught up in the mood and 38,748 counted fans made it a sellout. Depending on which report of the time chronicled the situation, it was said that between 10,000 and 20,000 fans were turned away, unable to purchase $1.50 grandstand seats or 55-cent bleacher spots. Tickets for the game featured a picture of a light bulb in addition to the section and seat numbers. Apparently, it was the fire department that made the call when to seal the gates.

Besides the loyal local rooters attracted by the first night game, an estimated 500 people from Vander Meer's home of Midland, New Jersey, bought a block of seats because the game was so close by. They were so thrilled by the first no-hitter they had a special little ceremony to honor him for that feat, presenting him with a gold watch. Among the pro–Vander Meer contingent were his parents, girlfriend, brother and sister-in-law. What it must have been like to sit with that bunch during this game.

The night was party as much as ball game. Besides Babe Ruth, four-time Olympic gold medalist Jesse Owens was on hand. As were a marching band and American Legion drum and bugle corps. The pre-game celebration took time and a big production was made of turning on the lights. As he had argued in Cincinnati, MacPhail was a proponent of night baseball becoming the panacea of the working man and cited how grand it had been for the minor leagues. He was scheduling the league-maximum of seven night games and anticipated raking in an extra $100,000 in ticket receipts due to increased attendance.

There was no louder or stronger voice supporting night baseball and MacPhail bent enough owners to his will that ultimately everyone came along (except the Chicago Cubs for a long, long time). Once, MacPhail had lights turned on in his park at 3 a.m. to illuminate a game between sportswriters. In a 1959 interview, while there were still many adherents for the majority of games being played in the sunshine, MacPhail said that was the polar opposite of the wave of the future. "Day baseball is now dead for all

Johnny Vander Meer was a southpaw who electrified the baseball world with his double no-hitters in 1938.

practical purposes," he said. "Sooner or later, the game will be played in its entirety at night, and, as I've said before, then baseball will squarely be in the amusement, entertainment business along with wrestling, midget auto racing and the trotting tracks."[3] It was not clear what category this introductory night game fit into, but there was showmanship involved, and then something MacPhail, in his controlling wisdom, could not have planned, a historical baseball game breaking out.

By the time of the first pitch, following the fanfare, it was already 9:20 p.m. This time the Reds were the visiting team, so they led off the first inning with the aim of dampening the pleasure of Brooklyn's big night. The Dodgers' starter facing Vander Meer was Max Butcher. Butcher was a big right-hander at 6-foot-2 and 220 pounds. He had a workmanlike, 10-year career, though often punctuated by losing records. Lifetime he went 95-106 with his best seasons occurring after he escaped the Dodgers and threw for Pittsburgh in the early 1940s. His finest season was 1941 when he finished 17-12. The 1938 campaign was Butcher's third with Brooklyn, but before the end of the season he was suiting up for the Philadelphia Phillies. Combined, he went 9-12 that year.

Cincinnati had basically the same lineup that competed in the no-hitter of June 11. Lonny Frey was the lead-off man playing second, followed by Wally Berger in left, Ival Goodman in right, Frank McCormick at first, Ernie Lombardi catching, Harry Craft in center field, Lew Riggs at third base and Billy Myers at short. Vander Meer batted ninth. The Reds' record was 26-21 at that point in the season, better than most had expected.

The Dodgers were pretty much stumbling along at 20-28. That day Kiki Cuyler, only recently cut loose by the Reds, was batting lead-off and playing right field for Brooklyn in what would be the last season of his career at 39. Pete Coscarart was next in the order playing second base. Left-fielder Buddy Hassett hit third, Babe Phelps was catching, followed by third baseman Cookie Lavagetto and first baseman Dolph Camilli, center fielder Ernie Koy and shortstop Leo Durocher. The future Hall of Fame manager, who was always a better fielder than hitter, and a bigger talker than fielder, was nearing the sunset of his playing days, though he did make the National League All-Star team that year. Butcher was last in the batting order.

Frey was the game's first batter. He was in the midst of a 14-year Major League career that began with Brooklyn in 1933, though he had his best years for the Reds, three times being selected a National League All-Star. He was a typical middle infielder hitter, not smoking many homers, batting above .250, but manning short or second capably. He greeted Butcher with a lead-off single. It was nice for the Reds to think they could start the game with a rally, it did not happen, even after Goodman walked and gave Cincinnati men on first and second with one out. They did not advance closer to home.

Vander Meer, whom some called "Vandy" for short, made short work of the Dodgers' first three hitters, retiring the side on a flyball, strikeout and ground out, a smorgasbord of variety, if nothing else for Cuyler, Coscarart and Hassett.

## 7. Vander Meer Pitches a No-Hitter—Another One 47

The top of the second provided nothing for the Reds, Butcher easily sidelining Craft, Riggs and Myers. None of them came close to reaching. Vander Meer got two outs on Brooklyn before walking Camilli. Although he did not score, Koy making the next out, Camilli's method of getting on continued to illustrate Vander Meer's weakness, a tendency to give out too many free passes. Each time a pitcher walked a man, especially early in an inning, the runner had every chance of haunting him by scoring.

Everything changed in the Reds half of the third. After he initially looked OK, Butcher imploded. Vander Meer hit a grounder resulting in the first out. Frey didn't do any better, so Cincinnati already had two down. Butcher really should have been out of the inning after Berger hit a ground ball to third. But after Lavagetto scooped it up he threw wild to first for an error and Berger was able to take second. Goodman walked and it was men on first and second for Cincy. McCormick, who had been pretty much dormant at the plate in Vander Meer's Bees no-hitter, stepped in. Boom! McCormick smashed the ball out of the park for a three-run homer. Now Butcher was out of sorts. Lombardi walked, Craft singled to right, and Riggs scored Lombardi on another single, Craft steaming into third base. That made it 4-0 Reds and Butcher's night was over. Manager Burleigh Grimes sent him to the showers and brought in Tot Pressnell from the bullpen.

Pressnell was a 31-year-old rookie right-hander who won 11 games that year, but in a five-year, big-league stay won only 32 total. Myers was the Cincinnati hitter and Pressnell struck him out to halt the offensive rampage. The pleasant delay did nothing to interrupt Vander Meer's concentration in the bottom of the third. Cuyler worked him for another walk, but the other three men he faced made nondescript outs. Pressnell stayed in the game for Brooklyn and seemed comfortable on the mound in the top of the fourth. Vander Meer struck out and Frey grounded out. When Berger doubled to left, there were already two out. Goodman's routine second-to-first ground out did not bring Berger home. It was the Dodgers' turn in the bottom of the fourth and they had plenty of time to catch up, or even get a hit. They did not make progress on either front in that inning, Hassett, Phelps and Lavagetto making the outs with no base runners.

Continuing his good work in the fifth, Pressnell seemed on top of any batting tricks the Reds tried. After two straight ground outs, Craft worked Pressnell for a single to left. But with a misplaced sense of optimism, Craft kept going and was thrown out at second base trying to extend his safety. Vander Meer kept mowing down the Dodgers in their half of the inning, almost flippantly retiring the side on two ground outs and a foul pop to the catcher. Another no-sweat inning in the books without permitting a hit.

In the sixth, Cincinnati hoped to extend its lead. At 4-0, and the way Vander Meer was going, a win was looking pretty safe, but there is no such thing as a true safe margin in baseball. Riggs went down on a grounder to second and Myers struck out. Vander Meer was up with no one on, but he bunted anyway, and it went for a single. Frey gave it a shot with a fly to center, but it was caught and the score remained unchanged. Pressnell seemed to have the Reds' number. He had most assuredly put out the flames after Butcher departed.

Pressnell did nothing on the offensive side in the bottom of the sixth, though, when he came to the plate. He grounded out to third. Cuyler worked Vander Meer for another walk, apparently someone in the Dodgers' lineup that day more patient than the others. Did this spell trouble? Grimes may have suspected so. He pinch-hit Gibby Brack for Coscarart. Brack was another latecomer to the majors, making his debut with Brooklyn the year before at 29. Although he was a lifetime .279 hitter in three seasons, he was shipped to Philadelphia not long after this game. Striking out looking may not have been the impetus for the deal, but he missed his chance to break up Vander Meer's second no-hitter in this circumstance. A Hassett ground out and Vander Meer was out of the sixth.

Pressnell was still around for the top of the seventh and he induced a fly ball out from Berger to second base. But when he allowed a single to Goodman, Grimes replaced him with Luke Hamlin. Pressnell went 3⅔ innings, gave up four hits and one run, and slowed down the Reds' momentum. Hamlin threw right-handed and was usually a starter for Brooklyn. Although his record was only 12-15 that season, the next year was the greatest of his career. He went 20-13 at age 34 and led the NL in starts with 36.

Hamlin could not get out of the seventh unscathed in relief of Pressnell. He struck out McCormick, but Goodman stole second. Not wishing to allow Lombardi to do the kind of damage he was capable of, Grimes had Hamlin walk the big catcher intentionally. But the move failed when Craft singled, scoring Goodman. Hamlin got Riggs on a fly to end the inning, but the Reds lead was now up to 5-0.

Insurmountable? No. And maybe Vander Meer was tiring or feeling the pressure in the bottom of the seventh. Certainly, the Dodgers' turn at bat turned suspenseful. Phelps grounded out, but then Vander Meer walked Lavagetto and Camilli in a row. The young southpaw still had not given up a hit, but he was treading into dangerous territory. Two men on, one out. But then Vander Meer came through with a clutch strikeout of Koy and got Durocher on a grounder. Whew.

As the late innings began unfolding and Vander Meer held Brooklyn at bay, the home fans' devotion shifted gears. Rather than rooting for a middle-of-the-season, somewhat unimportant victory by their guys, the support began drifting to Vander Meer's favor. The spectators had chosen witnessing history over witnessing a routine win. Billy Myers opened the

## 7. Vander Meer Pitches a No-Hitter—Another One    49

top of the eighth inning with a surprise bunt for the Reds. Brooklyn third baseman Cookie Lavagetto got to it, but once he handled it, he committed an error on the throw to first. Safe. Vander Meer couldn't help himself in his at-bat, hitting a grounder that forced Myers at second. Frey struck out, so it seemed possible Hamlin was going to recover. But then came Berger with his big bat and he belted a triple to center. Vander Meer came around to score to make it 6-0. Goodman ended Cincinnati's at-bats with a strikeout.

In the bottom of the eighth, outs running out, if not time, Hamlin was lifted for a pinch-hitter. He went 1⅔ innings, allowed two hits and the one run, and it was unearned. Stepping into the batter's box was veteran Woody English. Once a reliable hitting shortstop for the Chicago Cubs, English came to Brooklyn the season before. He ended his 12-year Major League career at the conclusion of this 1938 season at 32 after appearing in just 34 games due to a steadily declining batting average. This was a sort of last hurrah in a big moment for English. He could not win the game with one swing, but he could break up a no-hitter. English struck out. Cuyler flew out. Johnny Hudson, who came in to play second base after Brack pinch-hit for Coscarart, also struck out. Vander Meer was looking as sharp as at any time through eight innings as the suspense built. The fewer the chances Brooklyn had left the louder their fans shouted for Vander Meer.

A new pitcher, Vito Tamulis, faced the Reds in the top of the ninth inning. Tamulis, who pitched a couple of years for the New York Yankees at the start of his career, had his best big-league stretch this year, going 12-6 for the Dodgers after an unhappy 0-3 intermediate stop with the St. Louis Browns. He showed well in the Reds' half of the ninth, setting down McCormick, Lombardi and Craft in order.

Vander Meer had to face a minimum of three more Dodgers as the hysteria and drama built around him. He was one inning from immortality, but many pitchers over the decades took no-hitters into the bottom of the ninth and lost them. If there was any easing of pressure at all it could be attributed to Cincinnati's six-run lead. Buddy Hassett was leading off. This was the third of a four-year stretch at the start of his career that Hassett was a .300 hitter. There was no reason to pinch-hit for him. In the midst of the growing hubbub, Hassett took a swing at the plate—and grounded the ball back to Vander Meer on the mound.

Then temporary insanity took over Ebbets Field. Vander Meer reverted to Bad Johnny and walked Babe Phelps. Phelps, whose given name was Ernest Gordon Phelps, may have shared a nickname with Babe Ruth, but was no power hitter, averaging five home runs a season over his 11-year career. But he was a fine hitter, who also finished with a .310 lifetime average. Vander Meer walked him. Lavagetto, who may have felt a desire to atone for some of his sloppy fielding, also waited Vander Meer out for a walk. Grimes pinch-ran Goody Rosen for Phelps, but the Dodgers had runners on first and second, one out.

Stunningly, Vander Meer then walked Dolph Camilli to load the bases. This was almost too much. Did he have an attack of nerves? Or was Vander Meer picking the worst time ever to display his periodic penchant for wildness? McKechnie called time and made a visit to the mound to talk. There was no way McKechnie was going to take Vander Meer out of the game given his pitcher was on the cusp of doing something never seen before. But McKechnie did have Bucky Walters warming up in the bullpen in case of extreme emergency. Not knowing what to expect, many fans yelled at McKechnie, "Don't take him out!"[4] The manager did feel a soothing chat might help and Vander Meer did not mind the quickie pep talk. "I was rattled in the ninth with the bases full," Vander Meer said. "Bill McKechnie ran out, slapped my back, and said, 'Hell, kid, they're more scared of that ball than you are. Pour it in there!'"[5]

Ernie Koy came to the plate attempting to end the no-hitter and drive in some Dodger runs. Koy was as much football as baseball player when he was younger, playing fullback for the University of Texas. He turned down the chance to play pro football with the National Football League's Brooklyn Dodgers, the name, of course borrowed from the popular baseball team. Although Koy chose baseball over football, sons Ernie Jr., and Ted, both won football national championships at his alma mater and both played professional football. The elder Koy signed with the Yankees and was mired in their farm system because there was too much talent ahead of him on the big-league roster. He was a 28-year-old rookie with these Dodgers instead in 1938 and did well, batting .299, with 11 home runs, 76 runs batted in and 15 stolen bases.

What followed was probably the messiest play of the game. There was a single out, with bases jammed, when Koy, who had sprinter's speed (he said he ran the 100-yard dash in 9.5 seconds), smashed a hard-hit ball at the Reds' Lew Riggs covering third. "I came up in the ninth inning after Vander Meer had walked the bases full," Koy recalled years later. "There was one out and I hit a line drive to third base. Lew Riggs booted the ball, knocked it down, and then threw home for the force out."[6]

Riggs somehow prevented the run. Koy was safe at first, Camilli went to second and Lavagetto made it to third. But Lombardi put the all-important tag on pinch-runner Rosen. After all of that, Vander Meer still wasn't out of it. The bases were still loaded and he needed one more out. Before everyone in the building had a heart attack, Vander Meer cajoled Leo Durocher into hitting a safe fly ball to Craft in center field, who (finally) tucked it away for the last out of the ordeal.

And the crowd went crazy cheering a visiting player. Vander Meer's teammates mobbed him. Everyone knew on the spot they had seen a once-in-a-lifetime baseball accomplishment—at least one that rare. In the locker room, fellow Reds pitcher Paul Derringer teased Vander Meer, saying, "You sure are making it tough for us pitchers."[7] In recognition both of his heritage and his new achievement, Vander Meer was almost immediately named the "Dutch Master."

In the clubhouse after the game, Vander Meer admitted to exhaustion, though it might well have been mental fatigue from all the pressure, more than physical weariness. After two consecutive no-hitters, Vander Meer, who did walk an unsightly eight Dodgers to accompany his seven strikeouts, said he actually had better stuff in that 4-1 win over the Giants earlier in the month than in either of his no-hitters. "They got a lucky hit off me in the ninth," he said of that game against New York. "I was afraid the Dodgers would get lucky, too. Now I realize I was lucky. With all that wood swinging up there, you never know when a fellow is going to slice a peanut hit off you, or scalp the top of a ball for a (crappy) dribbler."[8] Looking into the future, shades of Jim Bunning.

Home plate umpire Bill Stewart, who called the balls and strikes in Vander Meer's shutout win, said baseball observers should remember the importance catcher Ernie Lombardi played in signaling for pitches in both no-hitters. "Give some credit to Lombardi," Stewart said. "Sure, Vander Meer had to pitch perfectly to get his no-hitter, but what about the guy who told the kid what to pitch? If Lombardi had guessed wrong on one hitter, if he had called for a fastball when a curve was the smart pitch, Vander Meer never would've made it. Lombardi's judgment was just as perfect and just as important as Vander Meer's pitches."[9] Stewart was on the right track in McKechnie's mind. He also praised Lombardi, who had gained more and more encomiums for his fielding as time passed. "Sure, he was great," McKechnie said of Vander Meer. "But it seems like everybody forgets that Ernie Lombardi had to catch two perfect games if Vander Meer was going to pitch them."[10]

Only a few months earlier, Vander Meer was an unknown quantity in spring training. Suddenly, he was the toast of the sport, an object of as much attention as the president of the United States, or the most famous Hollywood personage. Anyone who followed baseball understood how remarkable was what Vander Meer achieved. McKechnie, who had been around the majors since 1907, most certainly realized the spectacular uniqueness of the back-to-back no-hitters. "I cannot tell you how Johnny happened to be so good in those two games," said McKechnie of a pupil who was taking extra pitching lessons in Tampa. "It's beyond me and probably no one will know the answer. But I can say he's a fine pitcher and has the stuff."[11]

No one had more fun with Vander Meer's startling second consecutive no-hitter than the newspaper sportswriters assigned to write about the game. They were as much caught off guard by the historic moment as everyone else, but they had to live up to the occasion with their words. One writer led off his game story this way: "Miracles do happen."[12] It was a similar thought as the one expressed by sportscaster Al Michaels during the closing seconds of the United States hockey victory over the Soviet Union at the Winter Olympics in Lake Placid in 1980 when he said, "Do you believe in miracles?"

The writer continued his observation with this: "Events beyond all credulity are yet to be seen, Johnny Vander Meer, 23-year-old Cincinnati southpaw, has pitched two successive no-hit, no-run ball games, an achievement without parallel, and never to be exceeded until there is improvement upon perfection."[13] Never before, never again, immediately noted on deadline, a clarity of thought announcing it was beyond the ken that any pitcher would ever throw three no-hitters in a row. "In the 99-year history of baseball," continued the writer who suggested the fans inside Ebbets were "hysterical psychopaths" on game night, "there have been 115 no-hit, no-run games pitched by 105 men in the major leagues."[14] Only a few, it was noted, ever pitched two or more. That was before Nolan Ryan, Sandy Koufax and Bob Feller came along, though. As of 2020, and after 143 baseball seasons between 1876 and 2019, there have been 303 no-hitters. No one except Vander Meer has ever thrown two in consecutive starts, never mind (as the writer on the scene realized) thrown three in a row. Another publication called Vander Meer's double no-hit performance "a Meeracle."

All of those extra-large headlines and fancy descriptions would not be read until the next morning. However, upstairs in Ebbets Field, in a scene witnessed by only a few people, Dodgers chief operative Larry MacPhail, he of the bold innovations and outrageous temper, was throwing a fit. The future public chronicler of the outburst could not understand why. It was obvious the night baseball introduction was a huge success and the game itself, while not going the Dodgers' way, was producing one of the greatest results in baseball history. Rather than paying any attention to the game and its soon-to-be fabulous denouement, MacPhail was screaming at a bartender to get him an outside long-distance phone line so he could call someone in Zanesville, Ohio. MacPhail was hot on the trail of an individual named Ducky Holmes. This was a cockamamie story all-around. MacPhail was known for his tantrums, but this one didn't add up. The tale was being relayed by Harold Parrot, a long-time public relations official for the Dodgers, and one-time baseball writer.

Eventually, Parrot dragged the reason for MacPhail's meltdown out of him. He claimed this is what MacPhail said: "I found out today that four

## 7. Vander Meer Pitches a No-Hitter—Another One

years ago that son of a bitch (Holmes) released Vander Meer outright. Without permission, too. Except for that fathead, Vandy would still be a Dodger, and the whole show would have been ours tonight."[15] Vander Meer had signed with the Dodgers in 1933 and was sent to the Dayton Ducks, and not by Holmes. It was said Vander Meer was sold to the Boston Bees' Scranton team, though he later said he was declared a free agent. The obstacle of gaining a clear phone line aside, MacPhail would have had a great deal of trouble reaching Holmes on the phone at all to yell at him. Holmes died in 1932. Who knows if MacPhail ever figured that out when he calmed down?

Vander Meer was still hanging around the clubhouse long after MacPhail abandoned his quest and fans departed their seats. Sportswriters kept him talking. Plus, he was informed there was a crowd of fans in the streets waiting to surround him if he stepped outside too soon. One intriguing subject came up. Did Vander Meer have it easier, a better chance to throw a no-hitter, because the game was played at night under artificial light? These were newfangled lights in the 1930s, still comparatively experimental versus the more sophisticated ones in latter decades when someone could read fine print under them because they were so bright. "It was tough hitting against him," Lavagetto said sometime later. "It's always tough hitting against a fastballer under the lights. And the lights were new to us then. But Vander Meer was good enough that game to pitch a no-hitter under any conditions."[16]

Vander Meer accommodated all comers with their questions that night, lounging around soaking up the adulation, including his thoughts about the lights. "This was a tougher game than the one I pitched against the Bees," he said. "So I guess those lights really didn't make any difference as far as I was concerned. I only walked three against Boston in the daytime. I walked eight tonight, didn't I? I knew I had this no-hitter right from the start. I think that's what got me in trouble in the ninth. I was bearing down, trying to get those guys out." McKechnie's mound visit "relieved the tension."[17]

The single most astounding thing Vander Meer said in his post-game recitations was that during the game he had no idea that a second straight no-hitter would have been a singular achievement. Really. There were millions of baseball fans around the country who knew what Vander Meer was attempting to do, and probably almost all of the 38,000-plus ticket-holders in Ebbets Field, as well as his managers and coaches and probably all of his Reds teammates. "If I'd known it had never been done before," Vander Meer said, "it would have put more heat on me."[18] Well, yeah. Instead, he entered the Cincinnati locker room afterwards still oblivious, only aware he had pitched a second no-hitter that season, not that back-to-back no-hitters were unprecedented.

When Vander Meer at last departed the stadium, he still had no idea what manner of celebrityhood he had unleashed across the country. There was a day off scheduled for June 16. So when Vander Meer awoke the morning after the second no-hitter, he indulged in his favorite hobby. He went fishing. That was a brief respite. Suddenly, Johnny Vander Meer was so famous he couldn't duck the attention.

# 8

# Aftermath

When Johnny Vander Meer left Ebbets Field late on the night of his second straight no-hitter—actually, technically early in the morning of June 16 since the game did not end until about midnight—he almost surely thought the events were behind him and his next move was to prepare for his following Reds start in a few days. He never would have imagined that the accomplishment he so casually realized was so distinctive it would be appended to his name for the rest of his life. Forevermore, Vander Meer would be known as that guy who pitched two no-hitters in a row.

The attention ebbed and flowed for decades, but it never completely vanished. And it had barely subsided after a night's quiet. The next day, telephone calls flooded the offices of the Cincinnati Reds baseball team, mostly not merely to congratulate Vander Meer, but to make offers to hire him. He was a pitching man, but people wanted him to become a pitchman. He was being sought to pitch products, to not only lend his name to the Reds lineup, but to sign fresh contracts with corporations to endorse one thing or another. Suddenly, organizations that had not known his name earlier in the week, wanted to hitch their wagons to Vander Meer's shooting star. Even people who had known him his entire life wanted to become more closely associated with him, hoping his fame would rub off on them.

Vander Meer's home town of Midland Park, New Jersey, had turned out in force to see him pitch against the Dodgers, some 500 strong, and the proud patrons had already given him a gold watch to commemorate his first no-hitter at a time when there hadn't been a second no-hitter. Some town fathers, beaming with pride alongside his real father, likely thought, "How do we top that?" After all, somehow Johnny had topped that, his initial no-hitter, by doubling down.

Members of the sporting press descended on Midland Park, not only looking for Johnny, but intending to probe the hearts and minds of residents who knew him before to ask what made him tick. This is when they learned Vander Meer had gone fishing on some remote body of water with a friend named Orie Yonker. On just a few hours sleep, rising at 4 a.m.,

Vander Meer had slipped away to parts unknown, or at least unrevealed by family members. Big news could be had by sticking around anyway. Community officials were so taken by Vander Meer's fabulous pitching that giddy in the flush of the moment they were proposing changing the name of the town from Midland Park to Vander Meer, New Jersey. While a grand idea in the end this courtesy was never extended. Not that it would have been beyond the bounds of the possible since there is a Jim Thorpe, Pennsylvania, and he wasn't even from there.

It should be noted that some sportswriters were declaring the young Vander Meer, still in the early stages of his baseball career, had earned himself a rocket ship ride directly into the Hall of Fame. In 1938, the Hall of Fame existed on paper. The first stars had been elected, but the hall itself did not open until 1939 when Cooperstown, New York, beckoned with the first induction ceremony. There was no doubt Vander Meer had recorded a Hall of Fame achievement, but in its embryonic stages of existence, some writers may not have yet been clear on what the structure's entrance requirements were, or would become.

In Midland Park, applying discretion in dealing with the hordes of inquirers, Vander Meer's family provided some cautious answers about their boy, but then they also tired of the scene. Before that, Jacob, Johnny's father, showed off a piece of memorabilia he treasured, a declaration by *The Sporting News* calling his son "Baseball's No. 1 man of the year in the minor leagues."[1]

It took note of Vander Meer's 19-6 mark with 295 strikeouts for the Durham Bulls before the Reds were smart enough to bring him to the big leagues. The just-in-time scribe may have been the last one to pump Vander Meer's family for background information, "I'm very proud of him," his father said. "As long as he behaves himself, it's OK. If he didn't, I wouldn't care if he never pitched another game. I like to see Johnny get ahead, but I don't want to give you any story. Johnny does his own talking. And besides, it's almost 12 o'clock and I haven't fed the chickens."[2]

Attempts to interview the mother of Vander Meer's Kathy were less fruitful. Kathy seemed quite suspicious of the media, even way back then. "I'm the happiest woman in Midland Park, and maybe the world, too," she said. "But all I want to do is get away from you fellows. You make me nervous." Which would be the second time within about 12 hours she felt that way, saying the suspense of her son loading the bases was nerve-wracking. "In that ninth inning, I was shivering."[3]

Once the rest of the family scrammed, there was nobody left around Midland Park named Vander Meer to discuss the young phenom. So reporters unearthed his girlfriend, or "sweetheart" or "best girl," as they called Lois Stewart (who became Mrs. Vander Meer in a marriage of 50 years), to discover more about Johnny's psyche. "I've only seen Johnny pitch twice," said Stewart, who was in attendance at Ebbets Field. "It was wonderful to watch. I was very proud."[4]

A different New York newspaper got hold of a photo of Vander Meer with Stewart and ran that, although neither Stewart, nor any other Vander Meers were talking in the accompanying story. Instead, it focused on how Vander Meer almost was exiled by the Reds in 1937. Before all of the teacher-student help, there was some doubt the oddly-throwing, often-wild Vander Meer could make the cut.

The lead portion of one article read, "Johnny Vander Meer, the Dutch windmill, who is now valued at half a million dollars, was almost let go by the Cincinnati Reds last season because they didn't think he was worth the last installment of $7,500 on his purchase price. But Warren Giles, the Reds' business manager, gambled and the handsome lefty from Midland Park, New Jersey, paid off at 20-to-1 by pitching two consecutive no-hit, no-run games."[5]

The mention of a $500,000 price tag following Vander Meer's two memorable games, seemingly came out of nowhere. It was not likely bidders from other teams showed up on Giles' doorstep to make such an offer, and in 1938, no player would make a salary one-tenth as high. But then Giles got to talking. Discussion of Vander Meer's worth upon acquisition was explained by Giles, who said the Reds got him for $17,500 and another player. Giles did admit that Vander Meer's 3-5 record of 1937 was not particularly encouraging. "Last season, Johnny didn't look so good," Giles said. "He was wild. He couldn't get the ball over. He had a bad spring season. We had to make another payment of $7,500 on him. I debated whether we should make the last payment on him or let him go. I had to pay that $7,500 by April 15, or lose him. I didn't make my mind up until the last minute."[6]

Vander Meer might soon bring in huge sums of money in ticket sales whenever he pitched after establishing his name in such a manner, but Giles employed a different kind of math, calculating his theory based on the sale of star pitcher Dizzy Dean from the St. Louis Cardinals to the Chicago Cubs. "Now he is worth a half a million dollars when you figure that the Cubs paid $185,000 for Dean," Giles said. "Anyway, I wouldn't take any price for him. He is priceless."[7]

After following up his praise of Ernie Lombardi's pitch-calling with more praise of Lombardi's pitch-calling, manager Bill McKechnie, a bit stunned by Vander Meer's sudden emergence, said he lay awake in bed for quite a while after the second no-hitter. He searched his memory to think of a pitcher from the past to compare Vander Meer with. McKechnie said he was "trying to remember what old-time great pitcher he reminded me of. Remember, all of the truly greats were mighty big guys. Johnny hasn't the long arms of those fellows. His motion, however, reminds me greatly of Watson Clark, the old Brooklyn left-hander."[8] Who? Clark was a southpaw with dimensions of 6'1" and 175 pounds versus southpaw Vander Meer's 6'1", 190. Clark spent 12 seasons in the majors between 1924 and 1937 with a record of 111-97 with one 20-win season, but he was not a strikeout pitcher. He didn't walk many, either.

Although it wasn't clear how much of a compliment it was to be compared to "Watty" Clark, McKechnie didn't go off the deep end and compare Vander Meer to Cy Young or Walter Johnson just yet. Only a day had passed, but when Lew Riggs, Reds third baseman was asked about Vander Meer, he stated that success had not changed Vander Meer. "He's a fine kid," Riggs said. "We all feel the same about it. He hasn't a big head—and this thing hasn't changed him."[9]

President Franklin D. Roosevelt sent a letter of congratulations. Speaking of presidents, someone suggested the 1887 statue of President James Garfield in Washington, D.C., should be replaced by a statue of Vander Meer. Tampa, the spring training home of the Reds, named Vander Meer honorary mayor temporarily. Overnight, as word spread, and Vander Meer took off on his fishing trip with a state trooper friend to a lake about eight miles distant, those product salesmen chased after him. For lack of another starting place, they contacted the Reds. Giles intervened. Players did not have agents in the 1930s, either for contract negotiations or to help connect them with commercial ventures—with a few exceptions.

Babe Ruth was such a big name he had people knocking on his door and pestering him. He endorsed Old Gold cigarettes and Bambino Tobacco, underwear and chocolate, puffed wheat and Wheaties, gum and shaving cream, Louisville Slugger bats, Spalding baseball gloves and Remington shotguns. He was in a league of his own as a home-run hitter and a celebrity with a prominent name. Ruth did have someone acting on his behalf in Christy Walsh, who is regarded as the first sports agent. Walsh also represented Ty Cobb, Rogers Hornsby, Walter Johnson and others and was a skilled ghost writer, drafting as-told-to articles and books with his clients.

Actually, it was Lou Gehrig, Ruth's Hall of Fame teammate, who was the first athlete to be pictured on a box of Wheaties. Gehrig also took a Hollywood screen test to play Tarzan. Although he did not get the part, photographs of Gehrig lounging on his side wearing animal-skin attire while holding a wooden club, can still be found. The other big-name endorser of the time, going back to the 1920s, was football's Red Grange. His agent. C.C. (or Cash and Carry) Pyle, made the player a wealthy man once he gave up his college career at the University of Illinois and went on a national tour, and then had his name attached to a wide array of items, including soft drinks, candy, football dolls, and meatloaf. Ruth was the most famous name

## 8. *Aftermath* 59

in all of sports, if not in the country, so it was easy to capitalize on someone so well-known and popular who was ingrained in American society's consciousness. Pyle took a bigger chance with Grange, riding his shorter time in the limelight and shorter lists of accomplishments, but it worked out fine.

Vander Meer's situation was different. He had only just been thrust into the public eye because of one sterling achievement. He had almost no track record, so it would be wise to strike quickly to make deals—only Vander Meer pretty much ducked those making offers. Even more remarkable compared to the modern age, was that all responsibility for discussing opportunities with those salesman was given to Giles, the personification and symbol of the ball club. Such an arrangement would be viewed as crazy today. Giles and Vander Meer signed a contract that paid Giles $1 a year to represent him in these matters for as long as both were with the Reds. "I can't estimate how much has been offered to Johnny," Giles said very soon after the offers poured in. "Naturally, we will accept any sensible offer. But we are not going into anything that might detract from his record as a ball player. Johnny is a ball player, and that's all he wants to be. He doesn't want to be a freak attraction. He realizes that he must be careful about what happens to him at this time. So I will make the deals we both think are good for him."[10]

Especially viewed with hindsight from the future, the arrangement certainly seemed paternalistic. It would never have happened later, but Giles pretty much had the innocent Vander Meer pegged right. He really didn't care about any extra attention, or apparently, money. As one more illustration of just how large a national phenomenon Vander Meer instantly became, one piece of fan mail stood out. Addressed only to "Johnny Vander Meer, Midland Park, New Jersey," the return address was from Washington, D.C. It was a pleasant letter, dated June 17, sent to Johnny from J. Edgar Hoover. It read, "Last Saturday, although engaged in the Cash kidnapping case, nevertheless I did have time to glance at the sports page of one of the Miami papers and read the account of the thrilling no-hit game which you pitched against the Boston Bees, and then when I read of your second no-hit game in five days I simply could not resist dropping you this note to extend you my congratulations on this remarkable feat."[11]

Hoover continued in chatty fashion, saying he was always a baseball fan, even if he could not get to as many games as he would have liked because of work and he had been following Vander Meer's season. He informed Vander Meer that the Federal Bureau of Investigation team won the U.S. Government League championship the year before. It is not clear how many citizens knew such a league existed. Hoover added that the FBI team was doing pretty well in 1938, too, "although unfortunately we do not have any Johnny Vander Meers who are able to turn in two no-hit games within five days."[12] The director of the FBI also said he hoped he could be in New York when Vander Meer next pitched for the Reds against the Giants, "for I would be really thrilled to see you pitch a third no-hit game this season."[13]

Vander Meer was overwhelmed by the reception, completely surprised by the outpouring of well wishes, endorsement offers and seemingly other wild suggestions of ways he should be honored. "Yes, I've learned a lot about heroes," he said. "A fellow sure has to keep his head."[14] There it was, someone throwing out the idea that Vander Meer could extend the improbable into the realm of the impossible. Vander Meer had just established a ridiculously high standard and now people wanted to see him extend even that.

Has there ever been a more anticipated regular-season start in baseball history than Vander Meer's next scheduled mound appearance? Maybe when a pennant was on the line, but from an individual more than a team-standing issue, it would be difficult to think so. Vander Meer's turn in the rotation came around again on June 19 and it was against the Boston Bees again, although this time on the road. Vander Meer was carrying a 7-2 record and had won six games in a row at the time.

The game began shortly after 1:30 p.m. and 30,613 fans came out. Almost certainly, many of the paying customers wished to see what Vander Meer could do for an encore. He was wondering himself. At that time, there had been one minor league pitcher who had made the same kind of splash as Vander Meer, a thrower name of Clarence Wright hurled consecutive no-hitters in 1901. Some others have done it since. That afternoon in Boston, though, only Vander Meer was on fans' minds.

Cincinnati led off the first inning against Boston pitcher Ira Hutchinson and touched him for four runs right away, sending him to the showers after ⅔ of an inning. Vander Meer's first inning went more smoothly. He did walk Elbie Fletcher, but allowed no hits to the familiar Bees. Vander Meer retired the side in order in the second inning after the Reds failed to add to their lead. After making it through one inning cleanly, Hutchinson's replacement Dick Errickson started looking quite vulnerable himself in the third. Ival Goodman was hit by a pitch, Frank McCormick singled to center and Lombardi did the same thing. Harry Craft made it a trifecta with a third straight single to center and presto, the Reds had two more runs and a 6-0 lead. In the bottom of the third inning, Vander Meer walked Errickson, but got all three outs around him.

Vander Meer got a single himself leading off the top of the fourth off the hanging-in-there Errickson, but Cincinnati did not score. When Boston came up in the bottom of the fourth, Vander Meer had been through

## 8. Aftermath

three more hitless innings. Just enough time had passed to make spectators begin wondering if Vander Meer had yet more magic in his arm. Boston right-fielder Johnny Cooney led off and he grounded out shortstop to first for out number one.

Next up was Debs Garms, playing third base that day. Garms, who had a 12-year Major League career with a .293 lifetime average (though he led the National League in batting in 1940 for the Pittsburgh Pirates by slugging .355) and held the record for most consecutive pinch-hits of seven for 17 years, mostly split time between the three outfield positions, with some fill-in work at third. While possessing an unusual first name, Debs really was Garms' given name. When he was born in 1907, his family named him after politician Eugene V. Debs. It was Garms that broke the Vander Meer spell. He cracked a single to center field. There was not to be a third straight no-hitter. Indicating how much pressure he felt, after the game, Vander Meer said he felt the tension ooze out of his body and could have thanked Garms. "I think if I'd had a ten-dollar bill in my baseball pants, I'd have gone over to first base and handed it to Garms," Vander Meer said.[15]

Eventually, Boston even scored a run in the seventh inning before Vander Meer closed things out. Meanwhile, the Reds kept pouring on the runs and won 14-1. Vander Meer allowed four hits in all, and raised his record to 8-2. "I don't care what sport you're playing, you got to get the breaks," Vander Meer said. "But the real true answer to getting breaks is you got to take advantage of them."[16] Vander Meer got all the breaks he needed in his two no-hitters and then the odds and luck caught up to him when he was trying for a third straight.

# 9

# The Reds of 1938

For a short period of time during the 1938 season anyone who cared about the fortunes of the Cincinnati Reds was pretty much moonstruck over Johnny Vander Meer. Accomplishing something unique in the National Pastime meant that he was instantly nationally famous. Reds watchers were completely blinded by the bright light he threw off. It was not every day a phenom was born. Following the last-place season of 1937, suddenly having a new face to root for was refreshing. Heck, he was helping the Reds win more than anyone thought they would in 1938. And he was doing it in splashy fashion. Two no-hitters in a row indeed. Obviously, he couldn't keep that up. But even when his third try came around, Vander Meer teased the masses with another excellent pitching performance. He didn't get hammered when he finally allowed a few hits. He was not touched by lightning three times, but he still easily won the game.

After Cincy beat Boston, 14-1, on June 19, the Reds were 29-22 and in second place in the National League standings. Gradually, the tumult over Vander Meer's double no-hitters subsided and he became more or less just one of the guys in the pitching rotation. The nation's short attention span turned to other things. Following his slick spree, Vander Meer's record was 8-2 and he had won seven games in a row. For a week or so he made pitching big-league ball look easy (except for those walks). But baseball, with its long schedule, has a way of being a great leveler. No one bats .500. No one hits a home run every day. No pitcher strikes out every batter. And no pitcher keeps throwing shutouts or preventing every single batter he confronts from getting a base hit. Streaks all come to an end.

Gradually, and eventually, the sport's law of average caught up to Johnny. From mid–June on, even as he took the ball from manager Bill McKechnie as a regular in the rotation, Vander Meer was no longer a pitcher with superstar stuff. His supply of fairy dust ran out. He did his job and did it pretty well, but after the high of the no-hitters, even as Cincinnati played better than pre-season experts guessed they would, Vander Meer's name was no longer the one the curious begged for information about.

## 9. The Reds of 1938

Between the June 19 victory over the Bees and the end of the season, Vander Meer went 7-8 to finish with a 15-10 final record and a 3.12 earned average. If someone had told general manager Warren Giles and manager McKechnie prior to the season that Vander Meer would end up 15-10, they would have been happy. Vander Meer went from 3-5 to 15-10, so why wouldn't they be? But he also went from 8-2 to 15-10, so Vander Meer was not quite a .500 pitcher after the fuss, the excitement diminished. Still riding the early–June high, the righty beat the New York Giants on June 23 and the Pirates on June 28 before absorbing a loss to the Cubs on July 3. That was only 4-3. On July 10, Vander Meer won again, 3-1, over the Cubs, before losing three in a row before the end of July.

Vander Meer was proving to be very human, not an every-day miracle worker as the fans had anointed him. Other pitchers had better overall rookie seasons, though of course no one had stirred up as much temporary insanity because of a record-breaking performance. Everything crushed and rushed together so swiftly for Vander Meer, going from making the team to becoming a startling sensation, to just throwing like a regular pitcher.

It should be noted, that even at the instant peak of Vander Meer adulation following the conclusion of the second no-hitter in Brooklyn, it was Dodgers' general manager Larry MacPhail who said baseball would have to wait and see if the newcomer could sustain it. "Everybody, of course, is going to be asking whether he will last or blow up like a lot of other young pitchers who started out well," MacPhail said. "I don't know why he shouldn't last. But then, there have been a lot of baseball pitchers like him who have thrown their arms off in a pretty short time."[1]

On August 2, Vander Meer won his 12th game of the season, a 3-2 victory over the Philadelphia Phillies. That made the Reds 51-42 to the Phillies' 29-61. Clearly, the Reds were playing much better than they had the year before. They were in fourth place in the National League and people were wondering how far Bill McKechnie could take them.

Catcher Ernie Lombardi was having one of his special seasons. He was en route to a final .342 batting average (ahead of runner-up Johnny Mize's .337 for the St. Louis Cardinals) with 19 home runs and 95 runs batted in. Naturally enough, Lombardi had zero stolen bases that season and he walked just 40 times. But for a big man who swatted line drives, he didn't strike out much, fanning just 14 times all year. He was very much at the heart of the offense. Lombardi's average won the batting title, he was selected for the All-Star game, and in recognition by the rest of the National League of how important Lombardi was to Cincinnati he was chosen as the Most Valuable Player.

Lombardi won the Baseball Writers Association of America vote easily that season. The runner-up was Chicago Cubs pitcher Bill Lee (not to be confused with the future Bill Lee of the Boston Red Sox and Montreal Expos). "Big Bill" played between 1934 and 1947 and won 169 games during his career. In 1938, the two-time All-Star went 22-9. His wins, earned run average of 2.66 and nine shutouts all led the NL. Arky Vaughan, the Pittsburgh Pirates' Hall of Fame shortstop, who batted .322 and led the league in triples with 17, was third in the voting.

"I always considered Ernie the best right-handed hitter I've ever seen in my lifetime," said Reds teammate Harry Craft. "(Ted) Williams was the best left-handed hitter and Lombardi the best right-handed hitter. Look at all of the things he could do. He could hit with power, he could throw, and he was an exceptionally fine receiver. He was an outstanding catcher and he helped all our young pitchers."[2] Those included Vander Meer, Craft noted. Recalling Vander Meer's bouts of erratic wildness when he needed help, Craft credited the famed catcher for staying cool and aiding the young hurler. "I remember seeing Johnny Vander Meer so wild, he'd throw a ball two feet to the right of Ernie," Craft said, "and Ernie would just reach out and catch the ball bare-handed."[3]

Lombardi was one of those good clubhouse guys who got along with everyone, and was good-natured, but was also all toughness by nature. He did not complain and if his fingers took a beating, as catchers' digits inevitably did, he did his best to pretend nothing had happened. "Any time he'd get hit with a foul tip, neither our manager, Bill McKechnie, nor our trainer, would ever go near him," Craft said. "Ernie would simply reach down, get a handful of dirt, squat down again, and give our pitcher the sign."[4] In 1958, long after he retired, Lombardi, who spent 10 years with the Reds, was voted the most popular player in team history by fans. He was thrilled by that honor, reacting with glee and some nostalgic reminiscing.

"One of the greatest things that ever happened to me," Lombardi said. "And thank god I'm alive to enjoy it. Without a doubt, my 10 years playing for Cincinnati were the happiest in my major league career."[5] Lombardi gushed about the Reds and his experience in the town, from his arrival from Brooklyn and being assured he was the No. 1 catcher, to his success with the club, and the franchise's success when he represented Cincinnati. But the year he singled out as most special was 1938. "I led the league in hitting," Lombardi said, "but I'll never forget catching Johnny Vander Meer's two consecutive no-hitters. That was really something."[6]

Lombardi winning the MVP vote while playing for a fourth-place team was a rarity. Usually the leaders on pennant-winning teams capture that honor. But he was the key man on a Reds team that improved to 82-68 from a 56-wins, eighth-place team a year earlier. Although the team was not revamped, some of the personnel changes were notable. Vander Meer's

## 9. The Reds of 1938

extra dozen wins were critical. And first-baseman Frank McCormick finally got his shot. McCormick's .327 average was third in the National League, illustrating what a 1-2 punch he and Lombardi were.

The Reds showed flashes all season after a slow April. They won five out of six at the start of May, had another four-game winning streak in May, another four-game winning streak in June, put together a seven-game winning streak in July, two four-game winning streaks in August, and won four of their last five games in the regular-season. They did not scare the NL pennant-winning Cubs, but they were hardly an embarrassment. Fourth place, also behind the Pittsburgh Pirates and New York Giants, might not have seemed like something to scream about, but the Reds were only six games behind Chicago, compared to finishing 40 out the year before.

There were actually some killjoy critics who contended it was neither McKechnie's, nor Giles' triumph because departed GM Larry MacPhail had assembled much of the cast. McKechnie was gracious about the to-do. "What difference does it make as long as we win?" McKechnie said. "Certainly some of the men MacPhail brought in helped the club. Personally, I wish he had brought more in."[7] Well, under MacPhail, McCormick was stifled, and under McKechnie, he flourished. He was terrific in 1938, embarking on such a fine career that he became a borderline Hall of Famer, perhaps held back only because he didn't play his first full season until he was 27. Anyone who watched McCormick play that season probably had to wonder where he had been all along. The answer to that was that he had been stuck in the Reds' minor league system.

In 1936, McCormick clouted 211 hits with Durham as he batted .381. In 1937, he had his 24-game cup of coffee with the Reds while hitting .325. The rest of his season in the minors he batted .322. During his full season in Cincy he collected 209 hits, leading the National League. Early during his time in the bigs on a rain-delay day a few games into the 1939 season, McCormick informed sportswriters about his hitting philosophy. It was so basic it seemed anyone could follow his plan, even if they could not always hit as well as McCormick could.

"Never take your eye off the ball while at bat," McCormick said, "and swing on the first ball which comes over the plate in the strike zone. All my life I've hit the first pitch, or at least the first 'good' ball pitched to me. No one has told me to do so. I figured it out for myself when I was a kid playing on amateur teams that pitchers would try to get me in the hole—get ahead of me, as the saying is, by sneaking over a strike before I started swinging. So I began swinging on that first good pitch with excellent results and have followed that plan ever since. All last season, the National League pitchers kept trying to get that first strike past me, but they seldom did."[8]

Not every hitter possesses the discipline McCormick did. He said he enjoyed it when a pitcher tried to get him to bite on an off-the-plate first pitch, which happened constantly, and he refused to play along. He said if he ever devolved into guessing what a pitcher might throw he hurt himself and was not likely to be successful. "Hitting the first good one and following the ball with my eyes from the time it leaves the pitcher's hand, right up to the moment of impact with my bat are, I believe, the secret of what success I've had in hitting," he said. "Guessing is loaded with pitfalls. The fellow who guesses a curve is coming and crowds the plate so as to be able to reach it, often finds himself knocked silly by a fastball, driven into the dirt as he falls away to avoid one, or taking a wild swing and missing the ball entirely, or popping up."[9] It's not clear if McCormick's lighter hitting teammates followed his scientific classroom lesson, but other than Lombardi, none of them hit as well as he did.

In 1938, the Reds scored 723 runs, compared to scoring 612 in 1937. That was thanks to Lombardi's exceptional season, McCormick's partnership with him in the batting order, and the addition of Wally Berger as a regular. The 6-foot-2, 198-pound Berger made at least as big an impact on baseball consciousness as a rookie as Vander Meer. He was 24 when he broke in with the Boston Bees/Braves in 1930 and slammed 38 home runs. That was a Major League record for a first-year player and it stood for 57 years (until Mark McGwire of the Oakland A's hit 49 in 1987). Frank Robinson, the Hall of Fame Reds and Baltimore Orioles star, tied Berger before that in 1956, but that duo retained the National League record until 2017 when the Los Angeles Dodgers' Cody Bellinger hit 39. Pete Alonso of the New York Mets hit his 53 in 2019, blowing them all out of the water.

Berger twice more topped 30 homers in a season for Boston, and was an all-around player who bashed 242 home runs with a .300 lifetime average while becoming a four-time All-Star. He had incurred a shoulder injury and Boston traded him to the New York Giants in 1937 and after that short stopover he came to the Reds where in 99 games in 1938 he hit .307 with 16 homers, and was a solid run producer.

The outfielder had bounced around—or been bounced around—before he landed with Boston and felt he was being low-balled on salary after all of that with a $4,500 contract offer. "I held out immediately," Berger said. "They said we're giving you the standard increase over your minor league salary. 'You come up and show us what you can do and then we'll talk about what you can get the second year.' I finally agreed."[10]

Prove himself, he did, with that record-setting home run season. Although it seemed as if Berger was fading when the Reds acquired him, he seemed rejuvenated in 1938, perhaps because he was reunited with McKechnie, who had been his manager in Boston. Although Berger's home-run

## 9. The Reds of 1938

record brought him up in baseball discussions for years after he belted those 38 dingers, he pretty much suggested it just happened. "I never thought of records," Berger said. "I just liked to hit."[11]

There was another significant way in which 1938 differed from 1937 for the Reds. The pitching was upgraded. The squad allowed 634 runs, 72 fewer than the year before. It wasn't all about the emergence of 15-game winner Johnny Vander Meer and his no-hitters, either. Right-hander Paul Derringer was the real staff ace, going 21-14. And then in mid-season, Giles acquired Bucky Walters, who won nearly 65 percent of his decisions over the second half of the year. Derringer had been a lonely staple on the mound and now it seemed he was surrounded by gems.

# 10

# Paul Derringer and Bucky Walters

When he was at his best, Paul Derringer was one of the best pitchers in baseball. The 6-foot-3, 205-pound right-hander compiled erratic results over the course of his career. In 1938, at age 31, he was the Cincinnati Reds' top pitcher with a 21-14 record and a 2.93 earned run average. That season he threw 26 complete games and 307 innings, leading the National League in that category. It was his second 20-victory season for the Reds, and two more would follow.

This was part of a peak stretch for Derringer, who also suffered through some tough seasons, including a 7-27 year in 1933, which had to have been miserable. He began the campaign with the St. Louis Cardinals, his original team, and was 0-2 when shipped to the Reds. The 27 losses represented the worst in the league. But Derringer's earned run average of 3.30 wasn't bad at all while he was being saddled with the defeats. That is what later Derringer pointed to as an indicator he wasn't really hurling poorly so much has having bad luck hurled at him game after game. "You know," he said, "I look back on that season of 1933 as one of my best in the majors. They licked me time after time, but I pitched well. I think in about 19 games I was beaten when I allowed an average of about three runs per game. The Cincinnati club that year was terrible. I hate to say it, but I think it was the worst I ever played on."[1] Certainly, Derringer felt more of a sting about his pitching losses that year than he was letting on. The Reds were a last-place team with a 58-94 record that season, but they actually only won 56 games in 1937, a club that was comparably bad.

Derringer, who won 223 big-league games, came to baseball only gradually. There was farming in his youth and although his father grew tobacco in Kentucky, there were also dairy products in the family background. "I built up my strength and endurance when I was a kid in Springfield, Kentucky, where I milked 16 cows twice a day by hand," he said.[2] He played football, basketball and baseball in high school, but he was a catcher for his

## 10. Paul Derringer and Bucky Walters

Springfield High team until one day his coach asked him to take the mound as a replacement when the team was losing. After he struck out eight men, Derringer switched to the mound.

Later, Derringer relayed a tale to a sportswriter that he claimed famous Cardinal executive Branch Rickey told about him. "Branch Rickey used to tell a story about driving onto a road near my house and seeing a boy pushing a 400-pound plow by himself," Derringer said. "'Son, where do you live?' And then he would tell how the boy would pick up the plow with one hand and say, 'Right over there.'"[3] This was all well and good and it presumed that those in attendance at a sports dinner had never shown up at a football banquet during which University of Minnesota football coach Clarence Spears told the exact same story about how he discovered the great star Bronko Nagurski, who went on to become a Hall of Famer with the Chicago Bears.

Meanwhile, more likely keeping with the truth, Derringer, about 20 years old, was said to be throwing for a local mine club when a Cardinals scout happened by, thought he had raw talent, and signed him. Derringer spent four years in the minors before rising to the big club at 24 in 1931. He made a great impact for the Cardinals, finishing 18-8, and his .692 winning percentage was the best in the NL that year. Derringer was the first rookie pitcher to lead the National League in winning percentage. Derringer's 1932 wasn't quite as good—he went 11-4 with an ERA over .400—and St. Louis shipped him to Cincinnati as part of a multi-player trade. The key player going in the other direction was shortstop Leo Durocher. That horrible 1933 season followed, but although not rated as fabulous, Derringer recovered enough to go 15-21 in 1934 and in 1935 he was terrific. That year Derringer finished 22-13, his first 20-game-winning season, and he was chosen as an All-Star for the first of six times.

Over time, following his best seasons, when he had built a residue of goodwill with the Reds organization, Derringer would decline to sign the first contract sent to him leading up to spring training. Many years later, it wasn't always more money he was after, but extra time staying away from camp. "The reason I always held out," he said, "was because I felt that spring training was much too long, especially for guys who had been around as long as I had. It was great for the young fellows, but I didn't need six weeks in the hot sun to get ready. I didn't need all that running and all those exercises."[4]

As good as he was in many years, Derringer also had season-long slumps that didn't seem to make sense. After the 22-13 season, in 1936, he went 19-19 and his ERA went up by a half-a-run. It seemed on his best days, Derringer could get anybody out, no matter how good a hitter, and at other times the best hitters got the best of him. However, that season Derringer

**Paul Derringer rears back to throw. He won at least 20 games each year during the 1938–1940 Cincinnati Reds hot stretch, helping them win two pennants.**

pitched through injury. He had a hernia problem and underwent an operation at the conclusion of the campaign.

Derringer employed a fastball and curve as his best weapons over the seasons. Some of his most memorable pitcher-batter confrontations came against Hall of Famers. Of first baseman Johnny Mize, aka "The Big Cat," a lifetime .312 hitter who led the NL in home runs four times and in runs batted in three times, Derringer said, "He made you throw strikes." Of outfielder Paul Waner, a lifetime .333 hitter who won two league batting titles and twice each led the National League in doubles, triples and hits, Derringer said, "He was a great mechanic with a bat." Of Leo Durocher, who was recognized by the Hall of Fame for his managing, not his hitting, Derringer said, "Hit a lousy .230, but hit it all off me." Actually, Durocher batted .247 lifetime.[5]

When Derringer was being scouted by other teams, as well as the Cardinals, he almost made a last minute switch to the Cleveland Indians. At the time (1928 and 1929), Bill McKechnie was managing the Cardinals and played a role in keeping Derringer from signing with Cleveland instead. Several years later, they were back together with the Reds, McKechnie again as a manager, and Derringer as one of the most important players he had on his teams. McKechnie brought a reputation as a pitcher's friend to Cincinnati, and Derringer confirmed his view of working with the man many times. "If a pitcher can't win for McKechnie, he can't win for anybody," Derringer said. "McKechnie has always been more than fair to me and I try to be fair to him. It's worked out great for me and I only hope I've played some small part in Bill's success."[6]

The Reds were McKechnie's fourth National League club as a manager, which represented half of the league at that time. He had honed his style and it wasn't as if his personality was going to change by then, either. Everywhere he went, McKechnie was regarded as someone who was exceptional at handling a pitching staff. He was not a yeller or a nagger, but more of a nurturer, even when offering corrective advice. "If I'm terribly wrong," Derringer said, "Bill says to me, 'Let's discuss this,' or something like that in a fatherly way. And after we talk it over, we come to a mutual understanding about the whole situation."[7]

Derringer recalled one occasion when McKechnie got a message across to him in a unique way. Derringer acknowledged some people felt McKechnie was always serious and didn't have much of a sense of humor. But one day McKechnie's delivery of a remark was both humorous and a teaching moment. "I had a three- or four-run lead and was experimenting with a new pitch I was trying to develop," Derringer said. "I got too careless and boom! Somebody hit a home run off me. As I came back to the bench after the inning was over, he said, 'Hey, I'll punch you in that big nose of yours if you try that again.' He was kidding and I laughed secretly. But on second thought I reflected he might be on the square. Anyway, I didn't fool around with that pitch anymore."[8]

There is little doubt McKechnie helped rejuvenate the Reds in 1938.

Likewise, Derringer was a major part of the 26-game improvement in the victory total. He personally notched an 11-game improvement, going from 10 to 21 wins over the year before. On September 16, Derringer gave up eight hits, but no runs in a 2-0 triumph over the Philadelphia Phillies for his 20th win of the season. He lost twice after that, but in Derringer's final start of the season, he won his 21st, 7-1 over the Pirates.

The Reds were in transition, in hurry-up mode to rebuild following the disastrous 1937 season. General manager Warren Giles was in the market for fresh faces and good players who might fit. He did good work in the off-season and kept his eye open for talent even after the 1938 season began. No acquisition was more important than his June addition to the pitching staff of Bucky Walters. Walters was 29 years old and stuck with the can't-win Phillies, the worst team of the era. The 6-foot-1, 180-pound right-hander was 4-8 with Philadelphia a few months into the 1938 season. In giving up two players and $50,000, Giles was making a deal on potential, even if it was late-breaking potential. Walters did not have a record better than .500 in any year. And William Henry Walters hadn't even been a pitcher all that long.

When Walters, who was from Philadelphia, signed with the Boston Braves organization to play professional baseball in 1929, he was a third baseman. Within two years, he reached the majors long enough to play in nine games and bat .211. He got into 22 games the next year, but hit just .187. In 1933, then with the Boston Red Sox, he appeared in 52 games and batted .256. A year later, splitting time between the Red Sox and Phillies, Walters made it into 106 games, hit 8 home runs and batted .250. He was an average big-league third-baseman, and seemingly was starting to slump into a below-average hitter—and then the bizarre intervened. During that 1934 season, one day, and Walters was unaware just what happened, he suffered a bug bite on his ankle. There was speculation about the attacking insect, ranging from a mosquito to a beetle to a black widow spider. The impact was serious. Walters' ankle swelled hugely. He couldn't walk or hit and spent 10 days recuperating.

It was during this time period when Jimmie Wilson, the former catcher, and then the Phillies' manager, dreamed up the idea of trying Walters as a pitcher because he possessed a strong arm. "Why not make a pitcher out of Walters?" he said. "He has a great fastball and a powerful build. He should make a hurler."[9] This was Wilson's pet project. He had known Walters for quite some time. They even went back to growing up on the same street together in Philadelphia. Because they knew one another before just working together as manager and player, Wilson spent some extra time with Walters playing catch, and it was from those back-and-forths that he got the idea for Walters to try pitching.

## 10. Paul Derringer and Bucky Walters    73

"I used to warm Walters up before the game," Wilson said, "partly because we were friends, but mostly because of necessity. When you are the manager the players don't like to be seen with you too much because they are afraid they might be suspected of patronizing. Anyway, I found out something about Walters I hadn't known. I found he threw a hard ball that dipped. A sinker as we call it in the dugout. It was as good a sinker as I ever saw. Like every manager, I needed pitchers, except I needed 'em worse than most managers."[10]

Wilson began lobbying Walters about experimenting with pitching, but he resisted. He truly wanted to remain an infielder. "Nothing doing!" Wilson said of how stiffly Walters clung to the idea of remaining with the position that brought him to the majors. In the end, Wilson was proven correct about Walters' prospects of becoming better at pitching than hitting and fielding, but it was a battle. And it was a slow process.

Maybe this wasn't outright as brilliant a success as turning Babe Ruth from pitcher to hitter, but it was equally astute. This was a babystepping move. Walters started one game and relieved in another that year, going 0-0 with a 1.29 earned run average. The single game out of the bullpen came in the sixth inning after two Phils pitchers had been knocked out. He retired six men in a row. On the last day of the 1934 season, the Phillies had a double header. Walters played the first game at third base (going 0-for-4) and started on the mound in the second game. He hurled five innings against Boston, allowing eight hits and three runs, but only one of them earned. He struck out five and walked only one, though he also hit a batter. This small sample did not persuade Walters. Wilson thought he did OK, if not great, but nothing in Walters' brief performances changed the manager's mind about where his player's future lay. "Naturally, he didn't have that much success and the upshot was he was more determined than ever to stick to infielding," Wilson said.[11]

Still, that was a prelude to the 1935 season when Walters had a completely new job description coming out of spring training. Wilson basically tricked Walters into seeing things his way while they were in Orlando. The manager hatched a plot with coaches Hans Lobert and Dick Spalding to take Walters out to get him drunk by sharing six bottles of wine, while simultaneously battering him with logical arguments about why he should become a pitcher. Wilson sat out the initial part of the conspiracy, which took place at a road house, and then arranged to drop in later.

The way Wilson told it, Lobert said something like this to Walters: "What a sucker you are. What do you get as an infielder? Four thousand bucks tops? And you'll never get much more, as long as you're in baseball." Then Spalding tag-teamed him, saying, "That's right. Infielders are a dime a dozen. But pitchers, the kind of pitcher you'd be, get from $15,000 to $20,000. Don't be a chump." Then Wilson walked in and said, "What are you guys talking about? New ways we can blow games?" Wilson let his henchmen take the lead as he joined them for some wine, but holding back from the conversation for a while. Then he jumped in and said, "What's the use of talking to him? If he's satisfied to be a bush leaguer that's his privilege, isn't it?"[12]

At last these wily coyotes broke through Walters' resistance. Resistance weakened by the wine, he bristled over the attitude these guys were using to challenge him. "Is that so?" Walters responded to the bush leaguer crack. "I will tell you what I will do. Wilson, I'll pitch for you on this basis: 'Every game I win, you must give me a bottle of wine as a bonus.'"[13]

If Phillies fans were excited by Walters' shift, it was unclear because at that time there were not many Phillies fans. The team had been down for so long, and its prospects so regularly gloomy that the 1934 club drew only 169,885 spectators for the entire season to watch the last-place group finish 56-93. It would not be an exaggeration to suggest the team's supporters would be open to anything that hinted at positive change. As a life-long position player, Walters still had his doubts after the charade in the road house, but Wilson kept boosting his psyche. "I know you are going to be a pitcher and to show that I have confidence in your ability I am going to give you $25 for every game you win," Wilson said.[14] Somewhere between the drinking session and the start of the regular season the bonus had shifted from a bottle of wine per win to 25 bucks. Wilson did joke that it had been good wine.

Walters finished that season 9-9 and his transformation was going full blast. In 1936, Walters pitched in 40 games, starting 33 of them, and throwing 15 complete games. There were not so many huzzahs, though, because his record was 11-21, the most losses in the National League. Of course, he had the disadvantage of pitching for the lousy Phillies, who as a team went 54-100, in last place again.

Despite a mediocre 4.75 earned run average, Walters was looking more like a pitcher in 1937. His 34 games started was the most in the league and he finished 14-15. Maybe because they had to take someone from the Phillies, or because people felt sorry for him because he had to pitch for the perennially weak Phillies, Walters made his first All-Star team that year. Then, sitting on that uninspiring 4-8 start to the 1938 season, Walters received a reprieve. He was paroled from Philadelphia through the largesse of Giles and suddenly he was fulfilling Jimmie Wilson's prediction that he would be a pitcher, even if it was Cincinnati gaining the benefits.

Everything was different for Walters in Cincinnati. Master manager McKechnie, patron saint of pitchers, was the boss. The Reds were not stagnant like the Phillies, but on the rise. They provided more hitting support

## 10. Paul Derringer and Bucky Walters

for the pitchers. Walters got off to a slow start, losing his first three decisions, but then he began winning and winning. The first victory came in relief on July 8 against the Chicago Cubs, going 1⅔. Whether McKechnie sensed Walters was at a new comfort level or not, he started him the very next day. Walters tossed a complete-game, six-hit shutout. That probably gave him renewed confidence, and the team in him as well. That win really got Walters going with Cincinnati. He finished that second half of the 1938 season 11-6 for the Reds, so his overall mark for the year of 15-14 looked a lot better once broken down between locations.

While no other pitcher won more than seven games for Cincinnati in 1938, when the season ended, McKechnie was looking at a final stat sheet that showed Paul Derringer at 21 wins and 14 losses, making him one of the winningest pitchers in the National League, Bucky Walters, 11 wins and 6 losses with the Reds in half a season, and Johnny Vander Meer at 15 wins and 10 losses as a rookie, and known throughout the nation as the new pitcher who had set the record by authoring two consecutive no-hitters.

Looking ahead to 1939, McKechnie had to be optimistic about the arms he had on call and perhaps more arms that Giles might obtain.

## 11

# Johnny and the Players of 1939

After the two no-hitters, after the 15-10 final record of 1938, Johnny Vander Meer was a hot property. The season past was supposed to be only a taste, a tease, of what would naturally follow. Manager Bill McKechnie was counting on the southpaw to be one of the cornerstones of his pitching rotation for the 1939 season.

So was just about everyone else in baseball. Vander Meer was no longer an unknown. He was famous and just 24 years old. He made enough of an impact as a rookie that he was chosen for the National League All-Star team. Vander Meer was one reason why baseball experts believed the Reds had a shot at the pennant. The team's upgrade in personnel from the 1937 season filled in all of the key blanks. Holes were filled. The men who were left from that poor season were now surrounded by better players.

After the high of hurling the back-to-back no-hitters, though, Vander Meer was cautious about either pretending he knew it all, or that he was a guaranteed star. It actually seemed a bit surprising he did not sound more confident than he did, going off to spring training. He was quite aware that his tendency to walk too many batters could hurt him. "I am not a big-league pitcher yet," he said. "I have to learn to control my wildness. Control is the most important pitching attribute. A blinding fastball or a fast-breaking curve doesn't mean a thing if you can't signal your catcher the exact spot it's going to strike his glove."[1]

The three pitchers expected to shine at the top of the rotation were Paul Derringer, Bucky Walters and Johnny Vander Meer. General manager Warren Giles had plucked fresh talent. It was McKechnie who was publicly reticent about making grand predictions about how Cincinnati would fare. Even though he was from Pennsylvania, not Missouri (except for two seasons managing the St. Louis Cardinals), McKechnie behaved as if he was from the Show-Me state. "Ask me next August," McKechnie responded to sportswriters' inquiring minds about how he thought the Reds would

## 11. Johnny and the Players of 1939

finish. "Some of the new boys were all right in the minors, but that isn't in the majors. Yes, we don't know just what to expect from the youngsters."[2]

To his dismay and the shock of others, it never happened for Vander Meer in 1939. Almost as remarkably swift as his ascension was his stunning descent. Things went askew immediately, in spring training. The tutoring in Tampa of the year before was still lodged in his brain, but his head was not his problem. Nor was his left arm. Vander Meer got sick to his stomach, an ailment that leveled him. His illness was so debilitating he spent nine days in a hospital and lost 14 pounds. Although neither he nor Cincinnati officials realized it that soon, but essentially his season was headed down the drain.

The recovery time from the stomach problem meant Vander Meer had lost valuable conditioning. He did not pitch enough in spring training, and when he returned to the team, he was left in Florida as the Reds barnstormed their way to Ohio for opening day. Yet despite trying to make up for lost time and his body-weakening illness, the team chose Vander Meer to pitch the first game of the season.

Cincinnati entertained the Pittsburgh Pirates on April 17, 1939, at Crosley Field to mark the beginning of a fresh season. Some 30,644 fans turned out for the 2 hour, 16-minute game. Were they quietly hoping to see Vander Meer throw still another no-hitter? Probably not. He had come back to earth after mid-season in 1938, post-no-hitter frenzy, even if he did win those 15 games and demonstrate potential. But it was a different Johnny on the mound this next season. He looked quite hittable against a Pirates lineup that featured Hall of Famers Lloyd Waner and Arky Vaughan as starters and Paul Waner as a pinch-hitter. In hindsight, Vander Meer may not have been ready to compete in a real, count-in-the-standings game.

While he was not bombarded, neither was he sharp. Vander Meer tossed 2⅔ innings, gave up two runs on four hits, walked three and struck out only two. There was no crowd of corporate representatives waiting outside the park after this one to schmooze with Vander Meer and entice him to sign papers to sell products. Walters came on in relief and was hit even harder, with Peaches Davis and Lee Grissom combining to finish out the 7-5 loss. There were still 153 games to go, so no one was panicking. Except perhaps about Vander Meer, who it soon became apparent was having shoulder problems on his throwing side.

Unfortunately for Vander Meer, this was foreshadowing. Vander Meer was on his way to a 5-9 season with a 4.67 earned run average. Hardly what was predicted. He appeared in 30 games, only 21 of them starts. Vander Meer won his first game on May 13, a 2-1 good show over the Cardinals that was a complete-game, four-hitter with nine strikeouts. He also beat Boston and Brooklyn before the end of that month. Then he beat Boston again in mid–June. He was 4-4 after that victory, but 4-7 by the time the All-Star game came around. Not blind to the difference between the two Johnnys of the two seasons, one sportswriter wrote of Vander Meer that he "has lost his magic this season and is not regarded as a solid risk."[3] That was becoming more obvious by the day. Vander Meer was hurting.

The pitcher who back-to-back caught lightning in a bottle in 1938 to excite the nation really experienced only one brief shining moment in 1939. Almost as if it was payback for his brilliant feat of the season before, Vander Meer was named to the National League All-Star team. But he was no all-star at that point. He wasn't fooling anyone with his out-of-sorts showings that seemingly were thrown by a pitcher with a different arm. Teammate Derringer was the starting NL pitcher in the July 11 game in Yankee Stadium. Vander Meer did not play in the 3-1 loss to the American League. Johnny may have been an All-Star on his resume, but he rapidly became the forgotten man on the Reds' pitching staff, and surprisingly, they didn't miss him at all. All those pieces McKechnie did not trust were fitting together just fine, and it didn't take until August for him to recognize it. Cincinnati was 6-2 at the end of April and only 11-10 on May 14. The team was in third place that day.

And then everything jelled. A 4-3 win over the Phillies credited to Derringer, moved Cincinnati into a tie for first place on May 19. The Reds never moved out, resting in the top spot for the remainder of that month, all through June, July, August and September, right through season's end two days into October. The Reds clung to the tie for a few days, but as of May 26 they had a one-game lead. By the end of May, the Reds were 25-13, and then they got hotter. By June 20, Cincinnati's record was 37-18 and the club had a six-and-half-game lead in the National League pennant race.

Philadelphia, as usual during that time period, was awful, finishing last with a 45-106 record, 50½ games behind the Reds. Seventh-place Boston was 32½ games out. The Pirates finished 28½ out. At 77-74, the New York Giants at least had a winning record, but were still 18½ games behind. The Chicago Cubs never truly threatened, and neither did the Dodgers. After the Reds' lead ballooned to 12 games at the end of July, the Cardinals made a game run. In the end, St. Louis finished 4½ games out of first, never quite denting Cincinnati's runaway.

It really was a magnificent season-long performance with a couple of players reaching greatness as the 97-57 record was compiled. Vander Meer may have been the token choice for the All-Star team, a belated award for those no-hitters, but he was already familiar with a large percentage of the team. It seemed as if he brought almost all of his friends. Counting Vander Meer, there were seven Cincinnati Reds selected. Pitchers Derringer and Walters were involved. So were catcher Ernie Lombardi, first

## 11. Johnny and the Players of 1939

baseman Frank McCormick, second baseman Lonny Frey, and outfielder Ival Goodman.

McCormick, in his second season at 28, was the big stick. He was the big man on campus, bigger this season than Lombardi, the long-time fan favorite and reliable hitter. McCormick ascended to elite status in 1939, batting .332, with a league-leading 209 hits, a league-leading 128 runs batted in, and 18 home runs. That was his career-high average. That was one season when McCormick's production resembled his idol Lou Gehrig's, except when it came to home runs. Larrupin' Lou always hit more for the Yankees. Still, no matter what kind of season McCormick was having, he was not having comparisons between himself and Gehrig. "I'm only a first baseman," McCormick said. "He's the best."[4] Right then, McCormick was just about the best at first in the National League. But as good as he was in 1939, that's what the Reds were expecting from him by then.

It was not Lombardi's finest season, but he had a lot to live up to by that point. And, as evidenced by his All-Star selection, it wasn't as if he was flailing around striking out all of the time, either. Lombardi smacked 20 home runs that year, and drove in 85 runs, roughly his usual range. His average dipped to a still-fine .287, though it was a season average far below when he won the batting crown. He was far from over the hill yet, however. He was very much the trusted receiver in McKechnie's mind, appearing in 130 games, but the Reds had brought in back-up insurance, starting in 1938.

Catcher Willard Hershberger was not going to be the main man behind the plate, but he was a good enough hitter that he seemed an appealing prospect to sneak into the lineup or pinch-hit in other games. In 49 games in '38, Hershberger hit .276, though his home-run total was zero. Likewise, during the 1939 run, Hershberger got into 63 games and batted an exceptional .345 in 195 plate appearances. That year he also never hit a home run. His reputation as not any kind of slugger preceded him.

In 1937, Hershberger was playing for the Newark Bears in the International League, one of the greatest assemblies of minor-league talent, a squad that dominated the regular season, but fell behind three games to none in the championship series before rallying to win four straight games. Hershberger tripled at an opportune time when Newark came back in the finale. "They didn't think I could hit one that far," said Hershberger, who never did hit a big-league homer.[5] Hershberger actually was an accidental catcher. He was an infielder in the minors until one day his team's catcher got into a fight with a sportswriter and broke a finger punching the writer in the nose. Hershberger's manager asked him to try catching, and there he stayed.

At 28, this was Lonny Frey's first of three All-Star selections. He batted a career high .291 with 11 home runs and 55 RBIs, respectable for a second baseman, especially in that era when those who played the position were mostly counted on for their fielding. This was a very satisfying period in his career. Frey, whose given name was Linus, as in the future "Peanuts" comic strip character, was born in St. Louis and broke into the majors at 22 with Brooklyn as a shortstop. While he batted .319 in 34 games, he was nearly hooted out of town immediately. He had a sore arm and committed 18 errors, most of them of the throwing variety. "You couldn't believe the booin' I'd get in Brooklyn," Frey said. "I couldn't get the ball to first base."[6] The critical Dodger fans didn't believe in excuses. Frey survived three more seasons in Brooklyn, played one year for the Chicago Cubs, and became a Red in 1938, moving to second base just in time for some good years. He was in the lineup for both of Vander Meer's no-hitters.

Frey's keystone partner in '39 was Billy Myers. In some ways, Myers was lucky he got a chance with Cincinnati because he walked out on one with the Cardinals. Coming out of high school in 1928, Myers, who was from Enola, Pennsylvania, was assigned to a Lewiston, Pennsylvania, team which was only 60 miles from home. After that, he moved around to teams in Iowa and Florida, and when he headed to Avon Park, Florida, in 1929, his mother baked a goodbye cake for luck as he departed. But Myers swiftly became homesick. "The Cardinals put me in a room by myself in Avon Park in a hotel miles out of town," he said. "I stayed the first night, practiced the next morning, but by noon-time I was so lonesome I took the train back north at my own expense. I helped finish the farewell cake, too, I was back so quickly."[7]

That could have doomed his baseball career, but Myers returned to the Cardinals fold and played in a few cities in the minors. Myers broke into the majors with the Reds at 24 in 1935 after batting .313 in AA for the Columbus Red Birds the year before. He had never seen a big-league game until he played in one on opening day that season. Cincinnati lost, 12-6, to Pittsburgh, but Myers went three-for-five at the plate. He became captain of the team before his first year was out.

During that season, Myers, occasionally talked about his seven-month-old son Eddie, who had already received gifts of a catcher's mitt and a fielder's glove. "Let him pick his own position," Myers said.[8] Nearly two decades later, the Reds signed that baby boy named Eddie Myers to a contract as an infielder. He started in Class D in the Georgia State League. Eddie Myers was 19 and his father 42 when he inked that deal. "He's starting out just like I did, about the same age, with the same ambition—to be in the big-time one of these days. And I think he's going to make it, too."[9] Only Eddie did not reach those heights, never playing in the majors.

Billy Myers spent six of his seven Major League seasons with Cincinnati. In 1940, his last year in Cincy, Myers suffered an injured arm, cutting it five stitches worth as he tried to open a window. After one season with the Cubs in 1941, Myers joined the military to fight in World War II and did not play again. He said he was never really comfortable in Chicago and this time around he missed Cincinnati.

Billy Werber, who had been around, took over at third base in 1939. He was 31 and had already served time with the Yankees, Boston Red Sox and Philadelphia Athletics. More of a runner than a slugger, Werber did have a good year at the plate for the Reds, hitting .289. He also led the National League in runs scored with 115. A handful of seasons earlier he hit .321 with the Red Sox. He led the American League in stolen bases three times and catalogued one 200-hit season. Werber's high was 40 stolen bases in 1934, but with his speed felt he should have done more. "Well, I could run," Werber said. "Actually, in 1934 I kicked a water bucket and broke my big toe and I didn't know I had broken it. I played the last two weeks of the season with a broken toe on my right foot. The next year, I played the whole season with the aggravation of a broken toe. This was '35. I led the league in stolen bases (with 29) on that broken foot, but it pained me the entire year. I had to have it operated on."[10]

Werber was a teammate of Babe Ruth's in New York and loved being around him. Somehow, though, Werber's service with the Yankees did not overlap with any pennant-winning years. When he was originally scouted by the famed scout Paul Krichell, Werber agreed to join the Yankee organization if they paid for his last three years of college at Duke University. He was an All-American basketball player for the Blue Devils, the storied college team's first, and also a baseball All-American. He was 22 in 1930 when hit .339 for Albany in the Class A Eastern League and got into four games with New York.

By 1938, Weber was with the Athletics, but had an off-year, his average dropping to .259. Despite that, Werber felt he deserved a $1,500 raise. Philadelphia boss Connie Mack did not. Next thing Werber knew, he was sold to Cincinnati on March 16, 1939, well into spring training. Always an excellent fielder, Werber pushed Lew Riggs out of the Reds' starting third-base job. Werber played in 147 games, Riggs just 22, with only 43 plate appearances all season.

Werber was a veteran who brought a fresh spark to Cincinnati and he wasn't hesitant to unleash his personality. "When I got to Cincinnati, see," he said, "I didn't get down there until the day before they broke camp. I got down there on a Sunday and played seven innings against the Boston team and the next day spring training was over and we hit the road and started to come north. Well, it didn't take me long to determine in my own mind that the ballclub was a little dead ass. And after a bit, when I got to know the guys in the infield a little better I'd say, 'Bounce around on the balls of your feet! Fire that ball! Be a jungle cat!'"[11]

Werber said Frey had many liver spots on his body and the newcomer began calling him the Leopard. Then Myers got the nickname of Jaguar. When they asked who he was, Werber swiftly claimed the name Tiger—and he growled. That was how the Jungle Club was formed. Initially, in some of the teasing, McCormick at first base was left out and wanted in. Werber told him great hitting was all fine and good, but he had to hustle more fielding. "Well, he hustled," Werber said and requested, "Take me into the Jungle Club." Werber said he made McCormick buy him a beer and then anointed him Wildcat. Weber said McCormick then bragged to McKechnie that he had been accepted into the club and now had a big-cat nickname, too. "And that's what the Jungle Club was," Werber added. "I helped infuse a little life into them and I think it improved their play in games."[12] Maybe, maybe not, but it definitely seemed to improve morale.

That summer, on August 26, 1939, the first Major League baseball game was televised. The Reds were in Brooklyn to play the Dodgers at Ebbets Field. The game was shown on WX2BS, which later became WNBC in New York. Actually, there were two games since the teams played a doubleheader. Famed broadcaster Red Barber, by virtue of his connection with the Dodgers was involved in many firsts, from handling the first night game in Brooklyn to this milestone, to broadcasting the start to Jackie Robinson's career a decade later.

Only two cameras were used, and of course the picture was in black and white. Some of the video came across as blurry to the viewing audience if the action was fast moving. But then, there were not many people watching anyway. The home audience was estimated at 3,000.

The Reds won the first game, 5-2, with Bucky Walters pitching superbly for the Reds, as he did so often that season. He went all nine innings, allowed only two hits, and the two runs that scored were unearned. Cincinnati scored all five of its runs in the eighth inning. McCormick knocked in two of the runs with a double. The Dodgers won the second game, 6-1, no doubt making the majority of viewers happy since the local region was the only one in range.

In the opener, since the Reds were the visitors, they led off the first inning. The first player in the batting order was Werber, which meant he was the first player to have a televised at-bat in history. Facing Brooklyn pitcher Luke Hamlin, Werber hit a grounder to second baseman Pete Coscarart, who threw him out at first.

"I had no recollection of it at the time," Werber said much later. "I didn't know about it until after it was done. As a matter of fact, I didn't know about it until many years later. I didn't know about it until after I was retired and down here in Florida." Werber said he was playing golf at his club, perhaps 15 years earlier and was walking past the bag room. A teen

## 11. Johnny and the Players of 1939

working there called out to him and asked, "Mr. Werber, did you know that you were the first player ever to appear in a televised Major League ball game?" Werber replied that he did not know that and the young man said it was right there in the book he was reading. "Since that time," Werber said, "I've read it in several different places and people have called it to my attention."[13]

At 33, Wally Berger wasn't as potent as he was as a record-setting rookie in 1930, but he gave the Reds 97 games in center and right field with 14 home runs and 44 runs batted in during his final full season. Berger was proud of that long-standing 38-homer season in Boston, but said he was never consumed by statistics. "All I know is that I hit tape-measure home runs in every major-league ballpark I ever played in," Berger said. "I never thought of records. I just liked to hit."[14]

When Berger clouted his 38 home runs as a rookie, he did not lead the National League in that category. Before him, two rookies did accomplish that during the Deadball Era. Brooklyn's Harry Lumley led the National League in four-baggers in 1904 with nine. In 1906, Tim Jordan, who was a teammate of Lumley's that season with the Dodgers, or Superbas, as they were temporarily called, hit 12 to lead the NL as a rookie. Just the season prior to Berger's outburst, Dale Alexander cracked 25 home runs to set a Detroit Tigers team record as a rookie. Braves Field was regarded as a pitcher's park long before it became a football field for Boston University abutting the Charles River. One joke about how large it was came from Babe Ruth, who took one look at the 550-foot straightaway center and the seats 402 feet away along the right- and left-field lines and said, "Very nice. Where's the first tee?"[15]

Berger's blasts still found the fences, and sailed over them. Sometimes. Being located next to the Charles, often used as a course for rowers, brought strong winds blowing over the walls towards home plate. "I think I led the world in foul home runs," Berger said.[16] He naturally faced the best pitchers of his era, though primarily National League stars since he spent his entire career in that circuit. Berger did not always agree with how experts rated the finest throwers of his time, notably Dizzy Dean. While Berger thought Carl Hubbell was tremendous, and he had great difficulty with Dazzy Vance, he said Dean didn't bother him much. "Dizzy had no curve," Berger insisted. "Dizzy had a fastball. Period. It was a good fastball, but I could hit a fastball."[17]

One of Berger's regular outfield partners was Ival Goodman, who was chosen for his second straight All-Star team in 1939. After a five-year apprenticeship in the minors, much of the time spent as a catcher, Goodman spent 10 years in the majors, and was a fixture in Cincinnati for most of them, starting in 1935. He led the National League in triples his first two seasons, and in 1938 displayed a tremendous sudden outburst of power, smacking 30 home runs while knocking in 92 runs. His 1939 season was impressive, though different, while limited to 124 games. He slugged just seven home runs, but drove across almost as many runs with 84 RBIs, while batting a career-high .323 and posted a .401 on-base percentage. It was almost as if he were two high-level players with somewhat differing skills during those two seasons. Goodman, whose entire career was spent in the National League, impressed many of the American League players in 1939, according to an unofficial poll of top Yankees in attendance, including Joe DiMaggio, Bill Dickey, Lou Gehrig and manager Joe McCarthy, "Goodman… Goodman… Goodman," one scribe summarized their sentiments.[18]

Goodman, who said all he knew about his unusual first name of Ival was that an uncle had it before him, was appreciated on the Reds, as well. But McKechnie felt he could become great, rather than just very good, if he showed more aggressiveness. "There is only one thing that keeps Goodman from being a great ball player," McKechnie said. "That is that he lacks the initiative, or the brass, call it what you will, that a great ball player must have. He has everything else. He is a good hitter. He has strong arms and strong wrists and gets the bat around there with plenty of power behind it. He is a good hustling ball player and we miss him a lot when he isn't in the lineup. "He is the almost perfect ball player from a manager's standpoint. He's always in shape and even when you don't know where he is, you know he isn't doing anything he shouldn't."[19]

In all ways he was reliable, but McKechnie seemed to think if Goodman had more fire he could be an All-Star every year. Goodman probably would have disputed the analysis, given the way he felt about the game his whole life, growing up in Oklahoma after being born in Missouri. "I always liked to play ball," said Goodman, who was 26 before he reached the majors. "When I was a kid, I would rather play ball than eat." A little later in the same conversation with a writer he added, "I'd just like to say that that still goes."[20] He could afford to eat better, though, when playing in the majors than he had playing in the minors during the Great Depression.

The third regular outfielder, as the Reds chased their first pennant in 20 years, was Harry Craft. Craft's entire six-year, big-league career was spent with Cincinnati, and almost always roaming center field. Just an average hitter, Craft was a sturdily built 6-foot-1 and 185 pounds, a baseball savvy man who would later become a Major League manager. McKechnie did not count on Craft so much for big offense (he hit .257 in 1939, though with 13 homers and 67 runs batted in), as to cover deep territory in Crosley Field. Playing shallow because of his speed and tracking ability, Craft took runs away more often than he created them. He was described as a fielder that killed triples.

## 11. Johnny and the Players of 1939

Craft, originally from Ellisville, Mississippi, had his finest hitting year in 1938 when he batted .270 with 15 home runs and 83 runs batted in. He also caught the fly-ball out that completed Vander Meer's second no-hitter. The righty hitter and thrower was a latecomer to baseball. While attending Mississippi College, then Texas Christian, he started out on the track team, but didn't like that sport so much. "Give me a crack at baseball," he said.[21] That paid off. Growing up in rural Texas after his earliest youth spent in Mississippi, Craft did not play baseball in high school, only football. He played football and baseball in college and was observed by a scout for the Reds. "I signed a contract with Cincinnati for nothing," Craft said. "I signed just for the chance to play. It was the Depression and times were bad. I just wanted the chance to play."[22] The Reds needed good, young players and while Craft initially had future Hall of Famers Chick Hafey and Kiki Cuyler ahead of him in the outfield, they were wrapping up their careers. He also felt fortunate when McKechnie took over as manager. "Bill McKechnie was a good manager and a wonderful man. He was just a real class boy. He was great with younger players. You always knew where you stood with Bill. He called a spade a spade."[23]

In 1939, Lombardi, McCormick, Frey, Myers, Werber, Berger, Goodman and Craft made up a perfectly complementary starting lineup for a winner. McCormick played the most, in 156 games, Berger the least, in 97. Over a long season there will always be injuries or the need for rest, so other guys must contribute. Of course the Reds carried backups, besides Hershberger and Lew Riggs. Some were well-known, but just passing through. Others were needed more.

Outfielder Nino Bongiovanni hit .258 in 66 games. He was nicknamed "Bongo." The marvelously named Frenchy Bordagary, another outfielder, showed up in the box score 63 times that year, but batted only 197. In August, they were both traded to the Yankees for Vince DiMaggio, who had been acquired from Boston, but never suited up for New York. DiMaggio was on the losing side in Vander Meer's first no-hitter in 1938. Bongo never played in the majors again. DiMaggio only got into eight games for the Reds and hit .071.

Nearing the end of his 20-season Hall of Fame career, Al Simmons played in nine Reds games with a .143 average, also pretty much switching trains in Cincinnati. Lesser known, but more reliable at this stage, was Lee Gamble. Gamble spent parts of four seasons with the Reds and never hit a big-league home run. But in 1939, at 29, he played more than all of those others, competing in 72 games and hitting .267 in 236 plate appearances.

Then there was Les Scarsella, who pretty much had the finest free ticket to watch the Reds entertainment all season long. Scarsella, then 25, was the back-up to a player who never came out of a game. Scarsella was next in line behind McCormick at first base. He had been around, with a few gaps in the minors, since 1935, and in 1936 played well enough to be used in 115 games and bat .313. He was actually in McCormick's way. Scarsella grew up in Oakland, California, and as a young Italian-American idolized Ernie Lombardi when he played in that area, never imagining he would one day be a teammate of his. "Ernie was my hero," Scarsella said. "It's just the breaks some guys seem to get."[24]

Scarsella had an intriguing off-the-field background as an alternative career choice and talked about it right after joining the Reds. When he got the call to report from the minors in 1935, he was told to meet the Reds in Chicago for a game against the Cubs. "I was still kind of dazed when I checked into Wrigley Field," he said. "Before I knew what was happening I was out at first base and in a Cincinnati uniform. But there was no use in getting scared. You see, like my dad, I pack dynamite in the winter. No, I don't believe there's any danger if you're careful."[25] If he wasn't going to get a fright at a factory in that more dangerous industry, Scarsella's nerves should have been steady for his major-league debut.

Scarsella, whose wife Anna occasionally talked baseball on the radio, never thought he would make the majors after he signed, so becoming a full-fledged starter was more than he dreamed of accomplishing. His second season, though, was not quite as hot, with him hitting .246 in 110 games. And then he lost the first-baseman's job altogether. In 1939, when the Reds pursued the National League flag, Scarsella only got into 16 games with 15 plate appearances. He spent long hours on the bench.

Remarkably, so did Johnny Vander Meer. The sensation of 1938 was not in the regular rotation, especially in the second half of the season. So heavily counted-on during the 1939 pre-season, he became the invisible man. Unlikely as it seemed, Cincinnati had plenty of solid pitching without him.

# 12

# Johnny and the 1939 Pitching

By mid-season, Johnny Vander Meer had been reduced to irrelevancy. He spent as much time on the bench as Les Scarsella. The Reds really didn't know what to do with him. He was injured, to a degree, but not to such a degree he needed surgery on his pitching arm or anything like that. When he had his chances, he had been ineffective. Vander Meer went off to the All-Star game with his inglorious 4-7 record. On July 21, he lost a game in relief, then picked off another win on July 30. He pitched a complete-game, five-hitter over the Phillies, striking out seven in a 5-1 outing. The only glaring fault was eight walks surrendered, Vander Meer's wildness intruding even on an otherwise good day.

It was nearly two months later when Vander Meer was again involved in a decision. He started a September 19 contest versus Philadelphia, but nothing worked well. Officially, Vander Meer pitched zero innings. He did not retire anyone in the first, giving up four runs on one hit and two walks, ending a demoralizing season with a 5-9 record as his teammates played on. "I still think Vander Meer will be a great pitcher one of these days," said Reds manager Bill McKechnie.[1] Not at that moment, however. McKechnie kept giving Vander Meer chances that summer of 1939, but his arm let him down. Now the Reds had other priorities, such as clinching the National League pennant, and hopefully winning a World Series crown for the first time since 1919. Cincinnati's pitching situation had changed drastically in the year since Vander Meer made his mark, first with a winning streak, then with the consecutive no-hitters that drew so much attention.

The man on the mound drawing the major share of attention in 1939 was Bucky Walters. That season Walters was the best pitcher on the planet. He had served notice of promise when acquired by the Reds in June of 1938 and had gone 11-6 for the club. But the one-time third-baseman who had shown flashes with the Phillies was phenomenal during his first full season with Cincinnati. Walters was on his way to a 27-11 season and was so good, so dominating, that he was voted the Most Valuable Player in the National League. Walters threw 319 innings over 39 games, including 31 complete games with a 2.29 earned run average. He was tops in the NL in wins, ERA, innings, with his 36 games started and 137 strikeouts. He already had one All-Star pick on his resume, but this was the first of four straight selections for Cincinnati.

He should have bought Jimmie Wilson a car in thanks for twisting his arm (other arm) to convince him to take up pitching. And that would have been easy to do because Wilson was right there in Cincinnati with him. Wilson had been ousted as Philadelphia's manager after another poor season, although it would have taken the management powers afforded Moses parting the Red Sea for anyone to win with the Phillies at that time. Wilson joined McKechnie's staff as a coach and sneaked into four games for Cincinnati that season.

As it so happened, sportswriters who were reviewing Walters' career and taking note of his position shift, began asking about how it all came to be once he emerged as such a star pitcher. Wilson even caught one of Walters' wins a little bit later. The conversion became a periodic topic in the coming years after Walters' breakout. Wherever Wilson went, he was asked about why he chose to shift the infielder's role. "When I wanted Bucky to be a pitcher, I didn't bother him about his stuff, his curve, his fastball," Wilson said. "I wanted his spirit. I used to see him come into our clubhouse at Philly when we lost, and we lost a lot. But Bucky never quit. He'd walk in on a losing day and start throwing things around. He'd holler at guys. He'd walk around and call each fellow by name for what he did. I watched him. He wasn't putting on an act. He meant it. I figured that all anybody needed to be a pitcher was guts like Walters had. So I made him a pitcher."[2]

Walters won early and often in 1939. Even though he lost on opening day, Walters had two wins in the bank before the end of April, beating the Pirates twice. He picked up four more victories in May and four more in June. The wins were accumulating for Walters—and the Reds, as they made their move to permanently relocating in first place. He got even better in July. Walters was the winner in a 13-1 crush job of the Cubs on July 9, right before the All-Star break. He joined the other National League stars at the game on July 11 at Yankee Stadium, but didn't pitch there. Then he had to travel only a few blocks or so to rejoin the Reds for a July 13 game at the New York Giants. Walters shut them out, 7-0, on five hits.

The righty won eight times in July alone, including a second shutout, 4-0, over Boston on July 17. That was a four-hitter. One of the things that made Walters a success was the sinker ball that Wilson had noticed when the men were playing catch. It was a deadly weapon in Walters' hand, complementing his fastball and curve. "To me, this pitch is my natural fastball,"

Walters said. "I throw it with three-quarters motion, naturally. When I was a third-baseman, it was said that the ball I threw was 'heavy' and 'sank.' A heavy ball is a disadvantage to any player except a pitcher. Most of the pitchers' fastballs have a hop on them. Other pitchers, of whom I am one, have fastballs that sink. When I am at my best my fastball is sinking. When I am not, it is not doing as much and, consequently, is easier to follow. Occasionally, I throw more directly overhanded and my fastball does not sink. I usually try this when I think it might cross up a hitter."[3]

In another aspect of the game that had to give Walters some satisfaction, he even hit well in 1939. Coming to the plate 131 times, Walters batted .325. He hit just one home run, but he did knock in 16 runs. Walters was the ace of the Cincinnati staff in 1939, even eclipsing Paul Derringer. That was a mild surprise, though Derringer did not falter. It was more of a case of both of them being tremendous. Derringer went 25-7 with a 2.93 earned run average. His winning percentage led the league at .781, one of the few important categories Walters hadn't captured himself. When you have two regulars who combine for 52 victories you are basically more than halfway to a pennant. Walters' emergence caught baseball by surprise. Derringer was no surprise. He won 20 games the year before, but this proved to be the right-hander's finest all-around season at 32.

Derringer won the second game of the season and like Walters had two victories by the end of April. He picked off four more wins in May, including a 6-0 shutout of the Giants on May 24, a five-hitter with no walks. Derringer won three more games in June and that included another shutout, this one also 6-0, but over the Pirates. He surrendered only four hits with no walks that time. Just before joining Walters and Vander Meer at the All-Star game in July, Derringer added two more wins to his season total. With the Reds rolling, 21 games above .500, and their first-place lead at 8½ games, Derringer posted a third shutout, this time the Phillies being the victims. This was another five-hitter and once again Derringer, showing off brilliant control, did not walk a batter. By the time Derringer blanked the Phillies once more on August 23 with 10 widely scattered hits permitted, but still no walks, his record was 16-7.

Author of another five-hit shutout, this time of the Cubs, on September 3, Derringer cranked it up a notch. He piled up seven more wins before the end of September. That season, Derringer walked just 35 batters in 301 innings, making it tough for teams to score. However, there was one bothersome off-the-field situation that might have played havoc with Derringer that season. A court case was brought against him claiming he had caused bodily injury to a man three years earlier. In May, the New York Supreme Court ruled against Derringer. He faced a possible $25,000 fine and prison time. Only days before the All-Star game, the plaintiff backed off and a settlement was reached with the Reds helping Derringer pay. The threat of his being arrested in New York was removed. "Boy, I'm glad to get that off my mind," Derringer said.[4]

Derringer won his 20th game of the season, 7-2, versus the Chicago Cubs at Wrigley Field on September 10. That clinched his second 20-win campaign. He won number 25 on September 28, besting the Cardinals, 5-3. Although Derringer did walk a batter, he somehow allowed 14 hits, yet survived by giving up that few runs.

Walters and Derringer were the Big Two for the Reds. But it was supposed to be Walters, Derringer and Vander Meer as a Big Three. For all of Walters' and Derringer's greatness, the loss of Vander Meer in the rotation could have been fatal. This was not a deep pitching staff. In all, 16 men threw in at least one game for the Reds. It is not clear what to make of a 17th name listed under the team's pitching staff. Bud Hafey, an outfielder, has his name in that slot, but he never threw a pitch. The 16 is a very low number by the standards of 2020. During the 2019 regular season, the New York Yankees, who won 103 games, compared to the Reds' 97 of 1939, used 32 pitchers at least once. The World Series champion Washington Nationals employed 31 throwers. The Houston Astros, the World Series runners-up and American League pennant winners, used 26 pitchers in at least one game.

Hafey aside, several others were almost imaginary pitchers for the Reds in 1939, too. Art Jacobs and Elmer Riddle got into one game each, Jacobs for one inning, Riddle for two. Red Barrett appeared in two games, totaling 5⅓ innings. Jim Weaver and Pete Naktenis were inserted in a game by McKechnie three times each. It was three innings total for Weaver and four for Naktenis. Wes Livengood got into five games for a total of 5⅔ innings. Clearly, those six hurlers offered no assistance in replacing Vander Meer.

The potentially distressing circumstance for the Reds was that Vander Meer's five wins were sixth highest on the team. Johnny Niggeling went 2-1, pitching 10 times for 40⅓ innings. Only he had a yowser of an earned run average at 5.80, probably why he did not pitch more than that. Milt Shoffner also got into 10 games and finished 2-2, though his ERA was a more user-friendly 3.35. Hank Johnson threw in 20 games and had a nice 2.01 earned run average, yet still somehow ended up 0-3.

Peaches Davis, 34, whose given name was Ray, was also called upon 20 times. Davis did not reach the majors until 1936 when he was 31 and spent his entire short big-league career with the Reds. He did some good work for Cincinnati over the preceding three years, winning 11 games in 1937. Before that he had been marooned in the minors for seven years, once winning 19 games for Fort Worth in the Texas League before getting a long-awaited

## 12. Johnny and the 1939 Pitching

chance. But Davis wasn't as valuable to the Reds in 1939 as he had been. His record was 1-0, but his ERA was 6.46 and his Major League career ended when that season did. So it wasn't as if McKechnie did not mix and match and try several recipes when searching for aid for Walters and Derringer. The miracle was that he found it in unexpected places. The Reds won 97 games with just five pitchers winning as many as nine.

Probably the biggest surprise was the resurrection of Lee Grissom. Prior to Vander Meer's theft of all the headlines allotted to newcomer Cincinnati pitchers, it was Grissom who was supposed to be the find. He essentially vanished from the scene for two years, only to rise again in 1939 when needed. Grissom pitched in 33 games and went 9-7, and even if his ERA was a nothing-to-write-home-about 4.10 his 153⅔ innings were important. Whether he was more mature, healthier, or just what, Grissom's contributions counted, especially in May. In mid–May, the Reds went on a tear. They won 12 games in a row and 13 out of 14, moved into first place. They never relinquished the spot the rest of the season and Grissom won three games during the streak.

One pitcher who had been around with the Reds since 1936, but who kept failing to break through in a meaningful way, might have saved the season. No one saw his 1939 season coming. Lloyd Moore, nicknamed Whitey, pitched one game in 1936 and won it. The next season, in 13 games, he went 0-3. In 1938, his record was 6-4 with a 3.49 earned run average, meriting a closer look in spring training when life was collapsing on Vander Meer. Then, there he was, tapped on the shoulder by McKechnie more often than ever, going 13-12 with a 3.45 earned run average in 42 appearances. The 1939 season was Moore's moment in the sunshine. It was the high point of Moore's big-league career. While he spent parts of eight seasons in the bigs, Moore was never better than 8-8 again.

Whitey Moore did fine in his expanded role, but Gene Thompson did even more. Thompson truly earned the label of Where-Did-He-Come-From? Better known as Junior, the 6-foot-1, 185-pound righty had been laboring in the minors since 1935 after joining the Reds organization as an 18 year old. He became a keeper in 1939. One eye-opener in spring training was Moore and Thompson combining for an exhibition game no-hitter.

That showed McKechnie that Thompson had picked up tips on how to improve his curve, one of the pitches it was thought he needed work on. "McKechnie's stunt of having his pitchers throw curves as soon as they start warming up each spring," is what helped him, Thompson said. "This spring was my first real test of proper training and you can bet I appreciate it. No young pitcher can ask for a better break than I've been given this year. I've been treated with as much consideration as though my name were Vander

Meer, or Derringer, or Walters."[5] In one performance that season, Thompson did become the new Vander Meer. He was called Junior because he was literally a junior at birth and his father also played baseball, though he did not reach the majors.

At the beginning of the season, Vander Meer was very much in the team's plans. But as his physical ills mounted and his mound showings wilted, it was Thompson who stepped into the gap of opportunity. His first decision was a loss out of the bullpen to the New York Giants on May 2. He picked up saves on May 22 and May 25, though, McKechnie counting on him in relief. Thompson gained his first win on June 1, finishing a 13-inning victory over Boston. Vander Meer had started and did fine, but Paul Derringer's relief showing wasn't good enough.

It was nearly two weeks later when Thompson's next decision, another win, was registered, also in relief. On July 15, Thompson raised his record to 3-1. Vander Meer was pulled early and Thompson pitched six innings to beat the Giants. Giving up just three hits and no runs in that stint enhanced Thompson's status. On July 23, in Shibe Park, Thompson took on the Phillies in his first start. Although he allowed 14 hits, Thompson hurled an 11-inning complete game. Thompson did not keep Philadelphia players off the bases, but he did keep most of them from reaching home plate and won the contest, 5-2. It was now apparent Thompson had something going. Less than a week later he shut out Philadelphia on four hits and lowered his earned run average to 2.17.

Moore, Walters and Vander Meer won three straight after Thompson and in early August the Reds were 60-30 and 12 games ahead in the pennant race. As Vander Meer faded out of the picture, Thompson kept winning. On September 13, Thompson twirled a 3-0 two-hitter over the Dodgers, and the Reds were still 30 games over .500 at 80-50. As the season was winding down, a New York sportswriter took note of how Thompson had prominently injected himself into the Cincinnati pitching situation, writing, "After nearly a month of struggles, Bill McKechnie finally unearthed a pitcher who found out it wasn't against the law to win, even if his last name wasn't Walters or Derringer."[6]

Now completely backed by McKechnie's confidence, Thompson took a regular turn throughout September as the Cardinals hustled their way back into shouting distance of first place. On September 22, Thompson shut out the Pirates. On October 1, the next-to-last-day of the regular season, Thompson gave the Reds their 97th and final victory. He beat Pittsburgh once more, 9-1, for his 13th win, his record ending up 13-5, his earned run average 2.54. It was a special accomplishment for the rookie, who never dreamed of making the big-league club out of spring training. "I had no idea I would make the Reds roster," Thompson said. "But fortunately for me, and some other young pitchers, most of our pitchers who were going to be on the roster came down with the flu, which gave us young pitchers a chance to pitch in some spring training games."[7]

Thompson recalled it was his first exhibition game where he pitched the no-hitter with Whitey Moore. "This was probably one of the greatest moments in my life," he said, "because I can look back and I can think had it not been for the opportunity I got that day, I might not ever have pitched in the big leagues. That game was the first time I had ever had a big-league uniform on playing against big leaguers. I was astounded by the people I was playing against."[8]

Soon enough, Thompson was playing against all of the famous people in the National League. His timing was lucky, but he made the most of it for his career. But his timing was also lucky for the Cincinnati Reds that year because they needed a Junior Thompson so they could win the pennant.

## 13

# The 1939 World Series

Winning the pennant in 1939 meant a direct entree to the World Series. It would not be for another 30 years that Major League Baseball introduced playoff rounds. If you won the National League pennant, you were in. If you won the American League pennant, you were in. So the 97 victories that carried the Cincinnati Reds over the St. Louis Cardinals, their closest pursuers in the regular season, meant the Queen City, hard by the Ohio River, was going to host some World Series games for the first time in 20 years. This was not Chicago Cubs long, or Boston Red Sox long, droughts that would play out longer than the 20th century, but a generation had grown up without witnessing any kind of championship on the team resume.

The opponent, the team representing the AL, was the New York Yankees, as it so often had been since Babe Ruth was carelessly traded by Boston, since gargantuan Yankee Stadium opened in 1921, and a parade of all-time greats donned pinstripes through the 1920s and 1930s. That summer was no different. The Yankees overpowered the rest of the American League, compiling a stunning record of 106-45. The second-place team was Boston with an 89-62 mark, an almost-ridiculous 17 games behind the Yankees in the standings.

There was no doubt the Yankees would be almost obscene betting favorites over the Reds. But then, it should have been remembered that was pretty much the case in 1919 when Cincinnati last contended for a Series title, that time against the Chicago White Sox. In retrospect, given the rarely-remembered, regular-season records of the two teams that season, one might wonder why the Sox were favored. Chicago won the AL pennant by 3½ games over the Cleveland Indians with an 88-52 record. The Reds won the NL by nine games over the New York Giants with a 96-44 record.

The first World Series was played in 1903 and that first showdown was decided by a best-of-nine format. There was no Series in 1904 because the pennant-winning Giants, led by the grumpy John J. McGraw, refused to play. Every other Series between 1905 and 1918 required four victories to claim the championship. But for 1919, and through 1921, the round reverted to best-out-of-nine. The competition shifted back to best-out-of-seven in 1923 and has stayed that way forevermore.

More than a century later, despite court investigations, Major League investigations, books and movies produced detailing the situation, some of what occurred during the 1919 Series is still debated. The bottom line is that key White Sox players conspired with gamblers to fix games and lose them. This became known as "The Black Sox Scandal." The Reds won the title, five games to three, even as suspicions roiled the press box and some among watchers in the crowd. Although players were acquitted in a trial, which took until 1921, new Commissioner Judge Kenesaw Mountain Landis used his undiluted authority to exile eight White Sox players from the game, banning them from organized ball for life. Both a book and movie bore the name "Eight Men Out" in telling the story.

Some of the banned Sox players admitted complicity in the scheme. Some did not feel they had done anything wrong, playing to win despite their names forever being muddied within the sport. The players suspended for life were first baseman Arnold "Chick" Gandil, infielder Fred McMullin, not a key player, shortstop Charles "Swede" Risberg, pitcher Claude "Lefty" Williams, center-fielder Oscar "Happy" Felsch, third baseman George "Buck" Weaver, who always protested his innocence and for decades appealed for reinstatement to baseball, pitcher Eddie Cicotte, who was on a possible path to the Hall of Fame, and the famous "Shoeless" Joe Jackson, who was definitely on a path to the Hall of Fame. Jackson, a lifetime .356 batter, who in 1908 hit .408 for Cleveland, also felt he was not guilty of any wrongdoing and always contended he had played to win during the Series.

Landis was aware the Chicago trial of the hometown ball players was a sham and he took command to set wrongs right. "Regardless of the verdict of juries," Landis wrote in his edict, "no player who throws a ballgame, no player that undertakes, or promises to throw a ballgame, no player that sits in conference with a bunch of crooked players and gamblers where the ways and means of throwing a game are discussed, and does not promptly tell his club about it, will ever play professional baseball."[1]

While Reds players, managed by Pat Moran, believed they won the Series fairly, due to their own abilities, to some extent the shadiness of what surrounded the White Sox diminished the accomplishment in some eyes. Heinie Groh (.310 average), Edd Roush (.321 average), Slim Sallee (21-7 record), Dutch Reuther (1.82 earned run average) and the others, were always proud of the achievement. Why wouldn't they be? Until 1939, it was the only time in the 20th century the Reds had won the pennant and appeared in the World Series.

Many view the 1927 Yankees, termed the "Murderers Row," as one of the best baseball clubs of all-time. That team was loaded, but the Yankees under Jacob Ruppert's ownership and Ed Barrow's astute business and personnel manager (both would go into the Hall of Fame), had been loading up by then. Although the Babe's 60 home runs in '27 was a single-season record that stood for 37 years, fans forget that on his way to his career 714 home runs he hit 54 dingers in 1920 and 59 in 1921, punctuating the conclusion of the Deadball Era. In 1920, when he concussed those 54 balls out of the park, the closest any other team came to his individual total was the 50 clouted by the St. Louis Browns.

Until Ruth's arrival in New York, the Yankees (and under their previous nickname of Highlanders) had been nondescript. They won their first pennant in 1921, their second in 1922, but lost the World Series to the nearby Giants both times. They won their first crown in 1923, won the pennant again in 1925, and won the World Series again in 1927 and 1928. That was a first-look at a Dynasty. But even in the waning days of Ruth's career, they were as powerful in the 1930s. New York won the championship in 1932, and then under manager Joe McCarthy (another leader Hall-of-Fame bound) they won it all in 1936, 1937 and 1938. So the 1939 Reds were facing a juggernaut, a team hot for its fourth straight title. To illustrate the Yankees' potency that campaign, the team scored 967 runs while the pitching allowed just 556.

The one smudge on the near-perfect nature of the season was the sudden diminishment of Lou Gehrig's skills. Deemed the greatest first-baseman of all time, Gehrig, alongside Ruth, was part of the most dangerous batting duo in history. Gehrig had a lifetime .340 batting average with 493 home runs and 1,995 runs batted in. Five times he led the American League in RBIs, four times in runs and three times in homers, out-battling Ruth on those occasions. Famously, he set the Major League consecutive games played streak of 2,130 that stood until Cal Ripken of the Baltimore Orioles broke it in 1982 and continued on to set the still-standing record of 2,632 straight.

Gehrig's streak began in 1925, but ended early in the 1939 season. He appeared in just eight games at the end, with 33 plate appearances and hit a weak .143. His strength had deserted him mysteriously and he benched himself to end the streak. Soon enough, Gehrig and the public learned he was sick with an incurable disease. Until then, Gehrig had been called "The Iron Horse." But the great and powerful, admired and beloved Gehrig was suffering from amyotrophic lateral sclerosis, and his body had begun a wasting away process during the previous season when his performance began to slide. Diagnosed at the Mayo Clinic, the illness ravaging Gehrig came to be better known unofficially as "Lou Gehrig's Disease." Manager Joe McCarthy had sensed something was off with Gehrig, even before he

## 13. The 1939 World Series

knew. "I don't know what's wrong with him," McCarthy said, "but it isn't merely that he is slowing down as a player. There is something physically wrong with him, something that is robbing him of his power. He isn't popping up, striking out, or just getting a piece of the ball. He is hitting the ball squarely, but it isn't going anywhere."[2]

Things got worse from there and Gehrig removed himself from the lineup on May 2. When McCarthy asked why during their poignant conversation, Gehrig said, "For the good of the team." He raised the issue of quitting, but McCarthy told him to just take some time off. He would use Babe Dahlgren at first base, but the job was still Gehrig's.[3] Gehrig was given his fatal prognosis on June 19 and he promptly retired. On July 4, the Yankees held "Lou Gehrig Day" at Yankee Stadium. In one of the most moving sports-related speeches ever delivered, a reluctant Gehrig stood at a microphone before an adoring crowd. Even as he wiped a tear away, Gehrig referred to himself as the "luckiest man on the face of the earth."[4]

So as the Yankees blitzed the American League that summer, they did so without their leader, shocked by the knowledge of the paralysis and death at a young age (less than two years later) facing him. Gehrig went from an active player in the lineup to having his No. 4 jersey retired that July 4. The Baseball Hall of Fame building in Cooperstown, New York, had not opened yet, though classes had been chosen since 1936. In 1939, the waiting period for appearing on the ballot was waived so Gehrig could be considered. He was immediately elected in December, after the World Series, but coincidentally at the winter meetings in Cincinnati.

New York did not have Lou Gehrig in the lineup anymore for the World Series versus Cincinnati, but it hadn't mattered during the pennant race and no one thought it would matter now. Catching for the Yankees was Bill Dickey, a .302 hitter that year, who was headed to the Hall of Fame. Second baseman Joe Gordon would also end up in Cooperstown. Playing center, the successor to Gehrig as King of the Dynasty, was Joe DiMaggio. He merely batted .381 with 30 home runs and 126 RBIs during the regular season.

Those were just the Hall of Famers in the starting lineup. There was no shortage of good hitters in the rest of the batting order either. Third baseman Red Rolfe batted .329. Young Charlie Keller, just 22 and getting started, hit .334. And George Selkirk batted .306. Everyone in the starting lineup slugged at least 10 home runs and four of those players drove in more than 100 runs. Clutch Tommy Henrich got more than 400 plate appearances in 99 games and hit .277.

Red Ruffing was the ace of the pitching staff with 21 wins. But six other Yankees won at least 10 games. That included another future Hall of Famer, Lefty Gomez, who went 12-8. He missed some regular turns on the mound because of a pulled side muscle. Even a lesser-known pitcher like righty Steve Sundra was having the time of his life, going 11-1, splitting time as a starter and reliever. It was difficult to have a losing record with all of that firepower behind you, though a couple of pitchers did. Really, though, the Yankees of 1939 were almost absurdly deep.

The Series was scheduled to open October 4 in Yankee Stadium. There had been frequent rainfall in the Bronx leading up to Game 1 and sportswriters took note of the fact groundskeepers had left the tarpaulin on the infield. The Yankees, it was announced, were 3-1 favorites to capture still another championship. McCarthy tapped Ruffing to start, which was no surprise. Bill McKechnie gave the nod to Paul Derringer over Bucky Walters to start for the Reds. There was much talk about continuing gray skies and whether the weather would allow for an as-scheduled start. Cincinnati outfielder Wally Berger was nursing a sore foot, which had been stepped on, and there was speculation he might not be able to start.

One Cincinnati writer said the Reds would have to rely heavily on Derringer and Walters and "On paper, the Yankees, proven under fire as world title-holders since 1936, outshine the Reds in every department. Yet the outfit is weaker this year than for the last three campaigns simply because of the absence of 'Iron Horse' Lou Gehrig, first-baseman-slugger extraordinary since 1925."[5]

Before the games began, the Reds huddled and determined which players would receive full Series payout shares and others who would get smaller cuts. There were 26 full shares voted. The Yankees agreed on 30 full shares. Oddsmakers, fans, and writers were in agreement that New York was the stronger club. If Reds players were irked, they did not let on. They did not outright predict victory, but they believed they could win. Certainly, first-game starter Derringer did not sound cowed. "Well, they still use a ball and a bat to play this game, don't they?" he said.[6] In an odd ploy to obtain entry to Game 1, Derringer received a pleading telegram. It read: "Send me plane fare and an additional hundred bucks and I'll be on hand tomorrow to lend you my moral support. Your brother, Jim." A family plea so as not to miss the big moment? Not so. "Must be my phantom brother," Derringer said. He threw the telegram into the trash.[7]

Game 1 began on the afternoon of October 4 at Yankee Stadium in front of 58,541 fans, with Ruffing on the mound and the Reds at the plate first. This was the tightest game of the Series. Ruffing and Derringer matched scoreless innings through three. Cincinnati's Bill Werber, Lonny Frey and Ival Goodman presented no problem for Ruffing in the first. In the home half, Derringer controlled Frankie Crosetti, Red Rolfe and Charlie Keller. Frank McCormick singled for the Reds to lead off the second inning, but Ernie Lombardi hit into a double play and Harry Craft struck out. DiMaggio made a fly-ball out to start the second and Dickey and Selkirk struck out. Berger, who did start despite his achy foot, struck out in the top of the third. Cincinnati briefly got excited when Billy Myers singled to center, but Derringer hit into a double play. The only interruption to the parade of outs for Derringer was a Ruffing single in the bottom of the third.

In the top of the fourth, the Reds reached Ruffing. They didn't batter him, but put a run on the board when Goodman walked, stole second and scored on a McCormick single. That 1-0 lead felt good, especially after Derringer escaped the bottom half of the inning while yielding only a DiMaggio single. A Craft single in the fifth gave the Reds a fresh base runner, but again a double play cost them, Myers ending the inning. New York was itching to score and did so in the home half of the fifth after Gordon singled and Dahlgren, probably the least heralded member of the starting lineup, doubled down the left-field line to send Gordon home. It was 1-1.

It was three-up, three-down for the Reds in the sixth, and for the Yankees, too, in the bottom of the inning. No one up for the Reds in the seventh could solve Ruffing, but Derringer zipped through the next three Yankees hitters, as well. It was the same for both starting pitchers once more in the eighth, their stuff always ahead of the hitters, setting them down quickly.

Derringer, Werber and Frey made outs in the top of the ninth, unable to put a base runner on, unable, really, to scratch Ruffing. Extra innings seemed likely after Derringer retired Rolfe on a grounder to second to start the last of the ninth. But then Keller tagged a Derringer offering. Goodman tracked it to deep right-center and came close to catching the smash, but couldn't reach it. The ball bounced away and Keller didn't stop running until he was on third base with a triple. DiMaggio was next in the order and McKechnie decided he wasn't going to let one of the most feared hitters in the game beat him. So Derringer issued an intentional walk. The pressure mounted as Dickey entered the batter's box, but he ended things with a single to center driving home Keller. New York had not crushed Cincinnati, but still managed to win, 2-1, in just one hour, 33 minutes.

Game 2 was played barely 24 hours later, also at Yankee Stadium, and the announced attendance for this one was slightly larger, 59,791. It was obvious McKechnie would start Walters. McCarthy had multiple choices, but decided to throw Monte Pearson, who in previous New York championship seasons had won 19 and 16 games. The way things went in the Series on October 5, it appeared Pearson could have won 100 games if given the chance. Walters was supposed to be the big gun, but Pearson out-pitched him, throwing a complete-game, two-hit shutout with eight strikeouts. Yankee hitters held up their part of the bargain and New York won, 4-0, taking a 2-0 lead in the Series. Oh, that game lasted just 1:27. Barely enough time to buy a hot dog before it ended.

The Yankees, who totaled nine hits, scored three runs in the third and one in the fourth. Walters did not walk a batter and struck out five, and went all the way, but the third wrecked his outing. Dahlgren led off with a ground-rule double and scored on a meek ground ball. But then Rolfe singled, Keller doubled, DiMaggio singled and Dickey singled. In the fourth, Dahlgren (Him again?) hit a solo home run and that wrapped up the scoring for the day.

Dahlgren was no Gehrig and he would readily admit that. Yet his first day in the lineup for Gehrig during the regular season he stroked two hits and he produced one of his best all-around seasons. Moreover, when more eyes were on him than before or since, in this World Series, Dahlgren turned in the best imitation of Gehrig that anyone could have. After that game, Cincinnati scribes and headline writers picked Dahlgren out as a difference-maker. One sportswriter said Dahlgren was supposed to be "the weak sister" of the Yankees' lineup, but was stealing the show. The *Enquirer* headline used the same phrase after New York won its second game.[8]

The Reds trailed, but McKechnie was not conceding, even though his top two starters took losses. The Series was decided by the first team to win four times, not twice. "I still think we'll win," he said, "and that we'll lick 'em if we get started hitting. I'm going to take the Series game by game."[9] Perhaps "playing them one game at a time" was not yet a cliché. He admitted Pearson's performance was overwhelming, but that didn't mean the Reds were cooked. "Let's give credit where credit is due," McKechnie said. "All I can say is Pearson, Pearson, Pearson."[10]

The Series adjourned to Cincinnati for the next two games. The Reds players were certainly ready to vacate New York. They hoped returning to Crosley Field would produce the spark to avoid a four-game sweep. Of course, Crosley was much smaller than Yankee Stadium and that turned the ability to obtain tickets into a competitive sport around the Queen City. They were precious items and the *Cincinnati Enquirer* ran a small item about how one of the newspaper's ad salesmen nearly ruined his experience. The man, A.E. Breitenstein, went around town showing off his tickets, but at the end of the day, he accidentally threw them away with some other papers into a downtown receptacle. However, he retraced his steps and reclaimed them from a garbage can.

Reds management held out 4,000 standing-room-only tickets for last-minute sale on the morning of Game 3 with a limit of two per customer at a cost of $3.45 each. Bleacher tickets for additional Cincinnati games, particularly Game 4, the only other one guaranteed to be played at that point, would be available for $1.15 each. The gates would not open for Game 3 until noon, but fans began lining up for those standing room seats at 6 p.m. the evening prior.

## 13. The 1939 World Series

The atmosphere was electric in the streets for those hoping to witness the Reds' first home World Series game in 20 years. The campers wrapped themselves in blankets to ward off a night-time chill and some even built fires, as if they were in Yellowstone National Park rather than on a city street. After sunrise, when the rest of the city woke up, fans jammed the community. Taxi cabs doubled their usual rates. Parking prices were raised. Entrepreneurs who owned buildings across from Crosley, installed seating and charged admission for eager fans to try and watch action from high-rise windows, a la Wrigley Field in Chicago in the coming years. The mood was festive. The crowd flooded through the gates of the park early. Attendance was announced as 32,327 for the third game pitting New York's Lefty Gomez against Cincinnati's Junior Thompson. But some believed it was larger.

Under normal circumstances, if the season had gone as planned, this would likely have been Johnny Vander Meer's chance to pitch. But he never saw a minute of action in the Series. Gomez probably shouldn't have been out there, either, given his side issues. He talked McCarthy into using him instead of Oral Hildebrand.

During the sad moments after Gehrig had lifted himself from the Yankees' lineup, ending his consecutive games streak, Gomez, always a jokester, cracked wise, breaking up the mood for all the players, including Gehrig. Gomez said, "Hell, Lou, it took 15 years to get you out of the lineup. Sometimes I'm out in 15 minutes."[11] No one was laughing in Game 3 when that came true. Gomez surrendered three hits and one run in the first inning and was removed when he reinjured his side muscle.

McCarthy turned not to Hildebrand but to Bump Hadley when Gomez had to be removed. Hadley was a 34-year-old veteran right-hander who went 12-6 with a 2.98 earned run average that season. While never a superstar, Hadley (whose given name was Irving) won 161 games in a 16-year career, overall just a .500 pitcher, but someone who mixed outstanding seasons in with challenging ones for such poor teams as the Washington Senators and St. Louis Browns. Joining the perpetual Yankee winners was a gift for him and now he was unexpectedly in the spotlight. If fans did not know he transformed from Irving to Bump, the origin was oddly connected to him having the mumps. He did not have a bumpy road against the Reds, however. Summoned as an emergency fill-in, the 5-foot-11, 190-pound Hadley was exemplary. Picking up after Gomez's single inning, Hadley went the rest of the way, pitching eight innings, giving up seven hits and just two runs.

Although Thompson was just concluding his rookie season, he had seen enough activity not to feel too green, even in the daunting circumstances. This was a must-have game for his team, a likely make-or-break situation, down 2-0 in the World Series at home. Falling behind 3-0 would be bleak. But that's what happened. Hadley, who had already won a World Series game for the Yankees in 1936, pitched even better in this try for his second championship round win. It definitely beat having the mumps. He was a tad shaky in the second inning when Cincinnati used four singles to muster two runs, Werber and Goodman getting the run-scoring safeties.

Meanwhile, young Thompson, whose baseball life had so swiftly fast-forwarded, could not save the day. He went 4⅔ innings and the champs took him apart, scoring two runs in the first inning, two more in the third, and finally, three more in the fifth. All seven runs were charged to him in the Reds' 7-3 loss. Thompson walked the lead-off man in the game, putting on Crosetti. Two batters later, Keller, like Thompson a 22-year-old rookie, torched him for a two-run homer, blasting the ball over right field and out of the park. The Reds got their first run right off against Gomez, an Ernie Lombardi single scoring Ival Goodman and sending the left-hander to the dugout for medical attention. In the third, Thompson, who saw way too much of Keller, walked him. That set the table for DiMaggio, who smacked a second two-run homer off Thompson.

After a peaceful fourth, Thompson continued having difficulties in the odd-numbered innings. Rolfe reached on a single in the fifth, bringing up Thompson's least-favorite batter. Sure enough, Keller belted another homer. Thompson retired DiMaggio, but then Bill Dickey hit a solo home run. McKechnie then waved in Lee Grissom in relief. Although neither Grissom, who went 1⅓, or Whitey Moore, who tossed three innings, allowed another run, it was too late. "One of the things about the game of baseball is, when you're overmatched, you've got to admit it," Thompson years later. "That's the way that 1939 World Series was. I don't believe anyone was more overmatched than we were playing the New York Yankees. Those guys were absolutely awesome."[12]

There was no coming back for the Reds. At that point they would have loved to win a game, but they couldn't even do that. They made a good show of it, though, in Game 4, for the home 32,794 fans counted in the house at Crosley. Hildebrand did take the mound for the Yankees this time, without Gomez sneaking in for another chance. McKechnie went back to Derringer, one of his two horses that brought him this far. It was the only logical starting pitcher choice since Walters was less rested.

This game remained scoreless into the seventh inning, although McCarthy lifted Hildebrand after four innings with him throwing a two-hit shutout. Sundra followed and he hurled 2⅔ innings. He allowed three runs to the Reds, though none of them were earned. Derringer was sharp. He went seven full innings, and only at the end did the Yankees touch him for two runs. The first troublemaker was Keller, who launched still another home run. The sizzling Keller batted .438 in the Series. Although Derringer lived through the inning, Dickey also cracked a homer.

It was in the bottom of the seventh when the Reds rallied for the spurt that finished off Sundra. McCormick led off the inning with a grounder to Rolfe at third, who bobbled it for an error. That's why the runs were unearned. Al Simmons, who played such a limited role for the Reds this season, stepped up for a double and McCormick scored. Billy Myers walked and then back-up catcher Willard Hershberger pinch-hit for Derringer and stroked a single, scoring Simmons. Werber then drove home Myers with another single.

Walters came on in relief of Derringer for the eighth inning and shut off the Yankee run spigot. The Reds inched ahead, 4-3, in the bottom of that inning when Goodman doubled and Lombardi sent him home with a single. For the moment, Crosley fans were delirious. The boys were going to do it! They would play on. But the euphoria was brief. In the top of the ninth, the Yankees did what the Yankees do. Singles by Keller and DiMaggio, followed by a fielder's choice and an error with Dickey at-bat, knotted the game.

The Reds had last at-bats in the bottom of the ninth, a chance to end things right then. But the closest they came to breaking the 4-4 tie was a Werber lonely single. On to extra innings. That's when the sky fell on Walters, the National League MVP and winner of 27 games, and in peculiar fashion, on Lombardi, too. Crosetti worked Walters for a walk. Rolfe's sacrifice bunt moved Crosetti to second base. Keller swatted a grounder to shortstop, but Myers made an error. The next play was the heartbreaker and one of the strangest in World Series history. DiMaggio singled cleanly to right field. Crosetti scored easily and without controversy.

Goodman briefly mishandled the ball in right field. That was one of the two Cincinnati errors on the play given by the official scorer. Keller came charging around third going full blast to the plate as Goodman's throw sailed in. The ball beat Keller slightly, but the normally sure-handed Lombardi dropped the ball in attempting to make the tag. Keller was declared safe. But worse, Lombardi fell to the ground and stayed there, the ball lying nearby as DiMaggio, too, steamed all the way around the bases and scored on a single.

The uproar that followed was both immediate and long-lasting, tarnishing Lombardi's until-then sterling reputation. What happened? Why didn't Lombardi dive for the ball and prevent DiMaggio from scoring? There are multiple explanations. Famed sportswriter Grantland Rice was on the scene and was quoted decades later by a writer revisiting the situation. This is what he wrote at the time: "Senor Lombardi fell squarely on his broad back. The ball bounded out of his hands and lay at rest two feet from either hand. At this point, DiMaggio was just rounding third. Joe kept on traveling over the intervening 90 feet as Lombardi still lay at rest, a stricken being. The afternoon was insufferably hot and big Ernie was tired. He could have nailed Keller at the plate by holding the ball. He had no idea the roving DiMaggio was on his way to the plate."[13]

Almost instantly, Lombardi was vilified for his lack of movement. His nickname was "Shnozz" and writers said he took "a snooze" on the ground. One sportswriter accused him of being lazy. The real reason Lombardi was laid out was because in the collision with Keller he was hit below the belt and in the genteel choice of words commonly used at the time, no one wrote that he had been hit in that sensitive area.

DiMaggio later said, "Ernie was wronged" by the snooze label. "He WAS knocked out in a collision at home plate by Charlie Keller, who scored, and I saw immediately that something was haywire. I kept running and never stopped. Keller gave Ernie more than just a bump, as they described it. He put Ernie out of commission. Ernie said later in the dressing room he was not knocked out. You see, if he said he WAS dazed he would have been forgiven. But when he said he could see the ball right in front of him and didn't pick it up, well, the newspaper guys made him the goat."[14] Lombardi denied he had been knocked cold and refused to blame Keller for kicking him in the groin. Some years later, Lombardi said only, "It was an awful hot day in Cincinnati, and I was feeling dizzy. When Keller came in, he spun me around at the plate and I couldn't get up."[15]

It would have been so easy to tell the world he had been KO'd or passed out from the contact and the heat, but Lombardi never gave those excuses for the play, although it seemed certain he was abnormally physically affected by something, surely not simply cavalierly performing "Lombardi's Sit-Down Strike" as some sarcastic observers termed the incident.

After the bizarre, three-run scoring play, the Reds could not recover. Although both Ival Goodman and Frank McCormick wacked singles in succession to start the bottom of the 10th inning, they died on the basepaths and the Yankees won, 7-4. The winner's share from the Series for those 30 Yankees was $5,542 apiece and the full loser's share for those 26 Reds was $4,193 each.

Besides the memory of being the starting pitcher in a World Series game, and watching the Yankees beat him and his teammates around, Thompson long carried an image of an ill Lou Gehrig in his mind. He had pitched to a still fairly robust Gehrig in spring training, and like everyone else attuned to the sport, was aware of the end of Gehrig's consecutive games streak, and the moving ceremony at Yankee Stadium. But Thompson did not realize the extent of damage Gehrig's sickness was doing to his body until he saw him across the diamond at the World Series.

"It was a shock to see him in the late fall because I had not seen him since the spring," Thompson said 54 years later. "By that time he was shuffling his feet to stay up. It was sickening to see such a hulk of a man in this kind of shape. I saw Lou from our dugout and to stand up he'd have to hold on to something and shuffle his feet to move. It was sad. We just couldn't believe it that he had failed that rapidly. I can see him now. He was quite a player and quite a personality."[16] Gehrig was just 36 then, and should still have been in uniform, still helping his Yankees capture a fourth straight world title. Instead, he was a spectator.

In essence, that was what the mean analysts accused Lombardi of being in the clutch. It was surprising how so many who had always liked the man, respected his fielding, and admired his hitting, seemed to turn on him. Lombardi never lived down the play. In his later years he became bitter and reclusive and blamed the constant harping on this one home-plate incident for keeping him out of the Hall of Fame.

Walters, who was right there on the mound and barely 60 feet from the plate, defended Lombardi. "It was a silly rap," said the pitcher who took the loss in Game 4 as a result of that complicated play. "But the Yankees beat us four straight and they had to pick on something, I guess. You can blame part of the thing on me. I was pitching and I should have been behind home plate, backing up Lombardi. But the run didn't mean anything, anyway."[17] By that, Walters meant Crosetti had already scored the game-winner and the other two runs were gravy. "I hope Lombardi doesn't feel too bad about that." (But he did.) "It was played up so big. If a fellow was sensitive at all, it would really bother him, them trying to make a goat out of you."[18]

Vander Meer was no more of a participant in that World Series than Gehrig, present but not close to being inserted into the lineup by McKechnie. But those were his guys and Lombardi was his man. He resented the vilification of the great catcher and he also had his own replay of what really occurred, something not verifiable any more than other retellings because there was no such thing as television instant replay at the time. "I'll give you the true story on that," Vander Meer said of the infamous play. "The throw from the outfield came in on a short hop and hit Lom in the cup. You just don't get up too quick. Somebody put out the word that Lombardi went to sleep, took a snooze. He was paralyzed. He couldn't move. Anybody but Lombardi, they'd have had to carry him off the field."[19] A variation of the Keller-kicked-him-in-the-family-jewels theory.

Thirty-eight years had passed when Vander Meer and Walters spoke and Lombardi, still living, had not yet been chosen for the Hall of Fame, something those pitchers thought was a disgrace. "Lombardi belongs in the Hall of Fame," Walters said. "He did everything but run good. And he was a hell of a guy on the club. Everybody loved him." Vander Meer echoed that thinking. "How he's not in the Hall of Fame, I don't know," he said. "If you took a survey of every big-league pitcher, they'd tell you Lombardi was the last guy they ever wanted to face in a clutch situation."[20]

Cincinnati baseball fans enjoyed a 97-win regular season. They reveled in a return to the World Series for the first time in a generation, even if it resulted in a four-game sweep and the public humiliation of one of their favorite players.

But even in October, in the midst of the Series, there were hints the world at-large was on the verge of imploding, even if all of the warning signs were centered in Europe. A man had risen to power in Germany, introducing a new philosophy of hate disguised as nationalism. Adolf Hitler, one of the most evil men the world has ever known, was hell-bent on eradication of those who in his mind were not pure of ancestry, and his ambition was to overrun the continent.

In the same edition of the October 7 *Cincinnati Enquirer* that reported on the joyous massing of crowds to celebrate the Reds and to jam Crosley Field, were adjacent articles that hinted of portending tragedy. One story's headline read, "Nazis Hope F.R. [President Franklin D. Roosevelt] Will Intervene in Peace Effort."[21] Of course, there would be no need for a "peace effort" if Hitler had not inflamed tensions, made obvious his imperial aims, and stuck to renewing a Germany ravaged in World War I rather than building huge armies and arming his country to take on the world.

An appeasement was all a hoax anyway. In much the same manner Hitler had tricked Great Britain in 1938 into ceding Czechoslovakia without a fight.

On December 1, less than two months after the end of the World Series, Hitler's German army invaded Poland, triggering World War II. Baseball players, as most Americans did, probably thought this had little to do with their daily lives. The United States, ill-prepared for war at the time, strained mightily to stay out of the conflict for as long as possible. That position remained in place until December 7, 1941, when Japanese allies of the Nazis bombed Pearl Harbor.

In the wake of the invasion of Poland so soon after the loss in the World Series, it was likely few members of the Cincinnati Reds connected that international development with the probability that before the otherwise natural end of their baseball careers they would be wearing other uniforms belonging to different divisions of the U.S. Armed Forces. But such a day was coming.

For the time being, the Reds' pride had been dented. But now they had a sense of how good they were and how good they could become. The next challenge was to win another National League pennant in 1940, return to the World Series, and this time beat the American League team waiting for them.

# 14

# The 1940 Regular Season

The best that could be said of Johnny Vander Meer's 1939 season, merely a year removed from his great glory, was that he was on the periphery of the excitement. His ailments sidelined him from making much of a meaningful contribution to the National League pennant winners, other than his five victories.

Their performance during the regular season and gaining a spot in the World Series had certainly provided confidence to the Cincinnati Reds. If there was anxiety of a never-having-been-here type it had been erased by winning the flag. But the attitude of the franchise was not that a peak had been reached, but that the team was on the rise, would still get better. And now that the players had been there, they would be better prepared to cope with the hoopla of the World Series. Of course, it was simply playing on the biggest stage that the Reds found intimidating. Assuredly, the New York Yankees had something to do with the 4-0 sweep. But the Yankees could not keep winning forever, could they? Cincinnati was determined to test that theory.

Vander Meer had to arrive in spring training in Florida with a sense of hopefulness that things would get better for him than they had been in 1939. Under all definitions, Vander Meer was starting all over in Tampa. His brief star turn from tossing those no-hitters counted for nothing except as potential. He was like a rookie in his status, in a must-prove situation. The organization's expectations for him were lower. The big guns of the pitching staff, Bucky Walters and Paul Derringer, were in their prime. Junior Thompson was ready for year two. Sure, there would always be a place for a hurler who could make his pitches dance. But Vander Meer was just one of the hungry showing off their arms. "I'm going down there as a busher," he said. "I'm just trying to prove to Bill McKechnie that I have the stuff. And I'm sure that I can make the grade."[1]

McKechnie was not closing any doors, but he was cautious in investing too much energy in believing what Vander Meer could offer. The manager had basically won a pennant without him the year before. Could Vander

Meer be counted on? Would his arm hold up? Pitching arms are mysterious tools at the best of times. Vander Meer's had failed him a year ago. He was seeking to prove he could deliver the goods in 1940 the way he had in 1938. "His arm is all right," McKechnie proclaimed in Florida. "Yes sir, his arm is all right. He can wheel the ball in there just as he did before his arm went bad." What McKechnie was not sure about, he told sportswriters, was if Vander Meer's head was in the right place. He did not know if the setbacks Vander Meer faced had damaged his psyche. "You see, he had plenty of hard luck and maybe it shook his confidence. I'm pretty sure he has his stuff back again, but he'll need confidence to put it over."[2]

It is not clear if confidence was an issue, but wildness always was when it came to dissecting Vander Meer's work on the mound. He apparently did not regain McKechnie's confidence in spring training outings, though, because he was sent back to the minors. As the Reds embarked on the new season, firmly seen as contenders, if not favorites for another NL pennant, Vander Meer was not with the team. He'd been shipped to AA Indianapolis in the American Association. Used solely as a starter, Vander Meer appeared in 14 games, going 6-4 with a 2.83 earned run average. That was fine, but naturally enough there were other contenders in Cincinnati vying for rotation spots behind Walters, Derringer and Thompson. The competition was tough.

The biggest surprise success story was trade pick-up Jim Turner. Cincinnati swapped Les Scarsella and some cash to Boston for Turner, who was 36 that year. Turner had been a 33-year-old rookie with the Bees/Braves in 1937, winning 20 games with a league-leading 2.38 earned run average and 24 complete games. A native of Tennessee, Turner grew up on a dairy farm and in the off-season he delivered product, earning the baseball nickname "The Milkman."[3] "I won 20 games for the Bees last season," Turner said in the spring of 1938. "Maybe I was lucky. Some folks say it was a stunt that I will never be able to duplicate. Yet I don't know. It may be that life begins at 40, but I'm sure that a pitcher's life doesn't end at 30. I've heard a lot about this pitching record being a flash in the pan, but I can't conceive of any reason why it should be. Just take into consideration that I've been pitching professional ball for 12 years and that I had no more stuff in 1937 than in many of the preceding seasons. I'll be tossing them up to the same bunch of hitters that I faced last year."[4]

This was all well and good, but in this case the skeptics prevailed. A year later, Turner went 14-18 with an earned run average more than a full run higher. The next season he dropped to 4-11 with an ERA of 4.28. Boston was ready to sell. The Reds took a chance and the McKechnie influence figured into it. McKechnie was Turner's manager in Boston when he had that ground-breaking season. Somewhat remarkably, under McKechnie's leadership again in Cincinnati, Turner turned in the second-best year he ever had in his career, finishing 14-7. This proved all over again that McKechnie seemed to know what he was talking about in handling pitchers.

Whitey Moore was back, too, going 8-8 with a 3.63 ERA. But the other surprise major contributor was Joe Beggs. Beggs, whose nickname was "Fireman," hadn't even pitched in the majors in 1939. He spent the entire season in the Yankees' farm system, a victim of too much talent in the organization. In 1938, in a short stint, he went 3-2 for New York. In another astute front office move, Cincinnati parted ways with Lee Grissom to obtain Beggs. Used only in relief, Beggs went 12-3. Although the role of the reliever was in its embryonic stages, he finished 24 games with a 2.00 earned run average. Beggs, already 29, single-handedly made the Reds' bullpen one to be reckoned with that season.

A handful of other pitchers, Vander Meer included, showed up on the mound from time-to-time during the 1940 season. Vander Meer was promoted to the Reds from Indianapolis late in the year and did post a 3-1 record with a 3.75 ERA. By then, thanks to the others, the Reds had a Samson-like grip on first place, on their way to concluding the year with a 100-53 record.

There were some changes in the field, too. Wally Berger was at the end of his career. He played in just two games for Cincinnati and although he did bat .317 for the Phillies, he only played in 20 more games for Philadelphia before retiring at the end of the year. The Reds got no pop on offense out of the shortstop position. Billy Myers played in 90 games, but hit just .202. Eddie Joost, his best years ahead of him, showed up in 88 games and hit .216. Catcher Ernie Lombardi, seemingly unaffected (at least then) by the World Series–ending miscue, was his usual self on the field, hitting .319. Frank McCormick was better than ever at first. Lonny Frey at second and Bill Werber at third, were back in their customary slots, as were center-fielder Harry Craft and right-fielder Ival Goodman. Without Berger, however, there was room for someone new.

The new guy was Mike McCormick. Although he was called Mike, his given name was Myron, and as a 23-year-old rookie that season, the second McCormick in the lineup, batted .300. He could get on base, but his power was almost nonexistent. The righty-swinging McCormick hit just one home run that season and 14 total in a 10-year, big-league career. That was sort of the opposite of Berger, who was known for his home runs.

Several other guys contributed a little of this and a little of that. Back-up catcher Willard Hershberger hit .309 in 48 games behind Lombardi, who played in 109 contests that summer. Lew Riggs hit .292 in 41 games, though he came to the plate just 74 times. Outfielder Jimmy Ripple hit .307 in 32 games. In 31 games, Johnny Rizzo hit .282. Dick West only appeared in seven games, but hit .393. Morrie Arnovich played much more often, inserted in 62 games and taking 226 at-bats. He hit .284. One thing for sure was that McKechnie never should have run out of reliable pinch-hitting options.

McCormick Junior, as Mike or Myron might have been called with the Reds since no one, with the possible exception of his mother, used Myron, was a worthy addition. If anyone else veered into Myron territory he would say, "Call me Mike."[5] He was from Angels Camp, California, site of the discovery of the mineral in the California Gold Rush of 1849. A Cincinnati sports page headline writer had fun with that early in McCormick's stay with the team as one way to welcome him: "Mike McCormick, Born Where Gold Rush Started in '49, Looks like 'Pay Dirt' as Left Fielder for Cincinnati."[6]

McCormick was originally signed by the Cleveland Indians at 17, but Commissioner Kenesaw Mountain Landis ultimately ruled the Indians had violated the rules by keeping McCormick at minor-league Buffalo too long after his option ceased. He became a member of the Washington Senators organization, but was sent to the minors, in Indianapolis, a team the Reds were also connected with. Cincinnati bought McCormick's contract from the American Association club where they sometimes sent their own players, including Vander Meer. Mike McCormick was not related to Frank McCormick except through the commonality of baseball. At 6 feet tall and 190 pounds, he was strong enough looking to bash the ball to the moon, but as his career played out baseball people learned he only hit four-baggers when hurricane force winds were behind him. As an example of where McCormick's worth lay in the batter's box, besides an overall knack for getting on base, he led the National League in sacrifice hits in 1940. In essence, that made him the anti-slugger.

The arrival of McCormick was timely for the Reds. During the course of the 1939 season, as successful as it was, eight different players spent time in left field. Not all of them were back to stake a permanent hold on the job, but McCormick stood out in spring training enough for McKechnie to give him every chance to get a grip on the role. In addition, Goodman and Craft were dealing with injuries, giving McCormick regular spring playing time. "This is your job, but don't blame me if you fail to keep it," McKechnie told McCormick.[7] Then in a series of nine exhibition games against the Boston Red Sox, McCormick batted nearly .400 and he kept it.

On opening day at Crosley Field, McCormick smacked a double in his first at-bat and then made two notable catches in the field to help the Reds win 2-1 over the Chicago Cubs and Bill Lee. Paul Derringer was Cincinnati's first-game pitcher and he won it. Although Mike McCormick did not score any runs, he did have a single, so it was a memorable debut. Starting

## 14. The 1940 Regular Season

out 1-0 meant the Reds were tied for first place in the National League. There were not many days all season—pretty much only during the first two weeks at the end of April, and then in the first days of May—when the Reds were not in first place in 1940. The Reds won their first three games of the season behind Derringer, Thompson and Walters, in that order. They were 6-3 when April turned to May and while they were 13-4 by May 9, they were in second place behind the Dodgers' 12-2. After, though, there was only one other day in May the Reds did not go to bed in first place. They completed the month at 25-10 with a two-game lead.

Cincinnati did not really have losing streaks that summer. There were only three days in June the team was not in first place. After losing to Brooklyn, 11-6, on June 15, the Reds' record was 32-17. But the Dodgers were sitting at 32-13, giving them a two-game lead in the standings. The Reds kept up their hot play and at the conclusion of June the squad's record was 41-21 and led the standings by 1½ games. At the All-Star break, following a 4-3 victory over the Chicago Cubs by Beggs, Cincinnati was 46-23 and in first place by a half game.

The annual All-Star event was played at Sportsman's Park in St. Louis. The Reds were only decently represented given their status in the league and compared to the previous year. Pitcher Paul Derringer was chosen for the fourth time and partner Bucky Walters for the third time. Lombardi was picked at catcher for the fifth time and the other Cincinnati player selected was Frank McCormick, for the third time. Six Dodgers were picked and five New York Giants. For the second year in a row, Derringer was the starter for the National League. He threw to Lombardi, too, with McCormick and Walters reserves. Derringer hurled two innings, gave up one hit, and got the win in the 4-0 National League triumph. Walters relieved him, also pitching two innings, and not even allowing a hit. McCormick went 0-for-1 at the plate, but Lombardi crashed a single in the first inning when the NL scored three of its runs.

Back in Cincinnati right after the All-Star break, the Reds edged the Dodgers, 6-5, on July 11 at Crosley Field to increase their margin in the standings by another game. Walters went the distance and did give up those five runs, though only three were earned. Cincinnati got the winning run in the bottom of the eighth on a pieced-together rally. Joost got things going with a lead-off walk. Walters bunted him to second base, setting up an intentional walk to Werber. Ival Goodman's single brought in the run.

That was a pivotal win. Cincinnati was never out of first place again for the rest of the season. The lead mushroomed from there. Cincinnati won five out of the next six games, lost one, and then won seven in a row. Going on a 12-2 spurt between July 13 and July 26 broke the pennant race wide open. By the 26th, the Reds had an eight-and-a-half-game lead on second place. Derringer won six games in July. The Dodgers began July with a seven-game winning streak, seemingly prepared to put the heat on the Reds after the All-Star game. But the Reds romped, and the Dodgers faltered between July 11 and July 26 going 6-11 with one tie. By season's end the Dodgers were still in second place, but 12 games behind the Reds with 88 wins. The next year, Brooklyn would win the pennant, so there might have been carryover from what the Dodgers did accomplish, much as the way the Reds matured between 1938 and 1939.

The pitching truly came through. Derringer won 20 games with a 3.06 earned run average. But Walters topped him again. Walters did not match his inimitable 27-win campaign of 1939, but he did win 22 games with a 2.48 ERA. Those guys were the leaders of the pack, expected to and carrying the weight of the responsibility without blinking.

Thompson improved on his rookie season, finishing 16-9, but this time it wasn't a surprise, just a continuation of his development. His earned run average was 3.32 and he hurled 225⅓ innings. He wasn't a strikeout guy, but he did fan more than he walked. He won his 13th game of the year with a four-hit shutout of Boston on August 24. He would have reached that level sooner, but had a bit of a win drought in July. Thompson made a strong impression on one scribe, who called him "the Reds' coming ace. He has youth, plus fine equipment, and size strength."[8] In the same article it was accurately predicted it was likely Thompson would complete the season with 16 or 17 wins.

Thompson captured his final three victories of the regular season in September. Thompson's 15th win of the year on September 12, was not as picturesque as many of his others, but the 9-4 triumph (he gave up 11 hits in the complete game, five coming in the ninth inning when New York scored all of its runs, to induce some nail biting) did eliminate the New York Giants from pennant contention. Thompson had two hits of his own, as well as two runs batted in. It was observed in one newspaper's game story that it was the fifth time Thompson beat the Giants in 1940. The season-capping 16th win was recorded with another shutout, this one a two-hitter, over the St. Louis Cardinals on September 25. It was obvious Thompson would be the third man for McKechnie in the World Series behind Derringer and Walters.

When Joe Beggs was acquired from the Yankees for Lee Grissom, the National League Service Bureau, the league's public relations arm at the time, said it was a swap of "Looney Lee" for "Sensible Joe."[9] It was noted that to that point in his career, mostly in the minors, Beggs had pitched 1,018 innings and walked just 248 batters, an average of only one per 4.11 innings. One might wonder if in the back of his mind Bill McKechnie was thinking about Johnny Vander Meer's penchant for bases on balls. The son of a steel worker, Beggs' father couldn't believe anyone would pay good money for playing baseball. Beggs was a born thrower, apparently. He was so good at throwing the javelin after only briefly dabbling in the event in high school, he earned a track and field scholarship to college and some thought he was a good candidate for the 1936 United States Olympic team going to Berlin. But Beggs chose throwing baseballs over javelins for his real commitment. He won 22 and 21 games in consecutive seasons in the minors for the Yankees' organization, but the team lost interest in him as he moved up.

In 1940, Beggs was a marvel out of the bullpen for the Reds. His final record was 12-3 and he started only one game among his 37 appearances. Practically no one hit him hard. Beggs won for the first time May 4, the victor in an 11-inning game. He picked off a couple more wins before the end of the month, but there were lengthy gaps between decisions. In a different era there was still more reliance on a complete game. The save statistic had not been invented for relievers and was only retroactively figured into the statistics of early specialists like Beggs. There was little doubt McKechnie grew to trust Beggs the more he used him in tight situations. Beggs won four games in September and added four saves.

Once the Reds beat back the Dodgers in July they just kept adding to their first-place lead. Everything was going as well as could be expected. The pitching had more depth than in 1939, the key hitters were hitting, and there wasn't a team on the horizon that could prevent them from winning the National League pennant. As long as there were no serious injuries to any of the most important players (fingers crossed), the Reds seemed to be on a comfortable cruise over placid waters.

And then something unthinkable happened. Almost all members of the team woke up to sunshine each day, but one player never seemed able to see through growing storm clouds, even if they were all in his head. Willard Hershberger was only the occasional starter backing up Ernie Lombardi at the catcher's spot. He was a very good hitter. Though he almost never banged home runs, Hershberger was batting .309 on August 3. Hershberger was 29. He stood nearly 5-foot-11 and weighed a few pounds under 170. He was in just his second season in the majors, but had impressed other baseball people with his savvy swinging. "A real good contact hitter," said Reds pitcher Junior Thompson. "In my business, that's the kindest thing we can say about a hitter. He gets the bat on the ball."[10] Gabe Paul, the long-time baseball executive for several teams, but the Reds' traveling secretary and public relations man in 1940, said of Hershberger, "As good a hitter as I ever saw at getting a man in from third with two outs. A hell of a ball player."[11]

What McKechnie and other players knew about Hershberger by then was that he was a somewhat twitchy guy, given to fits of melancholy, hypochondria, insomnia, and anger, often acting as a loner, sitting by himself on train trips to other cities, or even in the dugout. Despite his on-field success and despite the Reds' success, as the season progressed, Hershberger seemed more morose. The people around him worried. Then, in a fit of despair one day, he said to McKechnie, "My father did it and I'm going to do it, too."[12] "It" was commit suicide. Hershberger's father Claude, an oil field worker in California where Willard had grown up, killed himself in 1928, using a shotgun in the bathroom of the family home, his motive blaming financial woes. The gun was Willard's, taken on a hunting excursion into the woods. Rather than clean it and put it away that evening, he left the shotgun and shells leaning against a wall. His slumberless father picked it up and used it later that night.

The Reds blew a game on July 31 with Hershberger behind the plate when the Giants scored four runs in the bottom of the ninth inning off Walters. Hershberger blamed himself for calling the wrong pitches and became obsessed by what he considered terrible mistakes. The loss was virtually meaningless given the command Cincinnati had over the league, but Hershberger, often called "Hershie" by teammates, would not let go of the situation. He kept beating himself up with comments as other Reds told him to forget about it and calm down.

After the game, the Reds took a train to Boston to face the Bees in a series. All the way, before the team checked into the Copley Plaza Hotel, Hershberger kept repeating to third baseman Bill Werber that the late-inning loss was his fault. "I called for the wrong pitches," Hershberger told Werber. "If Lom had been in there, we wouldn't have lost. I've let the team down."[13] Werber tried to talk him down, constantly reassuring Hershberger that kind of thing happened in baseball all the time and reminding him the Reds had such a big lead in the pennant race it was a meaningless game.

The next day, August 1, the team was free. Werber and Hershberger met for breakfast in the hotel, took a walk, and then went to a movie. Hershberger kept up his moaning and focus on his performance in the previous lost game. Hershberger did not pay much attention to the movie. He left his seat and paced in the theater lobby. There was a double-header versus Boston on August 2. That morning, Hershberger went to a drug store and bought a bottle of iodine, which he intended to take to poison himself. He had considered slitting his throat with a razor, but his own shaver was an electric. He backed off from his suicide plan and went to the ballpark with the team. Lombardi was out with a sprained ankle. Bill Baker, the third-string catcher and Hershberger's roommate, caught the opener, which the Reds lost, 10-3. Hershberger went all of the way in the second game and went 0-for-5 as the Reds lost this contest, too, 4-3 in 12 innings, giving them a three-game losing streak.

In the sixth inning of the second game, a play occurred that alarmed McKechnie. The Bees' Max West lay down a bunt about 15 feet in front of the plate, but Hershberger never made a move for it. Whitey Moore was on the mound for Cincinnati and he bounded after the ball and threw West out. McKechnie ran out of the dugout and asked Hershberger if there was something wrong. Hershberger said, "You bet there is. I'll tell you about it after the game."[14] Infielder Lew Riggs knew Hershberger better than most of his teammates, who liked Hershberger fine, even if he did not often mingle with them, avoiding going out for drinks in a crowd, or even schmoozing much during down time. "He caught that game through instinct alone," Riggs said, almost making it sound as if Hershberger had been in a zombie-like state. "When he would come back to the bench, he would not say a word to anybody. I don't really believe he knew what plays had been made."[15]

Hershberger stayed in for the rest of the game. Immediately after it ended, however, McKechnie and coach Hank Gowdy led Hershberger to a spot in the empty stands at Braves Field for a talk. Once again Hershberger let loose with his self-flagellating beliefs that the loss of July 31 was all due to him. Once back at the hotel, McKechnie brought Hershberger with him to his own room. There the young man poured out his heart, told the manager his father had killed himself and that he was planning to do the same. "He cried like a kid," McKechnie said. "Seemed he cried an hour and then he told me he was worried about the club losing games he had caught. The poor kid. He was worked up particularly about that game in New York Wednesday night in the ninth inning. He said he thought he had called the wrong pitches. I told him everything was okay and he seemed all right."[16]

McKechnie kept soothing Hershberger and their conversation went on for hours. The games had been played during the day, and eventually the two men went out for dinner. When they parted, McKechnie thought Hershberger was in a much better frame of mind. Indeed, Hershberger had reassured McKechnie that he was all right and said he would be at the games the next day ready to go. Later, Bill Baker returned to his shared room with Hershberger and found him sitting in the dark smoking a cigarette.

The Reds were scheduled to meet the Bees in another double-header the next day, August. 3. That morning, Hershberger joined the *Cincinnati Enquirer* baseball writer Lou Smith for breakfast, then hung around the lobby. Other players were present and they said Hershberger seemed to be in a good mood. As time ticked by, the Reds readied for the games, taking taxi cabs in small groups from the hotel halfway across town to Braves field. As Hershberger made no move to go, several teammates urged him to get going. Second baseman Lonny Frey said, "C'mon, Hersh, let's go." Hershberger didn't budge, only saying, "Yeah, yeah, I'll be along." Paul Derringer was one of the last to leave at 11:55 a.m. "Aren't you coming, Hershie?" Hershberger replied, "Not yet. I'm waiting for a friend."[17]

All the Reds were gone, conscious of the time. Hershberger made no effort to join them. He went back to his room. When McKechnie inquired of his players about Hershberger's whereabouts they reported last seeing him in the Copley Plaza lobby. No one said he came with them. Recognizing this as a danger sign after his long discussion of the previous night, McKechnie had Gabe Paul call Hersberger. Hershberger picked up the receiver at 1:10 p.m., with an irascible greeting. When Paul informed him who it was, Hershberger said, "What do you want?" Paul said, "Bill asked me to call you. He's worried about you and he wants you to come to the ballpark." Hershberger replied, "I'm sick." Paul added, "You don't have to put on your uniform. Bill says you can come out and sit in the stands. He's concerned and he just wants you out here." Hershberger haltingly played along. "All right," he said. "I'll be right out."[18]

That was a lie. Hershberger had no intention of heading to the park to be with his teammates. He had just methodically waited for them all to leave. Sometime after he hung up the phone from talking to Paul, an estimated half hour, Hershberger took off his shirt and undershirt and used his electric razor to shave. Then he pulled together the hotel towels and made a sort of rug out of them on the bathroom floor. Then he reached for the sharp-bladed safety razor belonging to his roommate and cut his own throat.

As he had threatened, Willard Hershberger had committed suicide, if not by the same method, he had followed in his father's footsteps. And certainly not for the same reason, because he was not in financial straits. In fact, he should have been enjoying life on a championship team, making a good living playing baseball. But he was haunted by demons, miserable despite outward trappings of success. No one knew what he had done yet because everyone else was at Braves Field.

The Reds broke their losing streak with a 3-1 victory over Boston. Derringer was the winning pitcher. But although there was another game to be played, McKechnie very much had Hershberger in his thoughts. He learned the player had not come to the park as promised, so McKechnie asked a friend of Hershberger's named Dan Cohen, a Cincinnati shoe store owner, to go to the Copley Plaza and check up on him. Cohen went to Hershberger's room and knocked on the door. He received no answer. It took some doing, but Cohen talked a maid into letting him take a look inside because he was concerned for his friend. When he opened the door, he saw nothing, just neatly arranged items in the sleeping quarters. On a whim, he looked in the bathroom. He discovered Hershberger half leaning into the bath tub, a bloodied dead man. Horrified and distraught, Cohen returned to Braves

## 14. The 1940 Regular Season

Field seeking McKechnie. Riggs saw him, and instantly felt a premonition. "When I saw Dan Cohen running down to the bench during the second game, I knew that something terrible had happened to Hershberger," Riggs said. "Goose pimples broke out all over me and the fellows told me I turned white as a sheet."[19]

McKechnie turned the team over to Gowdy for the rest of the game, asking him not to inform the players about what happened until it ended. The Reds lost, 5-2, and then Gowdy got their attention in the clubhouse. "I want to tell you something," Gowdy said. "Willard Hershberger has just destroyed himself."[20] It was an odd choice of words, but nonetheless accurate. For most of the players it was an incomprehensible tragedy. Back at the hotel, a shaken McKechnie, who refused to look at the body, called them to his suite and talked to them as a group. He told the players about his long session with Hershberger after the games the day before and told them of the catcher's mention of suicide and of his father's. Several of the players cried as McKechnie talked them through it. McKechnie spoke for about a half hour to what he considered to be the best team in baseball. Although this was really no time for a rah-rah sports speech, he also knew as manager he had to hold the Reds together in a time of crisis. As they split up, McKechnie said, "The thing for us to do now is win the pennant and vote Hershie's mother a full share of the World Series money."[21]

Most of the Reds, and most others in baseball, were shocked by Hershberger's act. Only those closest to him in the dugout realized he was a man with many issues, but no one envisioned such a drastic action. One sportswriter quoted an unnamed former teammate, who recognized Hershberger had problems. "Hershie was one of those fellows who always thought he was suffering from something," the player said. "He took many medicines [that was true]. He was always shaking his head and blaming himself for mistakes that were made even by his teammates when he was in there. But he was as valuable to the Reds as any of the other regulars."[22]

As the leader of the team, McKechnie was sought for comment by the writers, but he spent time in seclusion before talking to them. Then he exhaled and met with them, doing his best to explain what he considered to be the unexplainable, and definitely was without a mental health diagnosis by a doctor. He was candid, but said Hershberger confided some personal problems to him that had nothing to do with the Reds and he pledged never to tell anyone else. He kept that promise, but did otherwise speak highly of him. "Hershberger was a highly intelligent, extremely high-strung boy," McKechnie told them. "I wish I knew yesterday what I know now—that he has always been subject to spells of extreme melancholia. Joe Beggs, our pitcher who played with him in Newark, tells me that at times the boy was bothered mentally."[23]

McKechnie recounted talking to Hershberger at the park and in his hotel room, saying that was for two hours and they had dinner together, the player eating "a fine roast beef meal." He said Baker urged Hershberger to join him on a ride to the park at 11:30 a.m., but Hershberger "said he would come out later because he wasn't working until the second game." McKechnie said after the time shared with him the night before his suicide he should have realized the right thing to do was keep tighter tabs on him on the morning of August 3. "He told me that he had been trying to get up the courage to kill himself. I thought it was just a passing freak because otherwise he didn't have a trouble in the world. He was a very clean-living boy. He wasn't interested in anyone except his mother, whom he idolized. He just built her a home in Three Rivers, California, and was very proud of it. He just bought himself a new car and he had no financial worries."[24]

In an adjacent room, several of the Reds were huddled, talking about Hershberger and his gun collection and how much he enjoyed listening to the radio. The writers, gauging McKechnie's overall distress, still did ask if he thought the tragedy would impact the club with the better part of two months left in the regular season. "It's too soon to say whether this will affect us mentally, so far as baseball is concerned," McKechnie said. "We certainly will miss Hershberger, however, for he was a dependable pinch hitter and an excellent catcher."[25]

The day after Hershberger died, the Reds had a third straight double-header to play against Boston. This peculiar scheduling resulted from three prior postponements, May 21 due to cold weather, June 24 because of rain and June 25 because of rain. Cincinnati lost the first game on August 4, 5-3, then won the second game, 12-9. Whether he was still hurting or not, Lombardi caught the first game. Baker caught the second game. In the high-scoring win, Jim Turner, the third Reds pitcher, got the victory by going 5⅓ and permitting just two runs. Frank McCormick, in the midst of a mighty year, almost beat the Bees himself in that one. He mustered four hits and six runs batted in.

Mercifully, the Reds had three days off after that, not resuming play until August 7 back in Cincinnati. The next day, August 8, as Bucky Walters beat the Chicago Cubs, 3-1, the Reds paid tribute to Hershberger in a memorial service at Crosley Field. There was a moment of silence and the American flag was lowered to half-staff. "We were shocked and saddened and terribly depressed," said Bill Werber, who was closer to Hershberger than many of his teammates. "Hershie was loved by everyone associated with the Reds."[26]

Between August 11 and August 23, the Reds staggered through one of their slowest stretches of the season, going 5-9. Whether that was a hangover from the Hershberger death or simply the law of averages of the long season, can't be told. But then the Reds began winning again and won the pennant going away. McCormick was the linchpin. In 1940 he batted .309 with 19 home runs and 127 runs batted in, along with 191 hits. A year after Walters won the National League Most Valuable Player award, McCormick did so. He won rather handily over St. Louis slugger Johnny Mize and his own teammates, Walters and Derringer came in 3-4 in the vote.

Actually, as sterling a showing as McCormick had in his 155 games, he felt he would have done better if not for some ills. "I had a funny crick in my back early last season that bothered me before the sun got hot," McCormick said when it was over. "At the same time I went into a batting slump that pulled me down to about .200. The pain came back this winter. When I went to Cincinnati for a routine checkup and X-rays didn't show anything wrong with my back, the doctors decided an impacted wisdom tooth might be doing the damage."[27] McCormick mostly did damage to other pitchers as the Reds recovered—at least on the field—from the Hershberger catastrophe.

Even Vander Meer played a part in the late going. Indianapolis had been restorative and he thought he was back to full strength, ready to be of assistance, although assistance was not desperately needed by this pitching staff. While still in Indianapolis, he said, "My arm is freer. I'm looser all over and my control is better. Give me a spot on the Reds and I'll stick." When McKechnie brought him back, the manager said nice things. "Johnny Vander Meer is back with us again after being treated in Chattanooga [Tennessee] for a kink in his pitching shoulder and I'm confident he will help us in our September campaign."[28]

Both men were right. Vander Meer did pick up three wins in September. On September 5, he beat the Pittsburgh Pirates 6-3, with a complete game. The result was good, but the process had some iffy moments. He gave up nine hits and walked five. The next time Vander Meer got the call was September 18 against the Philadelphia Phillies. This was a big deal because if he and the Reds won they would clinch the pennant. It was said general manager Warren Giles made the decision, ordering McKechnie to start Vander Meer. Junior Thompson later complained about the choice. Some pitchers thought it unfair for Vander Meer to get the honor of going for the pennant when Walters and Derringer had been stalwarts all season. He probably was including himself, too, without saying so. It was a legitimate point since Vander Meer could have pitched any old day.

No one realized what an epic the game would turn into. It went 13 innings and Vander Meer hurled 12 of them, containing the Phillies with three earned runs. He allowed plenty of base runners, though he struck out 10. Cincinnati won 4-3, with Beggs pitching the last inning in relief. Vander

Meer had actually scored the winning run, too. He doubled and chugged home on a Mike McCormick single.

"My biggest day in baseball," Vander Meer said.[29] He pitched those back-to-back no-hitters, yes, but in-between he had been injured and not played any major part in the Reds' 1939 success. But now he had this. It was the pennant-clinching win, but it also signified he was back, a Major League pitcher again, one who had conquered adversity. "What tickled me was I was throwing just as hard in the 13th as the first and I wasn't tired," Vander Meer said. "I knew my arm was back and I had a future ahead."[30] Vander Meer ended his season with a 3-1 record and a 3.75 earned run average. He did have a future. And the Reds had an immediate future of playing in a second World Series in a row.

## 15

# The 1940 World Series

The Reds were jubilant to be back in the World Series. An-unfinished-business mood definitely prevailed. In 1939, the feeling was pretty much a happy-to-be-here outlook. Getting back immediately said something about the quality of the team, and because of the Willard Hershberger suicide, its ability to overcome adversity. Carrying a 100-53 record into the post-season felt pretty special, as well. The only thing missing was the Yankees. After four straight world championships, the juggernaut had been grounded. Winners of the American League flag were the Detroit Tigers, with a 90-64 record. Detroit won the pennant by one game over the Cleveland Indians. The Yankees finished in third place. No one outside of New York was weeping. The rest of the baseball world was ready for a new champion.

The Tigers played in the World Series three straight times during the early days of the championship, losing three straight times, in 1907, 1908, and 1909 despite the presence of the great Ty Cobb. They fell to the Chicago Cubs twice and the Pittsburgh Pirates, then they didn't make it back until 1935. The Tigers were the most recent team not named the Yankees to win the crown. That year, with Hall of Fame catcher Mickey Cochrane as manager, Detroit beat the Cubs 4-2, in games. Playing at Briggs Stadium, the 1940 Tigers attracted 1,112,693 fans, the leading attendance mark in the American League. Manager Del Baker had a powerful hitting club, led by future Hall of Famers Hank Greenberg in the outfield and Charlie Gehringer at second base. Those were the staples, but there were other strong hitters in the lineup, too.

When it comes to discussing the Tigers of that era, the starting place is really Greenberg, who was a linear descendent of Babe Ruth. The right-handed hitting Greenberg is sometimes too casually overlooked when it comes to listing all-time greats. That is partially because he missed more than three seasons of his prime while serving in the military during World War II. Lifetime, the 6-foot-4, 210-pound Greenberg batted .313, but because of his shortened career his individual seasons shine more than his overall numbers. Greenberg led the AL in home runs four times, with a high of 58, within two of Ruth's single-season mark of the time, in 1938. In 1937, Greenberg knocked in 184 runs, though revisionists say it was really 183. Lou Gehrig once drove in 184 and the all-time record is 191 by the Cubs' Hack Wilson. Greenberg also won two Most Valuable Player awards. His career on-base percentage was .412 and slugging percentage .605.

The son of Jewish immigrants from Romania, Greenberg was also the subject of anti–Semitic taunts and was the best-known Jewish athlete in the country during his career. Once, when an important game fell on the Jewish New Year, in a highly publicized debate, Greenberg chose to play and basically won the game for the Tigers. Soon after, though, he sat out a game during the pennant race on Yom Kippur, the most important Jewish holiday on the calendar. The way Greenberg was baited, actually made him more observant as a Jew than he had been. "Sure, there was added pressure being Jewish," he said. "How the hell could you get up to home plate every day and have some son of a bitch call you a Jew bastard and a kike and a sheenie and get on your ass without feeling the pressure. If the ball players weren't doing it, the fans were. I used to get frustrated as hell. Sometimes I wanted to go up in the stands and beat the (crap) out of them."[1]

Cincinnati pitching was going to have to contend with Greenberg at the plate. Gehringer had been around much longer and was 37, but he had just completed his last All-Star season. Gehringer also had an MVP award on his resume and once won a batting title with a .371 average. Lifetime, Gehringer hit .320 with seven seasons of at least 200 hits. He was so consistent that Yankees star hurler Lefty Gomez nicknamed him "The Mechanical Man." Although much of his prime pre-dated the creation of the All-Star game, Gehringer was chosen for the first six of the affairs.

Greenberg had been a first-baseman, but shifted to the outfield to make room for Rudy York. York may not have been a ballerina around the bag, but he was such a terrific hitter he had to play. In 1940, York hit 33 home runs, drove in 134 runs, and batted .316. That was his best all-around season at the plate, though three years later he led the AL in homers and RBIs. Early on, just as York was becoming known to big-league scouts, he drew some favorable comparisons to Greenberg. "This York person has proved himself quite a powerhouse, even when compared to hard-hitting Hank Greenberg," a Detroit sportswriter penned. "He seemed able to hit the ball no matter where it is placed so long as it comes near the plate. And he has the power to give the ball wings once he gets hold of it. It must be said that he looks like a better ball player than Greenberg did the year he came up. However, Hank developed fast."[2]

Birdie Tebbetts, who had a lengthy career in the sport as a player, manager and scout for 53 years combined, was the Tigers' primary catcher that season, hitting .296. Tebbetts was a four-time All-Star as a player, rewarded more for his fielding and savvy than his power statistics. Pete Fox, .289, and Bruce Campbell, .283, split time in the outfield, but neither was a liability at bat. Mike "Pinky" Higgins, manning third base, contributed with the bat, too, knocking in 76 runs with a .271 average. Earl Averill, then 38, was nearing the end of his Hall of Fame career, but still hit .280 in 64 games that season.

Campbell was not as well-known as some of the other regulars, but he probably should have been. In 1935, stricken with meningitis, doctors only gave him a 50-50 chance of surviving. But he was back to the majors after that. The Philadelphia Sports Writers voted him "Most Courageous Athlete" for his comeback, and he didn't even play in Philadelphia, but for the Cleveland Indians.

Then there was the comparatively obscure Barney McCosky, also an outfielder. He was just 23, in his second season in the bigs and his performance that year had the Tigers believing he might be their next superstar. During the 1940 campaign, McCosky led the American League with 200 hits and 19 triples and hit .340. He did well, but not that well over the next seasons before entering the Navy for three years during World War II. When McCosky returned at 29 he was never quite the same caliber of player again, though his 11-season Major League career did end with a .312 average. McCosky did not have the easiest of lives. He was the youngest of nine children growing up during the Depression in Detroit after his mother passed away when he was only a year old. The family was so poor, McCosky once said, "Nobody had any money. We took mustard and ketchup sandwiches to school."[3] As a senior in high school, nutrition-deprived or not, McCosky hit an astounding .727.

Tiger pitchers knew they could count on good run support. But the pitching ranks were thin. The staff ace in 1940 was Bobo Newsom, a colorful figure who talked about himself in the third person. In a 20-year career, Newsom won 211 games (though he lost 222), was sometimes brilliant and sometimes uneven. Much like Babe Ruth, Newsom had trouble remembering people's names, so he called them all Bobo. In response, everyone else called him Bobo. Detroit was the sixth of nine teams Newsom pitched for in the days when there were only 16 in all. But he pitched for several of them more than once, as well. Newsom had three different stays with the St. Louis Browns and passed through the Washington Senators five times. It might be said Newsom never wore out his welcome since he could always go home again—to some home.

Along the way Newsom was a four-time All-Star. A three-time 20-game-winner, Newsom was also a three-time 20-game loser and four times in all led the American League in losses. Newsom, whose given name was Louis, had his best season in 1940, going 21-5. That year was one of his

All-Star seasons. He was already 32, but that might as well have been teenaged years in Newsom's odyssey since he did not retire until he was 45. Newsom was an innings eater, a true believer a starting pitcher should go the full nine innings once he was handed the ball.

During one of his numerous stops with the Washington Senators, Newsom was smacked on the knee with a line drive hit by Earl Averall, then with Cleveland, but in 1940 a teammate with Detroit. Washington manager Bucky Harris rushed out to see if Newsom was okay. Newsom said, "I think it's broke." Harris asked him if he wanted to come out, but Newsom said, "You kidding me? I said it was broke, I didn't say I was dead."[4] Newsom kept pitching and no one believed his characterization of the severity of the injury. But when he had the leg X-rayed, the kneecap was indeed broken.

Newsom was the lead actor on the staff, but Schoolboy Rowe went 16-3. The young Rowe was a gem during his early years in Detroit, When he won 24 games in 1934, his season included a 16-game winning streak. In the next two seasons, Rowe won 19 games each time. Then his arm went bad, he pitched infrequently, and returned to the minors. The 1940 season was a return to his best form and his record gave him an .842 winning percentage, the American League's best. Rowe may not have been quite as outgoing as Newsom, but he gave him a run. The 24-victory season provided much attention to Rowe and he was a guest on such radio shows as "The Eddie Cantor Show." In the middle of the broadcast, Rowe deviated from the expected script, suddenly blurting, "How'm I doing, Edna?" to his high school girlfriend.[5] The tag line followed Rowe for the rest of his career, players and fans shouting it out at him.

Tommy Bridges was next in line to take the ball when Baker was filling out lineup cards. Bridges spent all 16 of his Major League seasons with the Tigers and won 194 games. A six-time All-Star overall, between 1934 and 1936, the right-handed hurler won 22, 21, and 23 games, respectively. In 1940 he was a more pedestrian, if still-helpful 12-9.

A few other names are listed in the statistics under Tigers pitching for 1940, all of them stars at one point in their careers, but not that season. Hal Newhouser, just 19, went 9-9. A few years later he was the best pitcher in the American League, winning two Most Valuable Player awards, and he ended up in the Hall of Fame, but in 1940 he was far short of his peak. Fred Hutchinson later won a pennant as manager of the Reds. He was just 3-7 in 1940 at age 20 and all his best seasons were recorded after World War II. Dizzy Trout was already 25, but had the same record as Hutchinson that season, blossoming during the war years and immediately afterwards.

Surveying the Tigers' talent, the Reds could feel optimistic. Detroit's 90 wins were 10 less than the Reds notched and the Tigers did not have the aura of the Yankees. Winning it all this time around seemed quite doable.

It was also noted by the baseball world that the National League had not won the World Series since 1934. Those Gashouse Gang St. Louis Cardinals managed by Frankie Frisch and led by brother hurlers Dizzy and Daffy Dean, Joe Medwick, Pepper Martin and Leo Durocher beat the Tigers, and some of the same Tigers themselves, including Greenberg, Gehringer, Fox, Bridges and Rowe. Then the Yankees won those next four years.

On the eve of the 1940 Series, Cincinnati's Bill McKechnie said this group was the best team he had ever managed and rated it 25 percent improved over the 1939 pennant winners. In speaking with sportswriter Lou Smith, who was the one who ate breakfast with Hershberger on the day he killed himself, McKechnie said he believed the May trade that sent Vince DiMaggio to the Pirates for Johnny Rizzo was the last necessary piece of the roster acquired. "We're set now," McKechnie said. "I think he is just the man we need to give us that extra-base sock. And he fields good enough to get by."[6] Being "set" was not quite true. In late August, the Reds grabbed outfielder Jimmy Ripple off waivers from the Brooklyn Dodgers. In 32 games he gained McKechnie's trust by hitting .307 for Cincinnati over the rest of the regular season.

Smith did revisit the topic of Hershberger's demise in his World Series advance, writing, "This was a trying time for the boys. For a time it appeared as if they were going to crack up and blow their big lead. But the fatherly McKechnie never lost his grip on the reins. He guided them over this tragic hurdle. It required several weeks for the boys to snap out of it. But when they entered the backstretch, the Deacon applied the whip, so to speak, and his boys responded as only champions can, blasting through the backstretch and down the homestretch in one of the greatest finishes in the history of the National League."[7] Losing Hershberger was not insignificant. Besides the emotional turmoil provoked by his suicide, he had been an important player. Ernie Lombardi recovered from his aches and was able to play at his usual high level, at least part of the time. The gap between what Hershberger brought and Bill Baker did to the back-up role, was considerable, though.

Jimmie Wilson, who had already been the manager of the Phillies and converted Bucky Walters from infielder to pitcher, was on the Reds coaching staff. At 39, he was retired from donning the catcher's gear. But after Hershberger's death in August, he was activated. Wilson appeared in 16 games before the regular-season ended, able to hit .243 in 41 plate appearances. Theoretically, there would be no rush to play him in the World Series with Lombardi and his potent bat ready.

If the Reds harbored any doubt they were in for a war, the Tigers made it clear they came to swing when the Series began at Crosley Field on Wednesday afternoon, October 2, before 31,793 fans. Once again,

Cincinnati was festive, the fans excited to host a second World Series so soon after the 1939 wipeout. Two years in a row! This one has to be our turn, the Cincinnati baseball supporters had to be thinking.

At least until the second inning. McKechnie chose Paul Derringer as his first-game starter. The manager usually tilted Derringer's way over Walters when a big game was at hand. Del Baker went with Bobo Newsom, who was having a year. Crosley was all a-buzz at the start, but it doesn't take much to take the steam out of an optimistic sports crowd. An opposing team explosion does it every time. Derringer quickly set down shortstop Dick Bartell, McCosky and Gehringer in the first. The Reds briefly threatened in the home half of the inning when Mike McCormick doubled with one out. But Newsom polished off the following batters.

Things went sour very swiftly for Derringer and the Reds in the top of the second. Those Tiger bats began booming. Hank Greenberg led off with a single. Rudy York also hit a single. Campbell reached on an error and Derringer was in a pickle, bases loaded, nobody out. The fans were worried about the tense situation. This promised an early advantage to Detroit, but

**When the Reds won pennants in 1939 and 1940 and hosted two World Series, winning one, their home park was Crosley Field. It was tough to squeeze more than 34,000 fans in.**

it turned into much more than that. The next several batters were about to determine the outcome of the game. Higgins singled to center, scoring two men, and Billy Sullivan, starting at catcher, worked Derringer for a walk. Newsom stepped into the batter's box with a grand opportunity to help himself. But he grounded out to first base and Frank McCormick threw to Lombardi for a force out at the plate. That was only the inning's first out. It was also only a brief respite from the mounting damage. Bartell came up next and zinged a single to center, scoring two more runs. McCosky continued the parade with another single. When Newsom scored on that hit he had a 5-0 lead.

When McKechnie trudged to the mound to remove Derringer, there was still only one out in the second inning. Derringer's day was done after just 1⅓ innings. Whitey Moore came in from the bullpen and in a clever first move had Bartell picked off second base. However, shortstop Billy Myers dropped the ball for an error, essentially proof that nothing was going right for the Reds that day. Moore retired Gehringer and Greenberg without incident, but Detroit had feasted.

The Reds at last scored a run in the fourth inning after Ival Goodman doubled to center and Jimmy Ripple drove him home with a single to right. A dent. However, the Tigers quickly went to the repair shop. In the top of the fifth they reached Moore, who overall did an exemplary job over 6⅔ innings, striking out seven and giving up just two runs. These were the two. After York tripled, Campbell belted a two-run homer. The lead was up to 7-1.

Cincinnati added one more run in the bottom of the eighth. It was just an annoyance to Newsom. Bill Werber doubled and Goodman provided an RBI single. That was it. The final was 7-2, a thorough thrashing of the home team, and an impressive complete game from Newsom. That gave the Reds a five-game losing streak in the World Series, including 1939.

Being down 1-0 is a blip on the screen, going down 2-0 is the beginning of a landslide. The Reds absolutely could not afford to have that happen. The starting pitchers for Game 2 the next day, also in Cincinnati, were expected, Bucky Walters against Schoolboy Rowe. It is difficult to imagine the grim thoughts permeating Crosley Field and the Reds' dugout, though, when the Tigers jumped out to a 2-0 lead in the top of the first inning. There had to be momentary flashbacks to 1939 when the Yankees swept. For that matter, people had to wonder what McKechnie was thinking when Bartell led off the game with a walk and then Walters walked McCosky, too. Gehringer's single sent Bartell all of the way home and McCosky to third. Greenberg hit into a double play, but McCosky scored. With all 30,640 fans on the edge of a nervous breakdown, Walters struck out Rudy York.

The flip side of falling behind early was that it was early. Plenty of

Cincinnati at-bats to come. The Reds did not score off Rowe in the first inning and Walters, looking like himself again, set the Tigers down 1-2-3 in the second. Rowe was about to descend into misery in the bottom of the second inning.

Frank McCormick led off with a single. Ripple made an out, bringing up Jimmie Wilson. Wilson? Wilson. The old man was starting at catcher in place of Lombardi this day. It wasn't as if McKechnie was adding much speed, youth, or extra pop to the lineup by this switch. Wilson was on the edge of 40, had been retired, and if he was to hit a home run at this stage of life, it would most likely be by accident. No such heroics were forthcoming, but Wilson did single to right. This initiated an epidemic since Eddie Joost and Billy Myers followed with two more singles and the Reds had themselves a tie game. A bit of a scramble followed when Joost was caught off second base. Only it turned into an instant-replay type play of Game 1 when Moore had Bartell picked off and the move was spoiled by an error. Joost, too, lucked out and was safe on an error. It didn't help the Reds, though. Rowe made it out of the inning without any more problems. So it was 2-2.

That did not last very long. Walters handled the Tigers in the top of the third inning, but the attacking Reds got to Rowe again. Goodman reached first on a bunt single, but he need not have worked so hard for his safety. Two batters later Ripple ripped a home run out of the field on the right side. Now the Reds led, 4-2.

Walters was back to normal on the mound and Detroit did not touch him in the fourth. He got the first key hit in the home half of the inning with a double to left and the next teammate up, Werber, sent him home with another double. If they needed it, the Reds' confidence was restored. Before the end of that time at-bat, Cincinnati led 5-1 and Rowe was showering. The new pitcher for Detroit was Johnny Gorsica, another right-hander, who was a 25-year-old rookie. He went 7-7 during the season and the Tigers were high on his future. As it was, he never really had a better season, though he was exceptional against the Reds in this game. Gorsica did slam the door, pitching $4⅔$ and surrendering just one hit.

Detroit scored just once more, in the sixth. McCosky walked, and then forced at second by a Gehringer ground-out. Greenberg bashed a double for the run, but Walters ended up allowing only three hits in Cincinnati's 5-3 victory. Despite his key double, Greenberg sought to blame himself for the Tigers' loss in this one. "In the first inning, I foolishly hit at a bad ball. Naturally, I did not hit it well and the Reds converted it into a double play that spoiled our rally. I believe that if I kept the bat on my shoulder, the game would have changed. We probably would have gotten Bucky Walters out of there before the inning was over and Cincinnati would have had to bring in a less able pitcher. Also, we'd have given Schoolboy Rowe a bigger lead and things would have been different all around." In a response to Greenberg's explanation, a newspaper headline writer said, "But Hank Is Simply Too Generous."[8]

Game 3 was in Detroit on October 4, with no rest day in-between. Briggs Stadium was much larger than Crosley, so attendance for this show was 52,877. Tommy Bridges was the chosen starter for the Tigers, but rather than go with Junior Thompson, as it might be guessed, McKechnie picked Jim Turner for the Reds. The decision did not work out, although things went well for a time. The way the modern game is played, Turner would probably have been relieved while still going well rather than his boss waiting until he started to fade.

Cincinnati got off to a nice start. Bill Werber led off the game with a double deep to left field. After Mike McCormick struck out, Goodman singled to center to bring in Werber. 1-0, Reds. The Tigers tied it in the bottom of the fourth. McCosky and Gehringer singled and, ironically, Greenberg drove in his team's first run on a double-play ball. This swat was a mixed metaphor taken in the context of his disappointment expressed after the Game 2 loss. He certainly wasn't going to give the run back just because it was an offshoot of a double play. Things remained placid after that, with both starters throwing well, until the bottom of the seventh when Detroit blew up Turner.

Greenberg led off with a single and York promptly bashed a two-run homer. Campbell singled and Higgins also cracked a two-run homer. It all happened so fast that if a Tiger fan had gone to the bathroom he might have missed the crux of the game. By the time he found the entrance, McKechnie would have raced to the mound, pulled Turner, and had Whitey Moore loosening up on the field. Moore got two quick outs, but then he looked shaky, allowing a Bartell single and a McCosky double. Bartell held at third and was still standing there when the inning ended. But now the score was 5-1 Tigers.

Tommy Bridges began to look vulnerable in the top of the eighth inning. Singles by Myers, Werber and Mike McCormick bought the Reds a run. Joe Beggs came in to pitch the bottom of the inning, replacing Moore, but the strategy didn't work. Greenberg tripled to center and then, with one out, Campbell singled him home. Higgins doubled and that boosted Detroit's margin to 7-2.

The Reds made a game try in the top of the ninth. Bridges was still hanging in for Detroit, but Cincinnati hitters were discovering friendlier offerings. Ripple singled to right and Bill Baker, who had replaced Lombardi behind the plate in the sixth inning, reached on an error to start things. When Joost singled to center, the Reds had a run. Bridges collected two outs, but a Werber single drove in another run. But that was it. Bridges fanned Mike McCormick for the last out of the game and Detroit won, 7-4.

The Tigers compiled 13 hits off Reds pitching, Campbell getting three of them, but McCosky, Greenberg, York and Higgins all contributed two each. Now trailing by a game in the Series, the Reds were going to have to do something about that Tigers lineup if they wanted to win the title. In a best-of-seven series, trailing 2-1 can be a critical point. Victory in Game 4 for the club behind is not imperative, but it is urgent.

The fourth game in the Series was on October 5, also at Briggs Stadium and attendance was a rousing 54,093. McKechnie seemed to recognize the necessity of a triumph simply in his choice of Derringer to pitch so soon after he started the opener. He was essentially saying, "We're going with our best." Of course, Derringer should not have been tired because he was knocked in the second inning of the first game. Del Baker made somewhat of a curious choice to start Dizzy Trout, who had done little that season. Trout had looked good in an exhibition game versus the Reds in the spring.

Detroit's choice looked a little bit on the iffy side from the start. Trout walked Werber to open the game. Mike McCormick's ground ball forced Werber at second base, but McCormick was on first. Goodman ripped a double to deep left field and McCormick was able to come around and score. Two batters later Ripple was safe on an error and Goodman scored for a 2-0 Cincinnati lead after the first inning.

The Reds added another run in the third inning on three straight hits off Trout, singles by Goodman and Frank McCormick and a timely double by Ripple. That was all for Trout, replaced after two innings by Clay Smith. Smith was a 6-foot-2 right-hander originally from Kansas who had an extraordinarily brief Major League career. After going 0-0 for the Indians the year before, Smith went 1-1 for the Tigers in 1940 and never pitched in the big leagues again. It was 3-0 when Smith closed out the inning. However, the Tigers crept to within two runs in the bottom of the third. The main blow was a double by Greenberg, sending across McCosky, who had walked. Smith settled in for four innings of one-hit ball, but he gave up one hit and walked three. The Reds worked him for a solo run in the top of the fourth to expand their lead to 4-1. Werber walked, Mike McCormick doubled, and Goodman hit a sacrifice fly.

Derringer yielded one more run in the bottom of the sixth. Bruce Campbell scored on a Pinky Higgins triple. Archie McKain, a bit more seasoned than Smith, pitched the last three innings for the Tigers. He was 5-0 with a 2.82 earned run average over the season, all in relief. In this one, McKain allowed four hits, and the Reds added a run in the eighth inning. Werber singled and advanced to second when McKain threw a wild pitch. Mike McCormick singled and that brought Werber home with the last run of the game. Derringer pitched a complete game, permitting just five hits. The 5-2 victory was sweet, but Derringer was fortunate in that the six base on balls he issued could have hurt him more.

After the game, the scribes gave some heat to Baker for relying on Trout in such a big situation. He was forced to defend himself, saying, "I had to gamble. I had to gamble Saturday or Sunday and I figured the better spot was when we were leading the Series. Under the circumstances, if I wouldn't have picked Trout, who would I have picked? I didn't think Dizzy was so bad. He had some tough breaks out there. The big trouble was in our attack. It's no cinch that Newsom or Rowe would have shut out the Reds, or held them to one run, which is what any Detroit pitcher would have had to do to beat Derringer."[9] This was the seventh time in his career Derringer had pitched in a World Series game, but the first time he recorded the W.

With the Series knotted 2-2, Baker did give the ball to Newsom for Game 5. McKechnie put his money on Junior Thompson. Who else? Thompson had won those 16 games in the regular season. But this was Newsom's—and the Tigers'—day. In some ways, it was both a high point and a low point in Newsom's life. As he performed brilliantly, he was coming in with a backdrop of family tragedy.

Newsom defeated the Reds in the Series opener. That evening, several members of his family joined him for a small party in the Netherland Plaza, a Cincinnati hotel. About midnight, Newsom's 68-year-old father Henry Quillen began suffering chest pains. He had a known heart condition, but had seemed fine as he soaked up the celebratory atmosphere surrounding his son's victory. It was said this was only the second time the elder Newsom, from Hartsville, South Carolina, had witnessed Newsom pitching. In those days, major hotels had doctors on call, and the house physician checked out Newsom's father, and prescribed sedatives. The following morning, though, Quillen Newsom suffered a fatal heart attack in the hotel. The rest of the family escorted the body back to South Carolina, but Newsom stayed with his team and started Game 5 with grim determination.

The Reds' lineup was able to conjure up absolutely nothing against Newsom, managing just three hits while the Tigers, starting with Thompson, battered Cincinnati pitching for 13 hits and eight runs. Thompson lasted 3⅓ innings and gave up eight hits and six runs. Whitey Moore went ⅔ of an inning and gave up another run. At the end of the game, rookie Johnny Hutchings (2-1 during the 1940 season), threw an inning and allowed one final run to Detroit.

The only Reds pitcher who tamed the Tigers that day was Johnny Vander Meer. No-Hit Johnny, almost forgotten on the staff, hurled a satisfying three innings. Detroit did not score on him and he permitted just two hits. As usual, his total of three walks was a little high for the circumstances. But he got into a World Series, which he did not do in 1939, and overall acquitted himself well enough when handed the opportunity. His role was not terribly important that day since the Reds were spiraling down the drain in the game. But it beat being relegated to the minors and it beat being injured. At least, thinking back to his no-hitters of 1938 when his future loomed so bright, he could say, "Hey, remember me?"

Meanwhile, Greenberg smashed three hits and drove in four runs, Campbell also hit safely three times, and Bartell, McCosky and Gehringer had two hits apiece. The Tigers scored three runs in the third inning, four in the fourth and one in the eighth. Newsom also struck out seven Reds. After twice around with the National League champions, Newsom had given them two runs in 18 innings. He was at the apex of his game and had much to celebrate. Newsom, who was also called Buck, in addition to Bobo, had well-positioned the Tigers to capture the World Series. They led 3-2 and had two chances to clinch.

Ordinarily, Newsom was a light-hearted soul, usually joking and acting loose. But he had been quietly focused on his grief out of the public eye following his father's death and he was a no-nonsense pitcher when on the mound for his dominating shutout. When the game ended and Newsom met reporters, he began to cry. "It was the hardest game I ever wanted to win," Newsom said. "I felt great. Naturally, I didn't feel as good as I should have. I pitched this game for my dad. I hope he knows what I accomplished. I know in my heart he wanted me to win. This was the one I wanted to win most." Catcher Billy Sullivan reassured Newsom, saying, "Bobo, your dad would have liked this one."[10]

Once again, the Reds were in a dire situation, one of those win-or-go-home games. Actually, they were home. Game 6 was scheduled for October 7 at Crosley Field. There was no real debate about who would start for Cincinnati. Unlike Del Baker, McKechnie had two 20-game-winners at his disposal. This was Bucky Walters' big opportunity. He had lived through the 4-0 Yankees sweep and it had been the Reds' goal throughout 1940 to make up for it. Like Newsom, Walters already banked a win in the Series and he knew his team was counting on him to make it two. Detroit's starter was Schoolboy Rowe, the second man in the rotation all summer.

Walters knew exactly what he had to do—control the Tigers' big bats. Rowe wanted to follow in Newsom's footsteps. Baseball, though, is all about different arms on different days. Walters put down the Tigers 1-2-3 in the top of the first inning. Rowe could not do the same. He did not even make it out of the first. Bill Werber led off with a double. Mike McCormick's sacrifice bunt moved him to third and an Ival Goodman infield hit scored

## 15. The 1940 World Series

Cincinnati's first run so swiftly Rowe didn't have time to get depressed. That would come soon enough. Frank McCormick singled. Jimmy Ripple singled and Baker gave up on Rowe, yanking him after ⅓ of an inning and trailing 2-0.

Building a quick lead was just the type of pep talk the 30,481 fans in Crosley Field appreciated. Walters, too, no doubt. When he had to be, Walters was as masterful as Newsom had been the game before. This day Walters pitched a five-hit shutout and a Tiger body on third base was a rarity. He walked two and struck out two and was hardly threatened as his teams lengthened the lead. The two-run margin surrendered by Rowe was not a huge one, so Walters had to be vigilant. Johnny Gorsica, Rowe's replacement, threw well, working 6⅔ innings and giving up just one run. Cincinnati picked that off in the sixth. Ripple, who was hitting like Ty Cobb, singled. So did Jimmie Wilson, the unlikely participant because of Lombardi's continuing fragility. A mix of infield plays, capped by Walters hitting into a force out, led to Wilson scoring to make it 3-0. Not satisfied, after Fred Hutchinson took over for Gorsica, Walters belted a solo home run for a 4-0 lead. He had provided his own breathing room.

Walters polished off the Tigers in the ninth and the world was presented with the drama of a seventh game in the World Series. The Reds got to host it at their place, too, on October 8. Del Baker seemed to comprehend that the only way his Tigers were going to survive this Series was if Bobo Newsom pitched Game 7. Newsom had only one full day of rest, but he was clearly operating mostly on adrenalin, anyway. Rowe had failed at his shot, so Baker really didn't have a reliable Plan B. Derringer was not at all rested by the standards of the modern pitching game, but he was willing and after Walters' triumph to rescue the Reds, he was the one the team and the city were counting on. The pressure was intense for Newsom and Derringer, the stakes as high as they got in the sport. What awaited was magnificent theater.

There were only heroes on the mound in this showdown, no goats. Any hit catalogued off either hurler was prized. Any run scored was precious. Over the course of a mere 1 hour and 47 minutes, the 1940 championship was decided. The game was scoreless into the third running until the Tigers pushed the lead run across the plate on a combination of a single, a sacrifice, a walk, an infield single and an error. It wasn't as if Derringer was lit up by the Detroit power. It was almost an accidental run, but it still counted and the Tigers were up, 1-0. One might have expected Newsom to show more fatigue, but however he really felt, he was overcoming it.

Newsom mixed a hit in here and there, seven in all. Derringer gave up a hit here and there, also seven in all. But still that 1-0 score hovered as the game aged. The Reds half of the seventh arrived and still Bobo seemed to have their number, for a third time. Frank McCormick, the NL Most Valuable Player, doubled to lead off, a good sign. Ripple (him again) did the same, his double sending McCormick home and tying the game at 1-1.

Jimmie Wilson, again in the lineup instead of Lombardi, issued a sacrifice bunt and Ripple made it to third. Lombardi pinch-hit for Eddie Joost, but Baker wanted none of the star hitter and intentionally walked him. Given Lombardi's well-known lack of speed, McKechnie sent Lonny Frey in to pinch-run. Billy Myers then stroked a fly ball to deep center field, so far back for McCosky to run that Ripple was able to score on the sacrifice fly. Now the Reds led, 2-1.

Until only a couple of days before, Derringer had been an unlucky World Series pitcher. The beneficiary of this one-run lead knew he had only to out-maneuver the slugging Tigers for two more tries to erase any and all bad memories. But he had to wade through pretty much anyone with any punch whose uniform showed off that English D to make it to the finish line. In the top of the eighth, Gehringer could have shaken things up with his lead-off single, but Derringer plowed through Greenberg, York and Campbell without incident. There seemed to be less potential danger in the ninth, though any single swing of a Tiger bat could have tied it. Instead, Derringer induced ground-outs from Higgins and Sullivan. Earl Averill pinch-hit for Newsom and all he could generate was a grounder to second base. Third out. Paul Derringer won his second World Series game. The Reds did it.

It made sense that if Cincinnati was going to win four games to take the Series that two were won by Derringer and two by Walters. It made less sense that Jimmy Ripple, the last man added to the roster (Johnny Rizzo was basically nowhere to be found in October) was one of the most valuable fielders. Ripple batted .333 in the Series and scored the winning run in Game 7. Ripple was so late joining the team that in the pre–Series dickering, he was voted just a half share of the players' take. In the clubhouse afterwards, Derringer turned to him and said, "You ought to have two shares, Jimmy."[11]

The other least likely major Reds contributor in the World Series was Wilson. As a coach, Wilson had no expectations of playing during the 1940 season. He was activated for fill-in duty after Willard Hershberger killed himself. Then, late in the season, Lombardi, who had a tough year physically, sprained an ankle. Of course, so long ago there was no designated hitter position, so the ailing Lombardi barely had a chance to play in the Series. Wilson started six of the seven games and hit .353. Even before that, showing their appreciation for how Wilson had stepped up, teammates gave him a gold watch. Now he had become a clutch player for a World Series champion, even by using his legs on the bases despite muscle cramps and bruises. "Boy, am I a helluva base runner," Wilson jubilantly joked after the victory.[12]

Remembering their pledge from August when they lost Hershberger, the Reds fulfilled their announced responsibility and sent a winner's share of $5,803.62 to Hershberger's mother Maude.

When the game ended, the fans erupted in full-throated roar and the downtown area filled with happy supporters, marching through the streets. Newspaper writers suggested it was the biggest party Cincinnati had seen since November 11, 1918, when the end to the Great War, later renamed World War I, was announced. A more complex analogy, comparing reaction to some of the daring adventure and exploration efforts of the era, was offered by another writer, who said, "It looked like Lindbergh, just in from Paris, was coming up Walnut Street and had run into Admiral Byrd coming over Fourth Street."[13] The *Cincinnati Enquirer*'s front page headline, in extra large type, read, "Reds Are World Champions, Paper Blizzard Blankets City After Game."[14]

The *Cincinnati Times-Star*'s headline read this way: "Reds Win World Baseball Championship, Cincinnati's Downtown District Becomes Bedlam." An accompanying story noted, "Like New Year's Eve, election night and Halloween all rolled into one was the scene at Fountain Square late Tuesday as the flash came that the Reds had won the world's championship. Old-timers accustomed to jubilee and exhibition declared they never had seen the like."[15] When it came to the Tigers, losers by such a thin margin, there was only glumness. Manager Baker sought to be gracious in defeat, saying, "The best club won, I guess. It was a National League year. If we had to lose, I'm glad we lost to you, Bill. You're a great guy."[16]

Bill McKechnie became the first manager to win a World Series crown with two different teams. He already had the 1925 title on his resume from his stint with the Pittsburgh Pirates. "It was a clean, hard-fought Series," McKechnie said, "The best I ever saw in all my experience in baseball."[17]

When things simmered down a little, though the baseball writers were still seeking to explore every possible angle, someone brought up Vander Meer's future with the Reds. He had only been a bit player, but thinking back just two years, in his relief appearance he looked like his old self. A rumor was apparently going around that he might be traded to the New York Giants. McKechnie squelched it. "Vander Meer is not leaving the Reds while I'm their manager," McKechnie said, "and I've got another year to go on my contract. They'll have to get rid of both of us to get rid of Johnny. That's what I think of him. It's news to me that the Giants are after Johnny, but if they are, it's a case of good judgment on their part."[18]

As quickly as could be written after the final out, The *Cincinnati Times-Star* penned an editorial with the simple headline, "The Champions."

In part it read, "The grandchildren of the present generation of Cincinnatians will be hearing about the game in which the Reds won the 1940 World Series. There is credit enough to go around for all of McKechnie's men. They have earned the gratitude of Cincinnati and the admiration of fans all over the country by their uphill fight to victory."[19]

# 16

# The Year 1941

The glow of the Cincinnati Reds' 1940 World Series championship helped light the winter sky in the Queen City and manager Bill McKechnie and his players showed up for spring training in 1941 feeling they had it in them to win 100 games all over again and repeat as champs. There was no reason to think otherwise. They had basically dominated the National League, except for a few blips over the months, and they had overcome some serious problems. The suicide of Willard Hershberger was foremost among the difficulties put aside during the pennant run. Ernie Lombardi's physical ills created complications, too. Missing Johnny Vander Meer at full strength for most of the season was a detriment made up for by the top-notch pitching of Junior Thompson.

It was not always an everyday smooth ride to the pennant, but to win 100 games is a solid achievement by any team at any time. McKechnie took all of those things into account when he spoke to sportswriters in Florida. The Hershberger matter was essentially in the past. Lombardi was able to catch full-time again. And Vander Meer, two years removed from his startling double no-hit accomplishment, was throwing as well as ever. After two seasons of coping with injuries, wildness, time spent in the minors, being overshadowed by better-performing pitchers, and barely a factor in the Reds winning two pennants, in 1941 Vander Meer was once again one of the most solid pitchers on the staff. However, as the season unfolded, it became quite clear that the Reds of 1941 were not anything like the Reds of 1940.

It is often said that the toughest thing in sports is to repeat as a champion. The phrase is applied to baseball, football, basketball and hockey in the major North American team sports, and in many cases to individuals in other sports. Why this is so sometimes defies the belief of fans, who see essentially the same lineup intact (particularly before the advent of free agency in pro sports) and can't figure out why those same beloved players cannot replicate their showings of the year before. Often enough, injuries intrude. Other times, players suffer an abrupt decline in skills. They may have lived out their last hurrah and are being told by age it is time to retire. Outside forces can play a part, sometimes the matter being as simple as another team improving and surpassing the locals. And it may also be that intangibles that aided a club one year do not apply the next. It might be behind-the-scenes chemistry changing.

The Reds should not have been spoiled by success. Two pennants in a row and one World Series title do not constitute a dynasty. The Reds as a group were about to learn something Vander Meer had already learned the hard way—success is fragile.

Vander Meer had been encouraged by his 3-1 showing in September of 1940 and thrilled by his brief relief appearance in the World Series. Those two developments told him—and McKechnie—he should be able to throw normally again in 1941. "Last year I just couldn't throw right," Vander Meer said in spring training. "My arm hurt and I was tight. You know how it is if you try to walk on a sore leg. You favor it. Well, I was favoring my arm and you can't pitch that way. I'm fine now."[1]

Adding a healthy Vander Meer to the rotation should have been like getting a lifetime supply of free desserts for McKechnie and the Reds. But there were some other roster changes that affected the regular lineup. Ival Goodman, who was such a good clutch hitter, was reduced to playing part-time, appearing in just 42 games with a .268 batting average. Easing into his 30s, Goodman was never again a full-time player during the remaining years of his career. Jimmy Ripple, the few-month wonder outfielder, competed in just 38 games in 1941 and batted .216. Shortstop Billy Myers was gone to the Chicago Cubs, where he played in only 24 games and then retired. Catcher Jimmie Wilson was retired for good. Third baseman Lew Riggs, who had been eclipsed by Bill Werber, was gone, playing for Brooklyn.

In most cases, it wasn't as if replacing these previously prominent Reds was the wrong move since almost immediately their careers faded out, but the personnel switches were emblematic of inevitable change. It is virtually impossible to keep the old gang together year-to-year. There is no such thing as standing still with a sports team.

Yet the 1941 woes of the Reds were more pronounced and less predictable than roster changes. What McKechnie did not see coming—nor could he have—was a more or less wholesale diminishment in performance amongst the best and most reliable hitters and pitchers from the world title team. Off years are to be expected. But everyone all at once? That was unfathomable. An unlikely scenario played out where the stars were dimmed across the board. It was as if the entire team suffered from attacks of food poisoning all at once. Or if the Cincinnati water supply had gone bad. Viewed from afar, as a whole, it seemed impossible that a team so good

## 16. The Year 1941

in so many aspects of the game one year could as thoroughly disappoint the next. There were no hits of such a faltering in spring training. Every team looks pretty good and is optimistic when basking in the Florida sun at the same time the everyday citizen must cope with snow and ice. So there really was no way to see the 1941 collapse coming.

Despite his aches and injuries of 1940, star catcher Ernie Lombardi batted had .319 with 74 runs batted in. The next year, at 33, Lombardi was back in the lineup, playing in eight more games, but batting just .264 with 60 RBIs. Frank McCormick hit .309 with 127 runs batted in during the 1940 season and won the National League Most Valuable Player award. In 1941, he hit .269 with 97 runs batted in. At second base, Lonny Frey's average dipped from .266 to .254 and his stolen base total from 22 to 16. Myers hit just .202 in his 90 games in 1940 and Eddie Joost took over full-time at shortstop in 1941. Billy Werber went from a .277 hitter one year to .239 the next while covering third base. At one outfield spot, Mike McCormick went from hitting .300 to hitting .287. Harry Craft, who was never a strong hitter, posted a .244 mark during the Series year and was basically a wash at .249 the next year. Goodman's slot was mostly taken over by Jim Gleeson, who hit .233.

Morrie Arnovich, who hit .284 off the bench for Cincinnati in 1940, was gone to the New York Giants for his last year in the majors. Johnny Rizzo, who batted .282 in his limited stay with the Reds, was playing for Brooklyn.

In the championship season, the Reds scored 707 runs, a year later the total was 616. That may have described the difference in close games. The pitching staff limited foes to 528 runs in 1940 and gave up 564 a year later. Not a horrible difference, but any rise when matched up with a low-scoring offense, was not helpful. Probably the biggest surprise was the comparative declines of recent heroes of the mound Bucky Walters and Paul Derringer. During the 1939 pennant season, Walters went 27-11 with a 2.29 earned run average and won the National League Most Valuable award. In 1940, he won 22 games. But in 1941, while he won 19 games with a 2.83 ERA, his record was 19-15. That run support differential may have mattered. Derringer, 25-7 in 1939 and 20-12 in 1940, as well as being the World Series star with two wins, tumbled to 12-14, 3.31.

Worse, Junior Thompson, who made his debut at 13-5 in 1939 and won 16 games in 1940, was just 6-6 in 1941. He got into only 27 games as a starter and reliever. Those were the team's top three pitchers in the title year and only Walters among them was nearly as reliable. That wasn't all. The year before, Jim Turner was 14-7. In 1941, he was 6-4. Joe Beggs was 12-3 one year, 4-3 the next. One minute McKechnie was flush with pitchers, the next he was searching for help.

**Slipping into his uniform (note the heavy flannels), Johnny Vander Meer prepares for a game.**

Vander Meer was coming through with a timely comeback, but in a remarkable change of status, Elmer Riddle, 1-2 in 1940 (though with a good ERA of 1.87) in limited play, nearly took over the National League in 1941. The high point to his career before that was pitching one inning in the '40 World Series. The right-hander from Columbus, Georgia, wasn't even an especially young phenomenon. That season he was 26. Older brother

Johnny, more prominent as a minor-league catcher, was with the Reds in 1941, appearing in only 10 games, but hitting .300.

McKechnie saw potential in Riddle, but in the early part of the season used him in relief. When his main starters began to have difficulties, the manager handed Riddle more opportunities and he stunned baseball by winning 11 straight decisions in June and July, most of them complete games. Not that he was boastful about what he was accomplishing. "I guess maybe I'll do all right if my luck holds out," he said.[2] It held out well enough. That season Riddle was a spectacular 19-4, the record giving him a National League-leading winning percentage of .826 and a league-leading ERA of 2.24. Where did this all come from? Riddle gave considerable credit to Wilson, back in his coaching role, and the time invested in him during spring training.

"Jimmie fooled around with me a lot and taught me things," Riddle said. "He's smart. I guess the biggest thing I learned was to control my change of pace, to get a soft curve over the corner now and then. My control's a lot better on my fast one, too." Riddle featured an exceptional sinker, as well, that regularly baffled batters, but he did not sound like a hurler who had true mastery of it, actually sounding more like knuckleballers do when dissecting their favorite pitch. "I'll swear, I don't know what it's going to do. I just turn it loose and it does things. All I hope is it keeps on doing whatever it's doing. But I've been luckier than some of our pitchers. Sometimes I've been out there with a three- or four-run lead to work on."[3] He was just hogging all of the Reds' runs.

As is common when a fresh face breaks in without any standing, the attention multiplies and he is labeled a sensation. Riddle fit that bill. He was the object of so much heady focus from baseball writers, McKechnie got worried. Perhaps he was thinking back to the deluge of ink spilt chronicling Vander Meer when he threw his back-to-back no-hitters. "Yes, Elmer is quite warm," McKechnie said. "Need I say that I hope you will not whoop it up too much about his streak? We want Elmer to go on winning and there is nothing like publicity to jinx a fellow and bust his streak."[4] Riddle was 11-0 at that moment.

Riddle said not only did Wilson help him in spring training, but watching Walters and Derringer during the 1940 season was like an extended clinic, or a college graduate course. Then he had to practice what he absorbed, getting more chances to pitch in games. "Like with any kind of work, the more you pitch, the more you know," he said. "Before I came up with Cincinnati, I didn't do much pitching to spots. I just tried to throw it past 'em. Well, I'm not the fastest pitcher in the world, and if I try to throw it past 'em in the big leagues, they'll bust me. So I'm learning to use my head."[5]

Sportswriters in new cities wanted to interview Riddle when the Reds came to town. On one occasion a columnist sat down next to Johnny Riddle, who said, "Who me? You want Elmer, don't you?"[6] Actually, the writer knew whom he was talking to, he just wanted to get some background from Elmer's brother. Being 10 years older, Johnny never saw Elmer pitch in school, but eventually did become the younger's advocate, telling prospective teams how good he could become.

McKechnie said one item on Riddle's resume helped as a selling point to Cincinnati. Riddle was tapped to pitch an exhibition game against the Boston Red Sox at Fort Benning, Georgia, not far from his home and looked sharp in front of an audience of about 16,000 soldiers. "When he held hitters like those Sox, I was certain he was a good pitcher. Good stuff, good control and implicit confidence."[7] Rather quickly, once Riddle's winning streak expanded to the point of eight or nine or so and could not be resisted by the press, the writers started calling him "Elmer the Great" in print.

The 1940 season opened April 15, with the usual madhouse crowd of 34,900 at Crosley Field. The Reds lost to the St. Louis Cardinals, 7-3. They then lost three more in a row before tearing off five consecutive wins to ease any angst. But by the end of the month, Cincinnati was just 7-8, in fourth place and five games out of first. May was fairly dismal, including a six-game losing streak and a three-game losing streak. As the calendar was changing to June, the Reds were 19-23. This was a club that won 97 games in 1939 and 100 in 1940.

Cincinnati ended June at 36-33 (thank you, Mr. Riddle), but was 10½ games out of first place. A five-game losing streak in early August was painful, but later in the month the Reds seemed to lock in and started winning at a crisp pace. In mid-month, the Reds won 10 out of 11. September included a stretch of 12 wins in 13 games, but it was all too late to close the gap in the pennant race. This NL race belonged to the Brooklyn Dodgers, whose final record was 100-54. The Cardinals took second with a 97-56 mark. Cincinnati finished at 88-66, 12 games out of first. But the Reds were not going to be playing ball in October for the first time in three years.

While he could not celebrate team success, Johnny Vander Meer could be content that he was back, back in the rotation, back as a first-class pitcher. A record of 16-13 looked awfully good. Right from the beginning, overall, actually, Vander Meer looked awfully good. On April 22, he shut out the Chicago Cubs, 1-0, on four hits. The only Reds run was produced by Goodman, who had two hits and the lone RBI, driving in Werber in the top of the sixth. Cubs pitcher Bill Lee was just about as stingy, allowing just five hits. Vander Meer was just that tiny bit better. Vander Meer beat the Pirates before the end of April and won two more games in May.

On June 6, Vander Meer won his fifth game, equaling the most he had won in a season since 1938. This was no ordinary victory, though. No, it was not still another no-hitter, but he came close. Cincinnati beat the Philadelphia Phillies, 7-0, on another shutout by the southpaw. In this complete game, Vander Meer struck out 12 batters and walked just one—always something to be noted when he pitched. He permitted just one hit. It was on the road, in Shibe Park, with just 7,044 paid customers. It was also a night game, something still far from an everyday occurrence in 1941. The walk came early, in the bottom of the first, so there was no thought given to a perfect game. Center fielder Stan Benjamin was Philadelphia's lead-off man and he looked to be a possible rally-starter. Instead, he was thrown out, caught stealing, and there never were any Phillies rallies on this evening. The same proved true of discussion of a possible no-hitter because the Phillies got their hit in the bottom of the second.

In 1941, Danny Litwhiler was 24, and at the beginning of a very lengthy baseball career, not only as a player, but as a coach. While with the Phillies at this time, Litwhiler concluded his Major League play in a Reds uniform a decade later, some of that time spent as a Vander Meer teammate. In '41, Litwhiler batted .305, but he was the one who interrupted Vander Meer's no-hit bid. The ball didn't get past shortstop, but it was a single. Some contended the play should have been called an error on Joost. Intriguingly, Lombardi, who was the catcher in both of Vander Meer's 1938 no-hitters, and was behind the plate for this game, as well, thought the hurler was better this time out. "It was the best game he ever pitched," Lombardi said.[8]

One wonders what the reaction might have been if Vander Meer did record a third no-hitter. Every baseball writer would have revisited the back-to-backs of 1938 and when Vander Meer was scheduled to go again, half the known baseball world would have requested credentials, just in case Vander Meer could do it all over again, as far-fetched as those odds were.

On August 20, Cincinnati faced the Phillies again in Philadelphia for a double-header. Vander Meer got the assignment in the first game and shut out the Phillies, 2-0, on three hits. Riddle pitched the second game and he also shut out the Phillies, 3-0, giving up six hits. In all, Vander Meer threw six shutouts in 1941. Riddle threw four shutouts. Vander Meer struck out a league-leading 202 batters, the first of three times he would top the National League in that category.

There was no Cy Young Award given out in those days, rewarding a best pitcher in baseball, or a best pitcher in the National League and American League. But some baseball writers casually, if unofficially, called Riddle the Pitcher of the Year. Young, the winningest pitcher of all-time, with 511 victories, was still living. It was not until Young passed away in 1955 that Major League Baseball introduced the award named to honor the legend.

Riddle's year was eye-catching. Vander Meer's was satisfying. It represented a rehabilitation and rejuvenation. Together, with Walters' assistance, they had rescued the Reds pitching staff in 1941.

Later that year, on December 6, Riddle was driving on a foggy highway in Americus, Georgia, on his way home to Columbus, with Skeeter Newsom, a friend who at the time was an infielder for the Boston Red Sox. They came across a head-on collision between a passenger car and a bus with bodies strewn on the highway. The crash killed seven people and injured 12, many of them soldiers from Fort Benning, and others members of boys and girls high school basketball teams. Riddle and Newsom helped rush the injured to a hospital. "It was a terrible sight," Riddle said. "Girls from the bus were scattered all along the roadside, lying around on grass soaked with fog. We pulled one man still living from the car, loaded up our car, and hurried to the hospital at Americus."[9]

The accident that took the lives of five members of the Army took place on December 6, 1941. The next day, December 7, 1941, "a day that will live in infamy," as President Franklin D. Roosevelt told the nation, the Japanese bombed Pearl Harbor in Hawaii. Some 2,403 Americans were killed and 1,143 were wounded in the sneak attack.

This act of aggression dragged the United States into World War II, both in the Pacific to avenge the Japanese assault, and in the European theater against Germany and the Nazis. The coming seasons would play out profoundly differently than they likely would have without a world war raging. Players' lives and careers were disrupted. Players' lives were taken. Although baseball played on, the biggest news nationally was not of who might win the American League pennant, but how America was faring on the battlefield. News from the playing field was not paramount from 1942 through 1945 when life and death were the stakes, not a trophy.

## 17

# War Changes Everything

Some of the greatest players in baseball history took a leave of absence from their teams and their careers to join the Army, Navy, Marines, soon-to-be Air Force, and even the Coast Guard to aid the United States during World War II. Others spent time serving in what the government called essential jobs.

Bob Feller was a hot young pitcher for the Cleveland Indians from Van Meter, Iowa, who had burst upon the big leagues as a 17-year-old phenom with a blinding fastball in 1936. He would become one of the greatest pitchers of all-time and one of the most stunning of strikeout kings. He was 22 in late 1941, already a winner of 24, 27, and 25 games in consecutive seasons. Eventually he led the American League in strikeouts seven times and was an eight-time All-Star. His career ended with 266 victories and it was universally stated that he would have easily won 300 if he had not given over more than three full seasons to the military.

Feller did not wait to be drafted. The first moment he heard about the Japanese bombing of Pearl Harbor on December 7, he decided what he was going to do. Feller was actually in his car driving to Chicago to meet with Indians officials to negotiate a new contract when he heard the news on the radio. "I was angry as hell," Feller wrote many years later. "I'd spent almost six full seasons in the major leagues by then, with a record of 107 victories and 54 losses, and I had a family-related draft exemption, but I knew right then that I had to answer the call."[1] He became a chief petty officer in the Navy and was assigned to be a physical training instructor. He lobbied to go into combat, though, and was sent to the USS *Alabama*. He was part of an anti-aircraft gun crew and saw action in the North Atlantic and in the Pacific, off Tarawa, the Marshall Islands and the Philippines. Feller was in the Navy in 1942, 1943, 1944 and into 1945. He returned to the Indians in August of that year and went 5-3 the rest of the season. "Combat is an experience that you never forget," Feller said. "War teaches you that baseball is a game after all, a minor thing compared to the sovereignty and security of the United States."[2]

Feller was one of the biggest name baseball stars who were in the military during World War II. Others included Warren Spahn, Ted Williams, Joe DiMaggio, Hank Greenberg and Stan Musial. Spahn, the winningest left-handed pitcher in history with 363 victories, fought at the Battle of the Bulge. Williams served in World War II and the Korean War and flew combat missions. Jackie Robinson was in the military before he became the man who broke baseball's color line with the Brooklyn Dodgers in 1947. The great Yankees catcher Yogi Berra was part of the D-Day invasion at Omaha Beach. Even ahead of Feller, future Hall of Fame manager Billy Southworth became a highly decorated pilot for England starting in 1940.

More than 500 men with connections to Major League Baseball served in the Armed Forces during World War II. Many, many more minor leaguers did so as well—an estimated 4,000 at a time when there were many more minor leagues and teams in existence than in the present era. There were 52 military men who were either big-league players, or spent time in the minors, who were part of the Cincinnati Reds organization. Twenty-four of them were in the minors. Others would play for the Reds after the glory years of 1939 and 1940.

Some of them, though, were very familiar names to Reds fans who had been prominent between 1938 and 1941, and helped the club win those two pennants. Included on this list, including a coach, Hank Gowdy, were Johnny Vander Meer, Junior Thompson, Joe Beggs, Lonny Frey, Mike McCormick, and Dick West. West played in one game in 1938, eight in 1939, seven in 1940 and 67 in 1941. Others who suited up in 1942, but went into the military, were Ray Lammano, Bert Haas and outfielder Hank Sauer. Sauer got into nine games with Cincinnati in 1941 and seven in 1942. He spent all of 1943 in the minors and two years in the military. Of this group, some had been around for a little while. Some would not play in the majors again after returning home from the war, or at least not play as well. West never played for the Reds after 1943 and never played in the majors again after that season.

Somewhat amazingly, of all the players who served—and some of the big stars, such as DiMaggio, were well behind the lines in physical training roles—only two perished during the war. Elmer Gedeon and Harry O'Neill were the two big-league fatalities. Gedeon was born in 1917 in Cleveland. He won varsity letters at the University of Michigan in baseball, football and track and field and became a minor-league ball player in 1939. He appeared in five games for the Washington Senators batting .200, for his only Major League experience. He was in the minors again in 1940, but was drafted into the Army in January of 1941, almost a full year ahead of Pearl Harbor and prior to the Major League season. Gedeon became a combat pilot and flew B-26 missions. His plane was shot down over France and he was killed in 1944. O'Neill was also born in 1917, in Philadelphia. A catcher, O'Neill was a baseball, football and basketball star at Gettysburg College. O'Neill reached the majors with the Philadelphia Athletics in 1939, but was only a third-string receiver for Connie Mack. He was used in just one game on July 23, as a late-inning fielding replacement. He never even got a big-league at-bat. O'Neill enlisted in the Marines in 1942. He, like Gedeon, was 27 when he was killed by a sniper's bullet in March of 1945 on Iwo Jima.

Also serving during the war were 119 players from the Negro Leagues, including Hall of Famers such as Jackie Robinson, Leon Day, Buck O'Neil, Monte Irvin and Larry Doby. Doby followed Robinson into the majors as a pioneer, the first African American to play in the American League. O'Neil was a star for the Kansas City Monarchs, their manager, and the first black Major League coach in the 1950s with the Chicago Cubs.

The immediate question for Major League Baseball after the bombing of Pearl Harbor and Congress' declaration of war was whether the sport would even have a season in 1942. After the United States entered World War I, the 1917 season was completed as planned, even as most minor league play ceased. But there was some ratcheted-up pressure from the public for baseball to offer more assistance to the war effort in 1918 and do more than conduct business as usual. The sport cut the season short by nearly 30 games, most teams playing about 126 to 130 games. The World Series was won by the Red Sox, their last title until 2004.

General Enoch Crowder, who supervised the implementation of the Selective Service Act of 1917 (the draft), issued a work or fight edict to take effect on July 1 of 1918 whereby eligible men had to either join the military or contribute in some essential job. Baseball won an extension until September 1, when the regular season shut down. Then the Red Sox faced and defeated the Chicago Cubs.

The National Commission, which governed baseball before a commissioner was ensconced as the czar of the game in 1920, had ruled that other teams beyond the pennant-winners would share in World Series payouts. The Red Sox and Cubs threatened to mutiny and it took the intervention of American League President Ban Johnson to talk sense and prevent a boycott. Johnson told the players to get a grip, to gain perspective. They were only going to be out a few hundred dollars at a time when American soldiers were being killed in war overseas. He was convincing.

That was the precedent when the U.S. responded to the attack on Hawaii and shifted to war footing. Now baseball had a commissioner in Judge Kenesaw Mountain Landis, who took over his duties in 1920 and remained on the job in 1941. Landis reached out to President Franklin D. Roosevelt for guidance on whether baseball should even plan on having a 1942 season. Landis put the offer to cease play into writing, in part saying,

"If you believe we ought to close down for the duration of the war, we are ready to do so immediately. If you feel we ought to continue, we would be delighted to do so. We await your order."³ FDR promptly wrote back in a letter dated January 15, 1942. He said it part, "I honestly feel that it would be the best for the country to keep baseball going. There will be fewer people unemployed and everybody will work longer hours and harder than ever before. And that means that they ought to have a chance for recreation and for taking their minds off their work even more than before."⁴

However, it was made clear that there would be no special exemption from the draft for baseball players. They could play on if they wished, or enlist, but once summoned, their cases would be considered in the same manner as any other civilian male. Roosevelt's response came to be known as "The Green Light letter," giving his blessing for baseball to continue. The other professional leagues going at the time, the National Football League and the National Hockey League, followed baseball's lead. They kept their seasons going, too. The National Basketball Association, the youngest of the four chief North American team-sport leagues, was not founded until after World War II. Individuals who competed in those sports were routinely drafted or volunteered for service. There was a tremendous manpower shortage for team rosters and the absence of many of the country's most athletic players reduced the caliber of play. But at least there was some play.

World War II was to last much longer than World War I. Selected players like Feller and Hank Greenberg were out of baseball even before the start of the 1942 season. Play was affected, but much more so in the ensuing three seasons of 1943, 1944, and 1945.

Not every player departing the Reds roster before the 1942 season left due to a military commitment. While it must have been difficult to do so, Cincinnati parted ways with long-time catcher and star Ernie Lombardi. The Reds sold him outright to the Boston Braves/Bees. Whether management believed he was over the hill, the lack of speed on the bases seemed too much to overcome anymore, whatever reason was used to justify Lombardi's exile, it seemed as if the move was made too hastily. Lombardi was 34 that year, and was only making $10,000, so he probably wasn't breaking the bank. Boston got itself a good deal. The creaky receiver played in 105 games and led the National League in batting for a second time, hitting .330. He made the All-Star team that year and played several more seasons in the big leagues.

The new Reds catcher, though not a long-term solution, was Ray Lamanno, a 22 year old from Oakland, California, who played 111 games and batted .264. But he soon left for the Navy and did not return to the Reds until 1946. Frank McCormick still anchored first base, hitting .277 with 13 home runs and 89 runs batted in. He played all the way through the war years. Second baseman Lonny Frey was still hanging in there. He played 141 games and batted .266. He went off to war in 1944. Eddie Joost was a familiar face at short, though he hit just .224 in 142 games.

Mike McCormick was around, but played just 40 games. He went into the service shortly after the 1943 season began. Harry Craft's playing career was on the verge of ending after his 37-game stint in 1942. Ival Goodman got into 87 games, but was approaching the twilight of his career and his association with the Reds ended that year.

Three other members of the starting lineup were newcomers to the Reds. Bill Werber was gone, no longer the third baseman. Bert Haas, who had a few cups of coffee with Brooklyn, was the main man in 1942, playing in 154 games. But he only batted .239. By 1944, he was in the military. Gee Walker, who had some terrific hitting years in the past, was past his prime at 34 while playing 119 outfield games. His average was just .230, 123 points below his personal best season. Another regular outfielder in 1942 was Max Marshall, who played in 131 games, but only hit .255. Mike McCormick, Craft, and Goodman, all yeoman of the past, filled in much of the time in the outfield along with Eric Tipton, who got into 63 games and only came up with a .222 average.

There was no pop in the lineup whatsoever when manager Bill McKechnie searched for a pinch-hitter or a sub. Frank McCormick's 13 homers led the team and 12 from Lomanno represented the next leading amount. And the pitching wasn't much better. Paul Derringer's drop-off in 1941 when he finished 12-14 after three straight 20-win seasons, continued. He finished 10-11 in 1942, though his earned run average was a solid 3.06. He could blame his record on lack of run support. The Reds scored just 527 runs all year. Bucky Walters survived to the point of finishing 15-14, with an excellent ERA of 2.66. What of Elmer Riddle, the 1941 sensation? He plummeted to 7-11. Jim Turner, who only two seasons earlier won 14 games, was 38, and went 0-0 in three appearances. Whitey Moore got into just a single game, concluding his stay in Cincinnati, though he pitched in nine more games that year for the St. Louis Cardinals.

Junior Thompson went 4-7, though he could not know all his best pitching was behind him and he would soon be headed to the U.S. Navy for three years. Early on, though, he recorded a memorable game. On May 12, he beat the Dodgers, 5-1 at Ebbets Field. It was a near-no-hitter. Thompson gave up one hit and one run. Pinch-hitter Lew Riggs, the former Red, got to him with a double in the bottom of the sixth inning. "I figure the pitcher, not me, is on the spot," Riggs said. "Maybe a hit by me will mean his ball game. On the other hand, the fans and the players realize that mine is a tough job and I can't be expected to come through too often."[5]

The most unlikely success story on the mound in 1942 was 36-year-old Ray Starr, who finished 15-13 with a 2.67 earned run average and was selected for the National League All-Star team. Starr, who appeared in seven games for the Reds in 1941, going 3-2, had previously not pitched in the majors since 1933, and barely then. Mostly buried in the minors by the Cardinals organization, Starr persevered anywhere he could throw. As more and more players left big-league rosters, the need for pitching became acute everywhere and Starr at last stuck with a big-league team. "I think I could have been a winner up here since 1931, if they'd ever given me a chance," he said.[6] The 1942 season was an opportunity he made the most of, even if he was old enough to retire. "I'm not as fast as I used to be," Starr said. "I used to be as fast as (Lefty) Grove. Now I change pace on them."[7]

As a minor curiosity on the pitching staff that year, 19-year-old Ewell Blackwell showed up in two games. Then he promptly disappeared for three years in the Army before returning to baseball action and doing some great things for the Reds.

Given the guys that were coming and going, McKechnie was caught with an erratically playing daily lineup and an iffy pitching staff. The Reds were on their way to finishing 76-76 and in fourth place. Distracted by war news and an up-and-down team, Cincinnati fans lost interest. The season-long attendance was just 427,031, sixth out of eight teams in the National League.

It may have been a mediocre season for Cincinnati, but there was one notable personnel change. The team acquired one new face in an important role who had more impact on the club than most players who ever pulled on the uniform. The prominent right-handed pitcher Waite Hoyt won 237 games during a 21-year career and eventually was elected to the Hall of Fame for his artistry on the mound. He retired in 1938 and began a broadcasting career. In 1942, Hoyt became the Reds' play-by-play radio man and he kept the job through 1965, becoming a legend in his own time due to his own voice. Hoyt, was a close friend of Babe Ruth's, and a long-time Yankee teammate, and never seemed to run out of Ruth tales. Hoyt also never ran short of stories and ideas to fill dead air time during rain delays. He became famous for his talent at holding listeners' interest when there was nothing going on. Hoyt said he was astounded when he was younger and first encountered a working radio, shocked that a voice could come out of the little box. He became quite good friends with that box.

However, the pitcher who really did more great things for the Reds than any other in 1942, and who gave fans reasons to turn out, was Johnny Vander Meer. The southpaw was still only 27. He had already shown he had returned to health in 1941. But he was even better in 1942. For the second straight season Vander Meer led the NL in strikeouts, this time with 186.

He also won two more games than in 1941, finishing with a mound mark of 18-12. His earned run average of 2.43 sparkled. It was a challenging season for the Reds during challenging times for the nation. An overnight star in 1938, beset by injuries and trips to the minor leagues in 1939 and 1940, how many baseball experts would have bet the same Johnny Vander Meer would win 18 games in 1942?

# 18

# The Reds During World War II

Baseball during World War II was peculiar. Once it was decided that Major League ball would continue, teams managed the best they could to field reasonably talented squads. Many of the finest players in the sport were serving in the military—Bob Feller, Warren Spahn, Joe DiMaggio, Ted Williams—as were many of their teammates. The war was a brutal conflagration for the United States on two fronts, in Europe and in the Pacific. While the country was not ready for such a fight when Pearl Harbor was bombed, the military raced to catch up, manufacturers went into overdrive to provide the equipment fighting men needed. Likewise, manpower was drafted, recruited, hurriedly trained, and sent into battle.

The Great War, ending in 1918, was supposed to be the war to end all wars. Instead, it really became a vamp-till-ready for World War II, Germany under Adolf Hitler, the initiator. The dictator, one of the most vicious and evil men ever to trod the earth, sought world domination. Not content to build his own nation into a colossus, Hitler, guided by some internal sickness, wanted to wipe out entire races and peoples worldwide whom he claimed were inferior to the Aryan race.

Daily, war reports overshadowed everything else in the United States. World War II was a war that the public understood to be of the gravest consequence. The founding roots and precepts of the country were at stake. The Constitution. The Declaration of Independence. Life, liberty and the pursuit of happiness. This was an at-all-costs war. The idea of Nazi rule, or the Japanese's barbaric rule, were repugnant.

Baseball players were citizens first, Americans first. They signed up for the service in droves. Some, based on personal circumstances, waited to be called. In anticipation of what was to come, the first peace-time draft in the nation's history and the draft was renewed in 1941 when it was no longer peace time. Baseball men joined up by the dozens from each team, stars, bench-warmers, minor leaguers beholden to a club. Sacrifices of all sorts were made by the American people during the war. There was gasoline, meat and clothing rationing. There was a ban on the manufacture and sale of such goods as washing machines and vacuum cleaners. Americans not only had to cope with the war, they had to fund the war. In many job categories wages were controlled. As men lined up by the millions to go overseas, women took their places in the workforce.

Generally, baseball players were prime candidates for the service. They matched the logical demographic of being young, strong, athletic and likely more prepared for the hardships that might occur in training, travel and combat. Still, there were ways in which a professional athlete could be judged 4-F, not fit for service. Overall, not related specifically to athletes, there were many reasons why a man would not be accepted into the service. He might hold an essential job. That included farmers. Also, previously being rejected for service would count someone out. Those between 38 and 44 years old and working in a national service capacity were deferred. Deferments were parceled out if drafting someone would create a family hardship. There were conscientious objectors. Moreover, a candidate could be rejected for wide-ranging definitions under the categories of mental, physical or moral reasons. Some physical reasons could include cancer, "imbecility," insanity, epilepsy, brain, spinal cord, heart, lung, liver, kidneys or bladder illnesses.

When the country mobilized for war and many of his teammates began wearing the uniforms of the Army, Navy and Marines instead of that of the Cincinnati Reds, Johnny Vander Meer was prepared to go to war, as well. However, initially, Uncle Sam did not want him. Due to his coping with colitis, military doctors deemed him unfit for service. He had become the star of the Reds' pitching staff in 1942, and he was back for 1943, too.

There really was no way for Bill McKechnie to know what players he would have for that season. Some regulars were still around. But they could be drafted in June. It was almost like planning around the possibility of a season-ending injury. If someone did depart for the rest of the season for military service, it was the equivalent of a serious concussion or knee injury for the team. Of course, for the player-turned-soldier, it could become fatal.

In a less literal sense, baseball was limping along. Fans did appreciate the games, but attendance was down because so many other fans were preoccupied and distracted by the war, especially if they had loved ones serving and at risk. Issuing pre-season predictions was a less-exact science than usual since all teams faced the same situation of not being sure who would be available to play all year.

Crosley Field was not as busy a place in 1943 as it had been in 1939 and 1940 when the Reds were winning National League pennants. Attendance for the entire season was 379,112—seventh out of eight teams in the league.

That did not match team performance, though. The Reds were much better on the field that year than in 1942 when they stalled out at 76-76. This year, Cincinnati finished 87-67 in second place in the NL. It was actually the third-best record in baseball. The St. Louis Cardinals tore through

One of Johnny Vander Meer's teammates was Bucky Walters, a converted third baseman who won as many as 27 games in a season and a Most Valuable Player award as a pitcher and even briefly managed the Reds.

the National League with a 105-49 record. The New York Yankees, even depleted, went 98-56 to conquer the American League.

At 22, young Stan Musial recorded an astonishing season for the Cardinals. He led the National League in batting at .357 and also led the league in games (157), plate appearances (700), hits (220), doubles (48), triples (20) and on-base percentage (.425) while also hitting 13 home runs and driving in 81 runs. He won the circuit's Most Valuable Player award. Just about the only hurler in the NL Musial couldn't hit well seemed to be Vander Meer. "Vander Meer is one swell pitcher," Musial said. "He has great stuff and is just wild enough at times to keep you loose. Maybe I'll catch up with him yet."[1]

Vander Meer was swell part of the time, if not as often as he had been in 1942. Although he threw 289 innings—proving his arm, at least was not 4F—and his earned run average was 2.87, his record was just 15-16. The ace was Elmer Riddle, returned to health and form after a down year in 1942. Riddle excelled, much as he did in 1941, going a team-best 21-11 with a 2.63 ERA.

Bucky Walters was still in the rotation, going 15-15, although his earned run average had inched up to 3.54. Ray Starr helped out again, going 11-10. But stalwart Paul Derringer's run in Cincinnati was over. He spent that season with the Chicago Cubs, finishing 10-14. Joe Beggs, now in his early 30s, kept chugging along. He went 7-6, remaining a key option out of the bullpen with his 2.34 earned run average. If Beggs was on the mound in the late innings, McKechnie figured the Reds had a chance.

Though in 1943, Beggs had competition for most important arm out of the bullpen. Clyde Shoun, who had come over from the Cardinals in 1942, produced the best season of his life, going 14-5 with a 3.06 ERA. Shoun was born in Mountain City, Tennessee, in 1915 and excepting a 13-11 season in 1940 was not often relied on much by the Cardinals. The Reds traded Whitey Moore to obtain Shoun in time for him to appear in 34 games in 1942, though he only had a 1-3 record. A southpaw, Shoun's nickname was "Duster."

As seemed to be the case in recent years, the Reds had still another new catcher in Ray Mueller, who played in 141 games and batted .260. Frank McCormick, who maintained his presence throughout the war at first base for Cincinnati, resumed his .300-hitting ways at .303 after a couple of comparatively down years and was the team's leading hitter. He was chosen an All-Star for the sixth of eight times.

For the sixth season in a row, Lonny Frey owned second base. He gave the Reds 144 games, hit .263, and made the All-Star team. However, this was his final season as a player during the war years, though he did return to the Reds in 1946. Steve Mesner hit .272 at third base.

Gee Walker was again an outfield regular and again did not hit very well at .245. Max Marshall, who played in the majors only during World War II, had trouble at the plate in his 132 games, hitting just .236. Outfielder Eric Tipton played much more in 1943 than he had in 1942, getting into 140 games, and he hit better, with an average of .288. After a little bit of a floundering start with the Reds in 1942, Tipton was a solid guy for Cincinnati during the war years. The reason Tipton was a regular during that time period was because the Navy turned him down three times because he was color blind. When he tried the Army, that branch turned him down, too, due to punctured eardrums resulting from childhood measles. One baseball writer referred to Tipton as "4F in the Army, but 1A in a Major League manager's heart."[2]

Tipton had played college baseball and football for Duke University and liked to brag about a career-ending shot he blasted against the school's arch-rival. "In my last at-bat for Duke," Tipton said, "I hit a 400-foot home run with bases loaded to beat our traditional rival, the U. of North Carolina."[3] Tipton was called "Eric the Red" in college. Whether the home run had anything to do with it or not, Tipton was eventually inducted into the Duke Athletic Hall of Fame.

Since the Reds hit just .256 as a team with only a total of 43 home runs sprinkled throughout the roster (nobody in double figures and Tipton leading with 9), it seems remarkable the Reds were able to win so many games in 1943 and finish 20 games over .500.

After the season, in January of 1944, the Navy seemed to remember Vander Meer's existence. His presence was requested at a hospital in New York for another examination of his colitis. By then he was cured and cleared to be accepted by the service. He was told he would receive a notice within 90 days and he did, reporting for induction on March 3, 1944. He wished to be dispatched overseas into the fighting, but that was not the plan for him.

Rather than deploy Vander Meer to a combat zone, he was kept away from the action and used as a ball player, a major leaguer not in the major leagues, but pitching to entertain troops on R&R. As long as he was going to pitch, anyway, Vander Meer said he would prefer to be back in Cincinnati. He was in the service, but didn't really feel he was providing much service in his role. "But the thing I wanted most was to get into this thing [the war]," he said. "Everyone else was putting on a uniform and I didn't see why I should be an exception."[4] Once in the Navy, Vander Meer was out of the majors for the duration of the war, missing the 1944 and 1945 seasons in the big leagues.

Baseball soldiered on without Vander Meer, and so did McKechnie, mixing and matching lineups in 1944 after losing another of his top pitchers

## 18. The Reds During World War II

and again fielding a starting lineup with few legitimate hitters, even by the standards of war-time play. The Reds went 89-69 and finished third in the league that season, one-and-a-half games behind the Pittsburgh Pirates and both of those teams far behind those 105-win Reds.

Frank McCormick, who played in his 1000th game with the Reds in 1944, was the offensive king. Hitting like his best self of the past, McCormick hit 20 home runs, drove in 102 runs, and batted .305. Catcher Mueller knocked 10 home runs, gathered 73 RBIs, and hit .280. Tipton came to life with a .301 season and Walker flashed some old form, hitting .278. Even with McCormick's output Cincinnati as a team banged just 51 home runs.

The middle infielders stayed healthy, Woody Williams playing 155 games at second and Eddie Miller playing 155 games at short. Williams played so much he led the National League with 707 plate appearances and 653 at-bats, though he managed only a .240 batting average. Even though Miller's average was a subterranean .209, he was chosen for the All-Star team, one of seven times for a guy whose lifetime average was .238. Good fielder.

Except for a brief stay with Brooklyn in 1938, Williams' entire Major League career was with the Reds during World War II. The early stages of his career were interrupted after he was hit in the head by a pitched ball in the minors and suffered a fractured skull. Although he was never a terrific hitter for a sustained period, Williams had one notable batting feat attached to his name, something that made a good first impression when he joined the Reds in 1943. He tied a record by collecting 10 straight hits. They were spread among six pitchers in three games over two days. "You've got to have luck to get a string of hits in a row," he said, "but you also have to be seeing the ball good, and I was seeing it clearly."[5]

Given his weak stick, Miller had to be special in the field, and he was. He was enough of a glove man to establish records at the time and was mentioned in the same breath as renowned fielders of earlier days such as Joe Tinker. Some said he was the best NL shortstop since Honus Wagner, the Hall of Famer who most assuredly was a finer all-around player. During the time period, though lesser known later, he was favorably compared to St. Louis' Marty Marion. "And I'll tell you why," said Hall of Fame pitcher Waite Hoyt, who was a Reds broadcaster. "Miller is what I call a playmaker. By that I mean he will execute plays Marion won't make. If the Reds have an outside chance of making a double play on a bunted ball they'll try for it, and I've seen the Cincinnati infielders complete the play. It was successful because of the part Miller had in it. Eddie's a marvel at starting double plays. He gets the ball away from him in a split second."[6]

Pitching was a different matter for the Reds in 1944. True to his every-other-year showing of winning big, then hardly winning at all, Riddle went 2-2, battling shoulder issues. Ed Heusser, a 35-year-old right-hander who had last played in the majors for the Philadelphia Athletics in 1940, had the finest season of his career, going 13-11, with a 2.38 best-in-the-NL earned run average. In his only big-league season, Tommy de la Cruz, 32, a native of Cuba, went 9-9. Harry Gumbert, 34, a seasoned righty, went 10-8 for the Reds after starting the season 4-2 for the Cardinals. Lefty Arnold Carter, whose only Major League time was during the war, did a terrific job for the Reds, going 11-7 with a 2.60 earned run average.

Clyde Shoun, who proved to be a surprisingly good get the year before, wasn't as reliable overall, but finished 13-10. But on May 15, the veteran southpaw pitched the Reds' first no-hitter since Vander Meer's two no-hitters in 1938, beating the Boston Braves, 1-0. It was a pitcher's duel, too, with Boston's Jim Tobin giving up just five hits. On a hitters' afternoon off, it took just 1 hour, 19 minutes to complete the game, witnessed by only 1,014 paying customers. Only a walk to Tobin in the third inning prevented Shoun from hurling a perfect game. Tobin himself had just thrown a no-hitter on April 29 against Brooklyn. Shoun benefited from two running catches by Gee Walker in right field. Cincinnati's lone run came on a home run to left field in the fifth inning on a swat by Chuck Aleno, playing third base that day. "I wasn't shooting at a no-hitter," Shoun said. "I just wanted to win a game. There was no pressure—no pressure at all."[7] Shoun also stroked two of his team's hits. Only two days prior, in the same series, Bucky Walters nearly threw a no-hitter against the Braves. When Walters congratulated Shoun, the game-winner said, "Don't worry, Bucky. I had to pitch a one-hitter before I got mine. You'll get yours."[8]

Walters, experiencing a renaissance season, did everything but pitch a no-hitter in 1944, starting with that May 14 one-hit, 4-0 win. He walked none that day while the Reds helped out with 14 hits, Frank McCormick and Eddie Miller each clouting three hits. At 35, Walters started 32 games, threw 285 innings, recorded a 2.40 ERA, and finished 23-8. That led the National League in wins for the third time. This was also his last great season before his skills began to fade, and Walters' sixth and last All-Star selection.

It was obvious by mid-season the Reds were playing for second place, that the Cardinals would not be caught for the pennant. The issue then became whether they could hold onto second. Some said it all depended on whether or not Walters was superb enough. One Cincinnati newspaper headline in late July read, "Reds Wonder Where They'd Be Without Wonder-Man Walters."[9] That may have been a little strong, but it was emblematic. Walters won his 10th game by mid–June, sooner than any other pitcher in the league, and pitched six shutouts that season. It was interesting that his teammate, Heusser, who won 10 fewer games and pitched two fewer shutouts, edged him out for the ERA title by .02. But Walters was selected as the National League Pitcher of the Year, again with the proviso this was not a Cy Young Award.

Walters notwithstanding, the Reds did not hold on to second place. The season ended with an all–St. Louis World Series, those runaway National League pennant-winning Cardinals beating the St. Louis Browns in six games. That was the only pennant the Browns won in their half-century of existence.

As a memorable footnote to the Reds' 1944 season, the Reds signed 15-year-old Joe Nuxhall right out of his high school and put him in uniform for opening day. On June 10, Nuxhall was brought into a game the Reds were trailing 13-0 to the Cardinals, making him the youngest player in baseball history. He got into that one game, pitched ⅔ of an inning and gave up five runs. Nuxhall did not get back to the majors until 1952, but the southpaw was eventually a two-time All-Star and then became a legendary Reds broadcaster from 1967 until 2007. When he reminisced about his unusual debut, Nuxhall said that going from pitching to 14-year-olds to facing Stan Musial was scary.

World War II dragged on, stressing the populace, straining the nation's resources. Men went overseas to fight. Men went overseas to die. Men came of age and were drafted or enlisted. Resources grew thinner. Millions grieved over the loss of the youth of the country. Starting with the deficit of being victimized by the sneak attack at Pearl Harbor, the nation rallied, the military grew mightier. The toll was terrible, but the direction of the war on both fronts gradually tilted towards the Allies.

The D-Day invasion of June 6, 1944, began turning the tide in Europe. The last gasp of the Germans at the Battle of the Bulge led to Americans and allied countries finishing off the Third Reich. As their cities were shattered and manpower destroyed, the Germans' defeat became inevitable. The rebuffing and conquering of the enemy continued on parallel tracks. In August of 1945, the United States unleashed the atomic bomb on Japanese soil over Hiroshima on the sixth of the month and then another one over Nagaski three days later. The power in the devices essentially incinerated those cities.

It took only until August 15 for Japan's emperor to surrender. The war in Europe ended on September 2. By then, another baseball season was rushing to a conclusion. That summer even Bill McKechnie seemed to lose his magic managerial touch with the Reds. They plummeted, finishing 61-83, with 28 fewer wins than in 1944. Just 290,070 fans showed up at Crosley Field all year. The baling wire apparently unraveled. Cincinnati did not have a .300 hitter in 1945. No one hit more than 13 home runs.

Frank McCormick, who was as attached to the Crosley first-base bag as the bag was to the earth, hit 10 home runs, drove in 81 runs and batted .276 in 152 games and again made the All-Star team. Sometimes, it seemed if not for McCormick, the Reds would have had no punch at all. However, Eddie Miller, of all people, hit a team-leading 13 homers in 1945. In the context of Miller's career that almost seemed like a typographical error. Not that he did much with the bat otherwise, hitting .238 with only 49 RBIs and an anemic .275 on-base percentage.

The 1945 season brought another new majority shareholder in the catcher's position. Al Lakeman, 26, appeared in 76 games and hit .256. That was more than Lakeman played in any other of his nine partial seasons in the majors. Lakeman had occupied a seat on the bench off and on since 1942, seeing minimal activity. A native of Cincinnati, he was nicknamed "Moose." After coming up from Syracuse in '42, he got into 20 games with 43 plate appearances. It was a memorable occasion for the hometown boy, or perhaps he did not remember anything at all: Lakeman fainted in the third inning of his first big-league game. Some said the heat got to him. Others thought the pressure did. Maybe it was nerves.

Never much of a hitter, Lakeman's lifetime average was .203. However, he crammed a lifetime's worth of hitting excitement into one day in 1945. On September 9, Lakeman drove in the winning run against the Brooklyn Dodgers in both games of a double-header, a 6-5 decision in 10 innings and a 6-4 win in the nightcap.

Al Libke was a new guy in the starting lineup, taking over right field for 130 games. In the first of his two Major League seasons, he hit .283. Libke, 26, stood 6-foot-4 and weighed 215 pounds and should have provided more power. A converted pitcher for Seattle in the Pacific Coast League, as well as for the shipyard where he worked, Libke came to the Reds spring training camp "as crude as petroleum," in the words of his own team's press release, issued after catching on at his new position and coming through during the regular season.[10] Libke showed enough to the talent scouting McKechnie to make him a fan, at least for the time being. "It looks like he may develop into a real hitter and maybe he can be taught to field, just as many other outfielders," the manager said.[11]

No starting pitcher in the rotation had better than a .500 record in 1945. "Bill [McKechnie] knows pitchers better than anyone in the business," said coach Jimmie Wilson, "and is a marvel at getting the best out of them. But you can search me how he does it year in and year out. He's a wonder."[12] This was very true for 1944, but in 1945 nothing McKechnie tried worked and none of his guys performed as well as they had in the past. Walters retained a very good earned run average of 2.68, but his record was 10-10 and he pitched much less frequently. Heusser was 11-16 and his ERA went up by nearly a run-and-a-half. McKechnie tried to pull another rabbit out of his hat with the acquisition of Joe Bowman, 35, who after losing two games for the Boston Red Sox reappeared in Cincinnati and went 11-13. That tied for the team lead in victories.

A fellow named Boom-Boom Beck, at age 40, gave the Reds a 2-4 record in 11 games. He did not make nearly the impact as hockey Hall of Famer Boom Boom Geoffrion did in the National Hockey League. Beck's real first name was Walter, and he received his nickname for an unfortunate reason. One day in 1934 while pitching for the Dodgers at the Baker Bowl against the Phillies, Beck gave up several hard-hit drives off the wall that made a booming sound. Hence, the nickname. As he was being removed from the game for a reliever, and compounding the bizarre nature of the situation, in a fury, Beck hurled a ball deep off the outfield wall. Hack Wilson, who gained fame with the Chicago Cubs, but was playing outfield for Philadelphia at the very end of his career, thought it was another hit and fielded it.

Walters did not serve in the military during World War II, but between November of 1944 and January of 1945, he participated in a recreational program for the Special Services Division in the European Theatre and received a certificate of thanks from that office. Walters wrote a fairly substantial missive detailing his experience as part of one of five baseball groups, calling it "an honor and my good fortune."[13] This was part of a program for soldiers to relieve the intensity at the front lines, but Walters said the visitors probably got more out of it than the fighting men. In part he wrote, "It was marvelous to see how easily the fellows could laugh in the face of the hardships they are going through. Often, these doughboys were just out of their foxholes in the front lines—some going right back again."[14]

Walters and his baseball partners, who included Mel Ott, Frank Frisch, and Dutch Leonard, traveled to the front line area wearing military gear. They put on a show for soldiers that included showing a film of the 1944 World Series. They talked, told stories, answered questions and tried to keep it light. The group visited Americans in France, Belgium, Holland, Luxembourg and Germany and included talks to the 82nd and 101st Airborne, as well as hospitals. Sometimes they had to adjust plans because of changing battle circumstances.

Judge Kenesaw Mountain Landis had just died after spending 24 years as baseball's first commissioner. Someone asked baseball writer Roy Stockton, from St. Louis, who might succeed Landis and he told the crowd, "Maybe they're waiting for a big name to come out of this war." Walters said "Some doughboy, fresh out of the front line, dirty-faced, and needing a shave, jumped up right quick and hollered out, 'That's me, buddy!'"[15] Walters said the soldiers expressed support for baseball and other games to keep going, but were hoping the war would end soon so they could go home. "We weren't actors or comedians, but just talked about something they liked," Walters said. "And they like anything American."[16]

Before the end of summer in 1945, the war was over and the soldiers were starting to come home. That included the baseball players whose service meant they missed prime years of their careers. They were going to try and resume playing, hopeful there were still spots for them on their old teams and that their old skills were not too rusty.

# 19

# When Johnny
# —and the Reds—
# Came Marching Home

After missing two baseball seasons in the Navy, Johnny Vander Meer returned to the Cincinnati Reds for the 1946 season. He was 31 years old, not the young flame-thrower of 1938 when he tossed those two no-hitters. And these were not the same Reds of yesteryear. They were the same Reds in general terms, if not all the same bodies, as the losing Reds of 1945. That meant they were pretty lousy that season, finishing 67-87 in sixth place. The country was in a much better mood, though. Fans were anxious to see "real" baseball, not watered-down rosters. Even though Cincinnati attracted 715,751 fans, over 400,000 more than in 1945, that was still last in the league in attendance.

A glance at the roster indicated the Reds did not have much going for them, either hitting or pitching wise. Many of the best players had retired or gone elsewhere. Ernie Lombardi, one of the best catchers the Reds would ever have, was nearing the end of his career with the New York Giants, but still batted .290 in 88 games. Instead, Cincinnati relied on Ray Mueller, who hit .254 after not catching for two years.

The often-great, and always reliable Frank McCormick was gone, sent to the Philadelphia Phillies where he batted .284 in his final All-Star season. Bert Haas, who hadn't played in two years, was the first-baseman, hitting .264. It was not an upgrade. Bobby Adams played a bunch of second base, hitting .244. Lonny Frey was back from the war and hit .246, though he was more of a utility man than second-sacker. Shortstop Eddie Miller may have been brilliant afield, but batted .194 Young Grady Hatton, who would have a long career in different aspects of baseball, took over third base and hit better than just about anyone else with his .271 average. Hatton played from 1946 to 1960 and managed the expansion Houston Astros in the 1960s.

Al Libke was the best hitter among the outfielders at .253. Eddie Lukon hit .250 with 12 home runs. Dain Clay batted .228. The overall team average was a sad .239. Lukon was an interesting case. He was 25 and appeared in 102 games. That amounted to a serious comeback for him after his health was jeopardized with trench foot in the Battle of the Bulge in 1944. Except for two games in 1945, he did not play professional baseball between 1942 and 1946. Lukon was treated at a field hospital near the front approaching Christmas of 1944 and sent home after a doctor said, "Another bad case of trench feet. No more action for that boy. Too bad! They tell me he was a Major League ball player with Cincinnati before he went into the Army. Guess he can forget about playing ball for a living."[1]

When Lukon returned stateside he was in shaky shape walking around, never mind running. He rebuilt his strength and rejoined the Reds, who used him in those two outings at the end of the 1945 season. In 1946 spring training, Lukon showed more, made the team, and became a regular. He had a five-for-five game against the Chicago Cubs. "I just couldn't seem to coordinate earlier in the season," Lukon said. "I was befuddled part of the season. Nothing came easily. All of it was an effort. Things just seemed to clear up all of a sudden. My confidence returned with that clearing. I felt like a ball player again."[2] Overall, it was a pretty neat comeback story.

Most of the pitching staff had at one time or another in previous years thrown for the Reds. In addition to Vander Meer the main starters were Joe Beggs, who had one of the best records at 12-10. Bucky Walters did not make it through the entire season 100 percent healthy, but went 10-7 with a 2.56 earned average. Ed Heusser's earned run average wasn't half-bad at 3.22, but his record was half bad at 7-14. Young Ewell Blackwell was back from the war at a still-young 23. His record was 9-13, no doubt due to poor run support since his ERA was an excellent 2.45. Harry Gumbert, 6-8, and Clyde Shoun, 1-6, were two others who had performed at higher levels for the Reds in the past.

Bill McKechnie went into this season under-armed, and he did not make it all the way through to the end. Coach Hank Gowdy managed the last games, going 3-1. There were mixed reports in newspapers of McKechnie resigning or being fired. General manager Warren Giles, his long-time patron, is the one who let McKechnie go, if reluctantly. "In baseball, you are forced to bow to the will of your patrons," Giles said. "McKechnie, failing to win, had aroused their antagonism. He became the symbol of the club's frustration and I was forced to make him the scapegoat. Actually, I was more to blame because it is my job to bring in the players, and no manager, not even the best, can win without players."[3]

Although McKechnie did not manage again in the majors, he did serve as a coach, spending five years with the Cleveland Indians and a shorter stretch with the Boston Red Sox. His tenure with the Reds produced a record of 744-631, with two pennants and one World Series title.

In 1946, Vander Meer put together a 10-12 record with a 3.17 earned average and 11 complete games. His 204⅓ innings were the most on the staff. Discharged from the Navy in late December of 1945, Vander Meer was glad to be home, but disappointed to discover he was not in baseball shape. It took him much longer than expected to come around. "We had to build up our stamina again," Vander Meer said. "It was the same thing with our coordination. You only go as far as your legs take you."[4] That is often said about pitchers, though the casual fan does not always understand that. In Vander Meer's case, they were 31-year-old legs, but he beefed up their strength by running five miles a day at spring training in Florida.

Even if Vander Meer did not feel as strong as he wished to be, his stamina did pay off in one of the most memorable games of his life. On September 11, 1946, the Reds were visiting the Brooklyn Dodgers at Ebbets Field. The teams played 19 innings before 14,538 fans and neither one of them scored a run. After 4 hours and 40 minutes, with darkness falling, the game was declared a tie. The game would be made up nine days later, on September 20, with Brooklyn winning, 5-3.

Vander Meer was the Reds starter that day. He threw 15 innings, allowing seven hits, and struck out 14 men. Harry Gumbert pitched the last four innings. Brooklyn used four pitchers, with starter Hal Gregg hurling the first 10 innings and permitting the Reds just five hits. Shortstop Claude Corbitt had three hits in seven at-bats for Cincinnati that day, the most productive man at the plate. Cookie Lavagetto also had three hits in the game for the Dodgers. The game was more important to the Dodgers than the Reds. Brooklyn was chasing the Cardinals for the National League flag and Cincinnati was buried near the bottom of the standings. Ultimately, St. Louis beat out the Dodgers by two games.

While Vander Meer will always be specifically remembered for his no-hitters, this performance rates highly next to them. Dodger general manager Branch Rickey was an eyewitness, and although his rooting interest was for Brooklyn, he was impressed with Vander Meer, calling it "the best pitching performance I have ever seen. I know to what weakness Vander Meer was trying to pitch, and to see him hit those spots consistently with as much stuff as he had was wonderful."[5]

With McKechnie in exile, the Reds went shopping for a new manager and hired Johnny Neun. Neun was a part-time, big-league player from 1925 to 1931 with a .289 average and had been a short-term fill-in as manager for the New York Yankees in 1946, going 8-6. He was most famous for making a rare unassisted triple play on May 31, 1927, while playing third base for the

Detroit Tigers against Cleveland. He also had one game with five hits and five stolen bases.

Giles received a solid recommendation from his old Cincinnati cohort Larry MacPhail on Neun and reached out to him as the end of the 1946 approached, requesting a meeting in secrecy. They met off the big-league path in Lexington, Kentucky. Neun said Giles was forthright about the Reds' woes. "He glossed nothing over," Neun said. "He stressed the fact that I would have to do a thorough rebuilding. He impressed on me the important thing that he and Crosley and the fans did not expect anyone to rush in and perform a miracle."[6]

That was no lie. Although promised new faces, those new faces did not perform miracles in 1947. The Reds were better, though, going 73-81 and placing fifth in the National League. Outfielder Augie Galan was a solid journeyman and although closing in on his middle 30s, he hit .314. Cincinnati liked the looks of 28-year-old rookie Frank Baumholtz, who batted .283. They also got a glimpse of 22-year-old muscle man Ted Kluzewski, who would become one of the team's most popular stars of the next decade, even though in his mini-look at big-league pitching he batted .100 in nine games.

The search for pitching struggled on. Vander Meer was only 9-14 with a poor 4.40 earned run average. At 38, Bucky Walters was 8-8 with an ugly 5.75 ERA. He hoped he wasn't at the end, but he was very close to it. In fact, despite trying to hang on for a couple more years, Walter never won another game, finishing with 198 victories.

Cincinnati's new ace, new star, was Ewell Blackwell, at least for the moment. He very briefly wore the Reds uniform in 1942 and then, for the next three years, he wore the U.S. Army uniform. His return to action as a regular in 1946 was at best so-so. But he was the talk of baseball, the object of gushing compliments wherever he went in 1947 as he won 22 games, lost just 8 and handcuffed hitters to the tune of a 2.45 earned run average. Several things set Blackwell apart. He stood 6-foot-6, unusually tall for a pitcher at that time and weighed just 195 pounds, a combination which elicited some verbal excess among newsman. Blackwell's physique, it was once written, looked "like a fly rod with ears."[7] He threw with an unusual delivery, too, not overhand, but partially sidearm, and broke his pitches off abruptly. That earned the nickname of "The Whip." Such a harsh style made it likely it would take a toll on Blackwell's arm, but that was not a concern in 1947. He was too busy dazzling onlookers.

On June 18, the Reds hosted the Boston Braves for a night game at Crosley Field, which attracted 18,137 spectators—many more fans wished they were there. Employing his trademark fastball as his main weapon, Blackwell shut down the Braves 6-0 while pitching a no-hitter. He walked four in a game that took 1 hour, 51 minutes to play. "I realized my sidearm delivery was intimidating," Blackwell said, "and I took advantage of it any way I could. I was a mean pitcher."[8] Blackwell won 16 straight games during the 1947 season, causing a major sensation.

Right from the game's start versus Boston, Cincinnati provided run support, scoring three in the bottom of the first. The Reds added three more in the eighth, but Blackwell was never threatened. Baumholtz had four hits that day and first-baseman Babe Young, who had a less-renowned career, hit two three-run homers that day. Blackwell's season in its entirety, and this type of performance, had the baseball world buzzing about him. Bill McKechnie, by then the former Reds' skipper, was coaching with the Indians when he learned of Blackwell's no-hitter. It reminded him of Vander Meer's work in 1938. He sent a telegram to Blackwell that read, "Congratulations, but why the bases on balls?"[9]

Dixie Walker, nearing the end of an 18-year, big-league career, said of Blackwell's pitching gyrations that he "looks like a man falling out of a tree." Sly comments and compliments were easy to come by, including from American Leaguers who saw Blackwell in the All-Star game. "He's a hell of a good pitcher," said Joe DiMaggio. Lou Boudreau, player-manager of the Indians, responded to a question this way: "Is he good? Who is better? He is equal to anyone in our league. His speed is terrific. He is around the plate all the time. His curve is deadly and his sidearm sinker spectacular." Ted Williams chimed in, too. "I don't think he's any better than [Bob] Feller or [Hal] Newhouser, but he has a chance to be. I had an awful time seeing him get rid of the ball."[10]

Following the no-hitter, Blackwell was up for his regular turn in the rotation on June 22, the first game of a doubleheader against Brooklyn. This was quite a hitting lineup, many of the players who starred for the remainder of the franchise's stay in Brooklyn, already in place. Jackie Robinson, Carl Furillo, Pee Wee Reese and Duke Snider all played in that game, as well as Walker. But as the game entered the ninth inning, Blackwell had them all buffaloed. He was sitting on a second consecutive no-hitter, poised to match Vander Meer's unique feat of a decade earlier, an accomplishment no one believed would be equaled.

It had been a 1-0 game until the bottom of the eighth when the Reds added three more runs. Normally light-hitting shortstop Eddie Miller accounted for those with a bases loaded double. The top of the ninth inning brought Gene Hermanski to the plate. He flew out to left field for the first out. Blackwell was inching towards equaling Vander Meer. Until second baseman Eddie Stanky entered the batter's box and ground a single to center field. There went the no-hitter. Now Blackwell had to preserve the shutout and the victory. Al Gionfriddo made a fly ball out. Robinson caught up to Blackwell for another hit before Blackwell set down Furillo on a ground ball.

Afterwards, Blackwell, while appreciating the 4-0 win, said he thought he should have caught Stanky's hit. "I thought he had hit it harder than he actually had," Blackwell said. "When it's hit straight back at you, sometimes it's hard to judge just how fast it's moving. I made my move too quickly. I went down for it and came up thinking I had the ball. Well, I'm proud of that no-hitter [on June 18] and I guess missing Stanky's grounder cost me about $100,000 in salary and endorsements."[11] He might have been right about that. Even though Robinson did add a second hit, he later said it was no fun to bat against Blackwell. "When he's right, he's virtually unhittable," Robinson said. "And when he wheels that ball in from somewhere around third base, he's tougher than ever. I'd rather hit against any other pitcher in the game 10 times than face Blackwell once. He's just the greatest pitcher in the game."[12]

Not for long, however. Blackwell soon endured a trifecta of health misfortunes. He had a kidney operation and an appendectomy and then a sore shoulder that finished him off with a lifetime record of only 82-78 which did not do justice to his impact. The 22-win season was by far Blackwell's best. He led the National League in victories in 1947. But he almost immediately went into a tailspin, going 7-9 in 1948 and 5-5 in 1949. He rebounded to 17-15 in 1950 and 16-15 in 1951 and then petered out altogether. Somehow, even in those early sketchy years, Blackwell was chosen for the All-Star team regularly, six times in all. It was Babe Ruth, late in life, who observed Blackwell's harsh delivery and predicted disaster. "That young feller Blackwell in Cincinnati is wearing himself out. He's throwing too many curves. Someone ought to wake that kid up."[13] Even though Ruth said it in 1947, when Blackwell was at the height of his stardom, the Bambino was correct.

When Blackwell nearly equaled his feat of hurling back-to-back no-hitters, Vander Meer was his teammate, still with the Reds, and watching closely. He was rooting for it to happen, to make his own one-man club less exclusive, inching from the dugout closer to the field in anticipation. "I was up on the top step," Vander Meer said. "I wanted to be the first one out there to congratulate him."[14] Blackwell provided much of the excitement for the Cincinnati Reds fan of 1947. The team still had its losing record, for the third year in a row, and those hitters weren't hitting much. The organization wanted to believe the club was on an upswing. But that did not show up in the record in 1948. The Reds went backwards, finishing 64-89, somehow avoiding last place in the NL, but placing seventh. Some fresh talent did stand out, though, if not entirely considered new faces, they were new contributors.

## 19. When Johnny—and the Reds—Came Marching Home

Due to World War II travel restrictions, the Cincinnati Reds were unable to set up spring training in Florida. Instead, they used the Indiana University campus in Bloomington, Indiana. That worked to their advantage when they came across a student there named Ted Kluzewski who could really play ball.

Kluzewski took over first base and showed the first stirrings of the star he would become. He hit 12 home runs and batted .274, foreshadowing of the future. Soon enough "Big Klu" would become a four-time All-Star. He was the National League MVP in 1954. The best season in his 15-year Major League career came in 1955 for the Reds when he bashed a league-leading 49 home runs, accompanied by an NL-leading 141 runs batted in and a .326 average. Ultimately, Kluzewski's No. 18 jersey was retired by the Reds.

One of Kluzewski's most distinctive features on the diamond was the way he snipped the sleeves short on his jersey to provide some air for his bulging arm muscles. Originally, for comfort, not to show off, Klu applied the scissors work on his own. Then Cincinnati invested in specially made shirts for him. "They could never make a uniform for me that would give me enough room," Kluzewski once explained of his early days of modifying the shirts by himself.[15] When Major League Baseball outlawed the Klu look, it did so in a creative manner, approving a rule that said all players on the same team had to wear sleeves of the same approximate length. So unless all the Reds cut down their sleeves, Kluzewski had to conform. At the time of the discussions, newspapers got into the habit of referring to the clothing manner as the "Sally Rand Rule," named after the famous stripper. Only ball players had to cover up, not take it off.[16]

Kluzewski spent most of his career with the Reds, though in 1959, his late addition near the end of the regular season helped the Chicago White Sox win the American League pennant for the first time in 40 years, or since the Reds' triumph in the World Series over the Black Sox. Klu hit .391 in that Series, making many fans in Chicago. Much later, Kluzewski became the Reds' hitting coach, providing advice for the team during the Big Red Machine championship era of the mid–1970s. This was the period of Pete Rose, Johnny Bench, Tony Perez and Joe Morgan.

Klu said his wife Eleanor shot movies of him at-bat to study when he was playing that he used for self-teaching. He was a big believer in referring to film for the Reds when the procedure was new enough to be newsworthy. "I can tell a player what he might be doing wrong, but you can be much more convincing if you tell him and then let him see for himself by showing him a film clip."[17] Kluzewski, who would not have been hired as a fielding coach, died of a heart attack at 63 in 1988.

The Reds decline of 1948 did not sit well with the Cincinnati organization, and 100 games into the season, manager Johnny Neun was fired. The new manager was community favorite Bucky Walters. Walters managed 53 games and his record was 20-33.

One of Walters' pitchers was a right-hander named Howie Fox, who had been trying to make an impact with Cincinnati since 1944. In 1945 he mustered an 8-13 mark. In 1948, he went 6-9. In 1949, his 19 losses versus six wins led the National League in defeats. His one fine year was an 11-8 record for the Reds in 1950. Fox was out of the majors after the 1954 season. He pitched for San Antonio in the minors the next year and purchased a bar in that city. That same year, Fox and his bartender threw three people out of his tavern because of unruly behavior. A fight broke out on the street in front of the establishment, and Fox was stabbed to death. It was said the weapon was a seven-inch Bowie knife and he was stabbed three times. Fox died on October 9, 1955. The bartender was wounded.

Actually, in 1948, while Kluzewski was still learning his craft, the team's surprise big slugger was Hank Sauer. A sturdy 6-foot-3 and 200 pounds, the timing of Sauer's career was completely sidetracked by World War II. He made cameo appearances with the Reds in 1941 and 1942, and after spending all of 1943 in the minors, he went into the military. He was released early enough to play in 31 games for Cincinnati in 1945, then spent two entire seasons in AAA Syracuse. By the time the Reds kept Sauer around for 1948 he was 31. Whether he was mad at them or the ball, he crushed it that season, with 35 home runs and 97 RBIs. Sauer said he previously played a considerable amount of golf, but it interfered with his baseball timing. Once he parked his clubs he began swinging better with his bat. "When I quit playing it during the baseball season last year, I really went to town," he said.[18]

During the 1949 season, the Reds shipped Sauer to the Chicago Cubs, where he really blossomed. It took the better part of a decade of prep with the Reds' organization, but when Sauer slammed 32 home runs and drove in 103 runs in 1950 for Chicago, he made his first All-Star team. In 1952, Sauer's 37 homers and 121 runs batted in—for the Cubs—won him not only All-Star recognition, but the NL's Most Valuable Player award.

As time passed and Vander Meer still remained with the Reds, many of even his most illustrious teammates left. Vander Meer even out-lasted Walters twice. The first time when they were fellow pitchers in the rotation. The second time came when Walters departed as manager before the end of the 1949 season. The Reds were still bad, not getting anywhere. The team finished seventh at 62-92. Walters departed when Cincinnati was 61-90. Luke Sewell managed three games.

Walters followed up coaching with the Boston and Milwaukee Braves, managing the minor-league Milwaukee Brewers, coaching for New York Giants through 1957, then helping the Philadelphia Phillies with their farm system. Then he walked away from baseball, going into corporate public relations. "And I never want to go back to baseball," Walters said. "I had enough of it. I pitched with pennant-winners. I was in World Series games. I managed in both majors and minors and I've had enough."[19]

Once one of the younger players on the team, in 1949 Vander Meer was 34 and still going. He also acquired a new group as teammates, some more memorable than others. Danny Litwhiler started the 1948 season with the Braves, but finished it with Cincinnati, and played out the rest of his big-league career with the Reds through 1951. He spent 11 years in the majors, missing the 1945 season for military service. In 1942, while still with the Philadelphia Phillies, Litwhiler played in every inning of 151 games and became the first player to do so without committing an error. That was his only All-Star season and the Baseball Hall of Fame requested his glove. "The next year I made an error and they got rid of me," Litwhiler joked.[20]

While Litwhiler may have concluded his on-field days in the majors, he kept on contributing to baseball. Between 1955 and 1963, Litwhiler coached the Florida State University baseball team to seven NCAA tournament appearances and three College World Series. Then he coached Michigan State for 19 years. His overall record for 28 seasons was 678-445-9. Also, Litwhiler was the president of the United States Baseball Federation between 1978 and 1983 and he served on the technical committee of the International Association of Amateur Baseball.

Litwhiler was the guy who invented the radar speed gun to measure the velocity of pitchers' throws. He tried it out at Michigan State and his model is in the Hall of Fame in Cooperstown, New York, too. The first development of his invention was popularly known as the JUGS gun. Litwhiler developed the gun in 1974 after lengthy experimentation. His inspiration was a newspaper photo of a new radar gun police used to clock speeders in vehicles. He convinced a campus police officer to participate in a baseball experiment using the car's radar gun. Litwhiler showed off his radar gun in spring training of 1975 and it was well-received. "Earl Weaver went nuts," Litwhiler said of the Hall of Fame Baltimore Orioles manager. "He was shooting anything that moved."[21]

Litwhiler tinkered and experimented like some mad scientist with bats and balls and gloves for most of the rest of his life (he died at 95 in 2011), and claimed 100 baseball innovations, but the radar gun was his most significant one. Litwhiler was called the "Thomas Edison of baseball inventors," but he did not like the nickname. "I just love the game of baseball," Litwhiler said, "I always felt that if I made a new invention each year for my teams they would feel like they had an edge on the competition. Some of the inventions were better than others. But it got to the point where players really looked forward to what would be invented next."[22]

The 1948 season was a good one for Johnny Vander Meer. He was the stalwart pitcher by far on a bad team that finished 25 games under .500, despite being in his 30s and seemingly around the Reds for close to forever. He went 17-14 that year with a 3.41 earned run average over 232 innings. Of course, he did lead the National League in walks with 124, a statistic that was almost like a flashback reminder of his career-long weakness.

Cincinnati of the immediate postwar years was far from being a serious NL pennant-contender. Between 1946 and 1949, the Reds finished far below .500 every season. In only one of those years, when it appeared Johnny Neun had the club moving in the right direction, did the Reds win as many as 70 games. "In the years after the war," Vander Meer said, "the Reds were a pretty good Triple A ball club. The players all tried and did their best. It just wasn't good enough. We didn't have the horses."[23] Of course, if anyone outside the team made such a comment during those years, the players would have bristled. But the numbers didn't lie.

Vander Meer could not know, especially coming off such a strong season, that he would never pitch as well again over a season, or that at long last his time with the Cincinnati Reds was ending. A year later, the 1949 season, Vander Meer was no longer the real Johnny. His pitching line was 5-10 with a 4.90 ERA in 28 games. A decade earlier, after he threw his double no-hitters and the Reds were on the rise, capturing two straight pennants and a World Series championship, Vander Meer coped with tough times and poor records, but made a comeback. There was no coming back this time around, with Cincinnati, or to his own high-level pitching standards. On February 10, 1950, the Reds sold Vander Meer to the Chicago Cubs. The owner of one of the best-recognized individual feats in baseball history took his resume to a new town. Soon, Vander Meer would embark upon new adventures in baseball.

# 20

# Double No-Hit for the Rest of His Life

By the time the Reds sold Johnny Vander Meer to the Cubs, he had aching knees and a 35-year-old arm. Still, he was in demand. The Brooklyn Dodgers were said to be bidding for him, too. During his lone season in Chicago in 1950, Vander Meer was used more as a relief pitcher than a starting pitcher. He appeared in 32 games with a 3-4 record and only started six times. His earned run average was 3.79. The Cubs seemed to feel he was washed up and released him.

Vander Meer was still hopeful that he had something left and ended up receiving a tryout for the Cleveland Indians for the 1951 season. Cleveland manager Al Lopez was willing to look and judge for himself how Vander Meer might fit in. He was pretty sure it had to be as a starter because Lopez, aware of Vander Meer's history of walks, did not see him contributing as a reliever. "I told him he could work out with us and we'd see what happened," Lopez said.[1]

What happened was that Vander Meer made it into one game for the Indians and gave up six runs in three innings and never pitched in the majors again. Cleveland cut him loose and nobody else in the big leagues was after him. Vander Meer's lifetime record was 119-121 with a 3.44 earned run average. He led the National League in strikeouts three times, and of course he had those back-to-back no-hitters on his record, which everyone remembered. Still, having witnessed several pitchers do well in their mid-to-late 30s for the Reds, even if mostly during the war years when talent was diluted, Vander Meer was not prepared to call his arm kaput. In 1952, at 37, Vander Meer posted an 11-10 record with a 2.31 ERA for the Reds' AA team in Tulsa of the Texas League. His main role was to act as pitching coach and to pick up as many pointers as possible to become a manager. Wouldn't you know it, though, Vander Meer threw a no-hitter for Tulsa.

Vander Meer said he was "phasing out (of playing) and being groomed for a manager."² He did become a minor-league manager. He supervised the Reds' Class D team in Tampa and also the AAA Syracuse Club. And he gave it a whirl in the Three I League with Topeka. But he didn't feel the pay was worth it, leaving baseball and spending 20 years working in sales for Schlitz Brewery. Vander Meer became popular all over again a bit later when the baseball nostalgia craze hit, fans began collecting sports memorabilia, and old-timers were in demand for autographs, especially at card shows. Along the way, he began out-living many of his other prominent Reds teammates, although a few others aged alongside him.

Bill "Deacon" McKechnie, the leader of the Reds' 1939 and 1940 pennant-winners, was elected to the Baseball Hall of Fame in 1962, honored at least partially because he was the first manager to lead three different teams to the World Series. His teams won 1,896 games. The manager who did not drink, smoke or swear showed he could still be a leader of men. "Just treat them the way you'd like to be treated," McKechnie said was his philosophy.³ McKechnie died in 1965.

Catcher Ernie Lombardi had a very difficult time later in life after retiring from baseball in 1947 after 17 seasons. He was 39 and carried a lifetime average of .306. Although teammates and other baseball people believed he was a shoo-in for the Hall of Fame, years passed without his induction. Lombardi became increasingly despondent and bitter about the situation. He felt, and others did, as well, that he was being unfairly victimized by the exaggerated story of him failing to make the key outs at home plate during the 1940 World Series. Or if not that, his long-ingrained reputation as the slowest of runners. A new generation of sportswriters supported the notion that the Series thing played into the minds of some voters.

A low point came for Lombardi in 1953 when he attempted to commit suicide by cutting his throat. Visiting a friend's home with his wife, Lombardi sought to do himself in at 45, but was rushed to a hospital in serious condition. It had already been decided that due to depression, Lombardi was going to enter a California treatment center. His wife Bernice found him in the bedroom after he cut himself. When first aid was first applied, the medical people on the scene said Lombardi said he "wanted to die."⁴

Lombardi recovered, but as time passed he did not get much closer to Hall of Fame election. His bitterness at the Hall snub became deeper and he became more of a recluse. For a time he worked at the Candlestick Park press box for the San Francisco Giants, but then walked off the job and essentially disappeared, completely removed from baseball circles. In 1974, Lombardi, found by a journalist by accident, said, "If they voted me into the Hall of Fame I wouldn't accept. Not now. They've waited too long and they've ignored me too long. I was the National League batting champion twice. How many other catchers have won a batting title? If they elected me,

I wouldn't show up for the ceremony. That sounds terrible. But every year I see my chances getting smaller and smaller. All anybody wants to remember about me was that I couldn't run. They still make jokes."[5]

Lombardi died at 69 in 1977 and was buried in Oakland. Then, in 1986, Lombardi was elected to the Hall of Fame posthumously by the Veterans Committee. The class that year included Bobby Doerr, another old-time player from the Boston Red Sox, and Willie McCovey, the Giants slugger. Ted Williams, the great hitter, was on that veterans committee, and recalled Lombardi's hitting prowess from spring training matchups. "I'd always watch him and say, 'This guy can hit.' He was a natural hitter, a huge man who couldn't run, but who swung a really heavy bat, made great contact all the time and hit line drives."[6]

Pledges of ignoring such an honor never became a factor in terms of Lombardi showing up for a Hall of Fame ceremony because he had been dead for nine years when his selection at last occurred. He had generally been a gentle man and many were sad to see him become so embittered. On what would have been a marvelous day for the old star, sportswriters authored stories defending his play in the World Series. One San Francisco sportswriter who knew Lombardi later in life even pulled out a quote the catcher had made to him that illustrated his sadness about the whole issue. "I've dreamed of being in the Hall of Fame," Lombardi said. "But they keep passing me by. Just like life."[7] More than three decades have passed since Lombardi's induction and four decades since he died and current Hall of Fame visitors only know one thing about the man: That he was good enough to be recognized and honored as one of the select group of players chosen for the Baseball Hall of Fame.

Some of those Reds from Vander Meer's time lived very long lives. Second baseman Lonny Frey, who spent seven years with Cincinnati, was 99 when he died in 2009. Junior Thompson was 89 when he died in 2006. Jim Turner, who at one time was the Reds' pitching coach, but also was part of nine World Series championships for Cincinnati, once, but mostly with the New York Yankees, died at 95 in 1998. Those were the highlights of Turner's 51 years in professional baseball. "If I live to be 100, I would never be able to repay baseball for what it has done for me," Turner said when he turned 84.[8]

The former Reds third-baseman Bill Werber lived to be 100, eager to talk baseball with anyone who wanted to listen nearly until the end when he was residing in an assisted living facility in Charlotte, North Carolina. He was the oldest living Major League ball player when he died in 2009. Werber was a teammate of Babe Ruth with the Yankees during his 11-year, big-league career. Not for long, but long enough to observe the Big Fella, as Ruth was sometimes called, and to gain admiration for him as a great player and person. "If you were a stranger and I introduced you to him, he'd shake your hand and be taking you to dinner," Werber said. "He'd stand there while kids walked over his white shoes. He'd stand there an hour signing autographs."[9]

Werber was a key addition to the Reds when they improved enough to seize the 1939 pennant and the 1940 pennant and World Series. Werber secured the infield at third. "At the end of the year we won the pennant," Werber said of his Cincinnati debut season in '39. "I think I made a significant contribution to help them win the pennant."[10] He made it sound as if contract negotiation with Warren Giles was easy. Maybe it was because the front office was in a good mood. Werber was married for 70 years—longevity surrounded him. Once, a baseball fan–turned garbage collector–turned writer, found an ancient Bill Werber glove in the trash on his route and saved it, proud to uncover it, partially because it was in such good condition. He wrote to Werber and informed him how he came into possession of the mitt. Werber sent back the same letter with the comment "Amazing" upon hearing of how this stranger got the glove.[11]

Crosley Field, the home park of the Reds throughout the lead-up to their 1939 and 1940 triumphs, through World War II, and beyond, died before many of the players from that era, closing its doors in mid-season of 1970. The final Reds game was played there on June 24 when Cincinnati came back to beat the San Francisco Giants 5-4 on late home runs by Lee May and Johnny Bench. Wayne Granger pitched two innings of hitless ball to collect the victory.

It was a sentimental evening for more than 28,000 fans and the Reds players. "You bet it meant something," Granger said. "It meant something to every guy on the ball club. Everyone wanted to win that last game. I'll remember this for a long time. So far, it's one of my biggest thrills."[12]

Riverfront Stadium opened right away as the Reds' new home park. During a stretch of stadium building centered around multi-use, charmless construction, Riverfront was referred to as one of the "cookie cutter" stadiums along with Busch in St. Louis and Three Rivers in Pittsburgh. Subsequently, it was replaced by the Great American Ball Park, the Reds' current home.

Wherever Vander Meer went the legend of the back-to-back no-hitters of 1938 followed him. There were worse ways to be remembered. Some people suggested that he belonged in the Hall of Fame, but the Hall of Fame is not a one-note song. It is a career award. To be sure, Vander Meer's feat is remembered as a Hall of Fame–level achievement. But pitchers with lifetime records of 119-121 do not get elected to the Hall. In his later years, Vander Meer was interviewed about the accomplishment, which endured as unmatched throughout his lifetime and has out-lived him with no one else equaling the lightning-strikes-twice nature of the dual no-hitters.

## 20. Double No-Hit for the Rest of His Life

Smiling Johnny Vander Meer is greeted by Babe Ruth in June of 1938, after he pitched his first no-hitter, but before he went out and pitched his second straight no-hitter. Ruth was on hand at Ebbets Field as the Dodgers played their first home night game.

Routinely, as special anniversaries, the 25th, 30th, 50th arrived, some sportswriter somewhere contacted Vander Meer to reminisce, or combed historical archives, to bring the no-hitters back to mind for new generations of readers.

On the 50th anniversary of the second no-hitter, Vander Meer went fishing, just as he did on the night after he pitched his second straight special game. He left wife Lois to answer the phone that day. Other news agencies had reached out earlier and nailed him via telephone. At 73, in 1988, Vander Meer reminisced when he made an appearance in Cincinnati and talked to fans over the loudspeaker who were attending the game. "The fans were always great to me," Vander Meer said of his Cincinnati backers. "I had a lot of bad days, but they were still great to me." He said he enjoyed signing autographs for the fans. "I'll give you a tip on that—when you can't sign 'em anymore, you're dead. I enjoy being alive."[13]

The older he got, the more Vander Meer seemed to appreciate his achievement in a way he never did when it was fresher and he was younger.

He was still caught up in his career then, and coping with disappointments like injuries. As the decades passed, his perspective changed a little bit. It wasn't as if he would hate it if another pitcher pitched two consecutive no-hitters to join him in rare air. But he admitted he thought about what it would be like if he had company. "Every time somebody pitches a no-hitter, in a way I hold my breath to see if he'll pitch another one in his next start," Vander Meer said. "I thought Nolan Ryan and Sandy Koufax had a chance." Ryan pitched a record seven no-hitters in a long career and Koufax hurled four in a much shorter career. "It'll take somebody like that who throws hard, who can get 12 or 14 strikeouts. That reduces the number of other outs you have to get. I wouldn't mind seeing somebody do it. After all, it's been a great record for me, a great record for the game."[14]

An intriguing side matter to Vander Meer's second no-hitter was that it was not broadcast back to Cincinnati via radio by play-by-play man Red Barber, the voice of the Reds at that time. He was in the booth for the first no-hitter. However, at that particular time, the Brooklyn Dodgers, New York Giants and New York Yankees had a ban in place preventing visiting radio announcers from broadcasting games in their New York parks. This was coming to an end, but not soon enough for Barber, who could not work the game from Ebbets Field.

Decades later, while attending a broadcaster's convention, Barber re-created the game on a cassette tape through eight innings. Then, at another event, 41 years after the no-hitters, Barber was a speaker and off the top of his head essentially broadcast the bottom of the ninth when Vander Meer loaded the bases on walks and was trying to wiggle out of the problem he had initiated without surrendering a hit.

For this audience of other broadcasters, Barber launched into his own version of the call he did not get to make in 1938. "Now, on the brink of greatness, unprecedented greatness, he's gone wild," Barber said, bringing the crowd back in time with him. "There's no one warming up in the bullpen. It's going to be Vander Meer going all the way. It has to be. He pitched a no-hitter four days ago at Cincinnati against Boston, and tonight is his night. His father and mother are here. The girl he's going to marry. They're all here. And this crowd is now for him. They've turned their backs on their ball club, the Dodgers. They want him to do it." Then Barber wrapped it up, host of his own reality show: "It's no balls, two strikes, three on. It's a high fly ball going to medium center field. Harry Craft comes under it, sets, and takes it, and it's a double no-hitter for Vander Meer."[15]

When Johnny Vander Meer reached his 60s, he began having health problems. In December of 1974, he was having heart pains and feared a heart attack. He entered a hospital in Tampa, where he made his retirement home, was taken into intensive care and given a thorough examination. It was determined he did not have a heart attack, but had a blockage of the main artery to the heart. "He is feeling much better and there is no heart damage," his wife Lois said.[16] When Vander Meer was released from the hospital he began taking medication. He also lost 22 pounds to drop to 200, not too far above his pitching weight. He also went back to work for his long-time employer Schlitz. "I am feeling better than I have for a long time," he said.[17]

Despite the weight loss and medication, Vander Meer remained closely monitored and his activities restricted. His initial hospital visit was scary, and he was cautioned. He adopted a healthier regimen and his medication for angina remained a long-term thing. "My athletic days are over," he said in 1977 when he was 62. "I can't overdo anything. The best exercise I can do is walk, which I try to do every day, a mile or two, according to how I feel. What I'm trying to do is avoid surgery." When the doctors identified his chest pains, he said, "that will make you see the light."[18]

By then, he was on leave from his job, pending retirement scheduled for the end of that year, concluding a two-decade connection to Schlitz in which he flew 60,000 miles annually. "The doctor doesn't want me traveling under pressure. If I do too much, I get pains in my chest."[19] One thing Vander Meer did have energy for as he aged was watching baseball. He followed the game closely on cable television, paying closer attention to teams that had wide reach on television. He kept close tabs on the Chicago Cubs, Atlanta Braves and New York Mets in particular. He was always quizzed about his contemporary players in the big leagues, former Cincinnati Reds teammates, as well as the no-hitters. He once rated Bill Lee of the Cubs, Hall of Famer Carl Hubbell of the Giants, Dizzy Dean and Paul Dean of the Cardinals, and Hal Schumacher of the Giants, as the best hurlers of his time period.

"I'd say every club had one or two [good ones]," Vander Meer said. "We were kind of blessed. We had [Bucky] Walters and [Paul] Derringer. We were built around pitching there for a few years." He was quietly very active in organizations that aided former Major League players in financial difficulties. He was an active participant in sports card shows, as well, enjoying mingling with other old-timers. When autograph requests came to him at home (and he said he got a lot of mail), he charged a fee with the money going to help those older players.[20]

There is no mystery about singling out Johnny Vander Meer's greatest accomplishment. Those two no-hitters made him a much more memorable figure than he otherwise would have been. It would be easy to say the double no-hit fame was his greatest thrill in baseball, but he said that was not so. It really was just making it to the big-time, coming out of the minors and realizing he was in the majors. "I think the biggest thrill in my career was when I got to Cincinnati and got my own locker with my name over the top of it and my uniform and all of my equipment in it. That's something I dreamed of."[21]

Sometimes it is obvious in an individual's life—whether it is welcomed or not, planned or not—that one thing closely identifies him in the public eye. Vander Meer's enduring back-to-back no-hitters on the Major League stage was one of those such things. For the pitcher that defining moment occurred when he was a young man, just 23 years old, but it was clear that twirling consecutive no-hitters was a deed that would stick to him, whatever else he did in life, would likely be mentioned in the first paragraph of his obituary.

Baseball people will almost surely always talk about those two days in the man's life. Taking note of the 80th anniversary of the no-hitters in April of 2018, one sportswriter delved into the topic for his readership. Comment was made by Chuck Stevens, 99, who was then the oldest living former major leaguer. "Guy walks in and throws two no-hitters," said Stevens who was in the minors when Vander Meer did so, and actually died only a month after the article appeared. "It's unbelievable. I thought it was astounding and everybody else did." The same story quoted Major League Baseball Historian John Thorn with an interesting perspective that was almost sarcastic. "Two consecutive complete games are pretty rare," Thorn said of present-day play.[22]

When Johnny Vander Meer passed away in 1997 at 82 with a cause of death being listed as an abdominal aneurysm, the ante was raised even from forecast expectations. Not only did many newspapers print stories that referred to his two straight no-hitters, in one way or another they even made it part of the headline. In what could be referred to as famous last words, the *New York Times* used a quotation from the pitcher about how his 1938 accomplishment became tattooed to his identity. "At least once a day I hear about my no-hitters," Vander Meer said many years after he pitched them. "It's just something that's caught the public's imagination."[23]

# Chapter Notes

## Chapter 1

1. "See in Grissom, Reds' Pitcher, Another Dizzy," *Brooklyn Eagle*, February 21, 1937.
2. Faber, Charles F., "Lee Grissom," Society for American Baseball Research, no date.
3. Williams, Joe, "Reds' Pitcher Wows Fans, Wins One Game, A Holdout Marcels Hair For Movies," *New York World-Telegram & Sun*, March 21, 1937.
4. "Something to Give Away: Screwball Title," *New York World-Telegram & Sun*, March 21, 1940.
5. Powers, Jimmy, "Vandy Inherited Arm From Dutch Bowlers," *New York Daily News*, June 17, 1938.
6. Ballew, Bill, "Johnny Vander Meer Discusses His Baseball Career," *Sports Collectors Digest*, May 25, 1990.
7. Ballew, *ibid.*
8. "M'Phail Quitting Club, Effective On November 1," *Cincinnati Times*, September 18, 1936.
9. "Former N.L. President Giles," *The Sporting News*, February 24, 1979.
10. "Former N.L."
11. Spink, J. Taylor, "Three and One, Looking Them Over," *The Sporting News*, October 5, 1939.
12. Spink, *ibid.*

## Chapter 2

1. Graham, Frank, "Setting the Pace," *New York Sun*, February 1, 1938.
2. Stinson, Mitchell Conrad, *Deacon Bill McKechnie: A Baseball Biography*, Jefferson, N.C.: McFarland, 2012, p. 70.
3. Stinson, *ibid.*, pp. 96–97.
4. Stinson, *ibid.*, p. 121.
5. Stinson, *ibid.*, p. 163.

## Chapter 3

1. Powers, Jimmy, "Grove Shows Vandy How To Control Ball," *New York Daily News*, June 19, 1938.
2. Johnson, James W., "Johnny Vander Meer," Society for American Baseball Research (no date).
3. Powers, *ibid.*
4. Johnson, *ibid.*
5. Kieran, John, "Sports Of The Times: A Threatened Red Uprising," *New York Times*, March 19, 1938.
6. Kieran, *ibid.*
7. Kieran, *ibid.*
8. Kieran, *ibid.*
9. Kieran, *ibid.*
10. Kieran, *ibid.*

## Chapter 4

1. Swope, Tom, "M'Cormick, Recruit First Base Star, Gift To Cincy From Persistent Letter Writer," *Cincinnati Post*, April 21, 1938.
2. (No byline), "McCormick Is Certain He'll Stay In Majors," no newspaper, National Baseball Hall of Fame Library Archives, October 3, 1937.
3. Schumacher, Gerry, "Gehrig Incentive And Hard Work Marked McCormick's Ball Success," *New York Journal and American*, July 30, 1938.
4. Schumacher, *ibid.*
5. Schumacher, *ibid.*
6. Schumacher, *ibid.*
7. Schumacher, *ibid.*

## Chapter 5

1. Holmes, Tommy, "Purchase Of Lombardi Makes Robins A Team Of All Nations," *Brooklyn Eagle*, January 29, 1931.
2. Zanger, Jack, *Great Catchers of the Major Leagues*, New York: Random House, 1970, p. 125.
3. Zanger, *ibid.*, p. 123.
4. Zanger, *ibid.*, p. 125.
5. Zanger, *ibid.*, p. 128.
6. Zanger, *ibid.*, p. 130.
7. Rosenthal, Harold, "Two Capricious Characters Join Hall Of Fame's Elect," National Baseball Hall of Fame Archives, 1986.
8. Reuters, Joel, "MLB Power Rankings: Cecil Fielder And The 25 Slowest Players In MLB History," Bleacherreport.com, April 17, 2011.
9. Reuters, *ibid.*
10. The Old Scout syndicated sports column, "Lombardi Uses Grip of Golfer In His Batting," August 4, 1936.
11. The Old Scout, *ibid.*
12. The Old Scout, *ibid.*

## Chapter 6

1. Johnson, James W., Double No-Hit: *Johnny Vander Meer's Historic Night Under the Lights* (Lincoln: University of Nebraska Press, 2012, p. 1.
2. Bloodgood, Clifford, "A Good Man Is Goodman," *Baseball Magazine*, August 1936.
3. Francis, Bill, "Make His A Double," baseballhall.org.
4. Johnson, James W., *ibid.*, p. xviii.
5. Johnson, *ibid.*, p. 5.
6. Johnson, *ibid.*, p. 16.

## Chapter 7

1. Johnson, James W., *Double No-Hit: Johnny Vander Meer's Historic Night Under the Lights,* Lincoln: University of Nebraska Press, 2012, p. 8.
2. Francis, Bill, "Make His A Double," baseballhall.org.
3. Holland, Gerald, "Who In The World But Larry," *Sports Illustrated*, August 17, 1959.
4. Stinson, Mitchell Conrad, *Deacon Bill McKechnie: A Baseball Biography*, Jefferson, N.C.: McFarland, 2012, p. 169.
5. Francis, *ibid.*
6. Van Blair, Rick, "Ernie Koy Recalls Life In the Big Leagues," *Sports Collectors Digest*, October 15, 1993.
7. Francis, *ibid.*
8. Johnson, *ibid.*, p. 97.
9. Frank, Stanley, "Botcho Lombardi Rated Master-Mind Following Vander Meer's No-Hit Job," *New York Post*, June 17, 1938.
10. Johnson, *ibid.*, p. 97.
11. Johnson, *ibid.*, p. 97.
12. Frank, Stanley, "Vander Meer On Pinnacle," *New York Post*, June 16, 1938.
13. Frank, ibid.
14. Frank, ibid.
15. Parrott, Harold, "MacPhail: A Roaring Bull with Golden Touch," *The Sporting News*, June 26, 1976.
16. Johnson, *ibid.*, p. 98.
17. Cannon, Jimmy, "Vander Meer Tells Story," *New York Daily News*, June 16, 1938.
18. Johnson, *ibid.*, pp. 98-99.

## Chapter 8

1. Sann, Paul, "Johnny's Home Town Wants Name Of 'Vander Meer,' New Jersey," *New York Post*, June 16, 1938.
2. Sann, *ibid.*
3. Sann, *ibid.*
4. Sann, *ibid.*
5. Cannon, Jimmy, "Debated Final $7,500 Vander Meer Payment," *New York Journal and American*," June 17, 1938.
6. Cannon, *ibid.*
7. Cannon, *ibid.*
8. Cannon, *ibid.*
9. Cannon, *ibid.*
10. Cannon, *ibid.*
11. J. Edgar Hoover personal letter to Johnny Vander Meer, June 17, 1938.
12. Hoover, *ibid.*
13. Hoover, *ibid.*
14. Van Blair, Rick, "Ernie Koy Recalls Life In the Big Leagues," *Sports Collectors Digest*, October 15, 1993.
15. Keller, David N., "Oh, Johnny, Forgotten Baseball Legend," *Timeline*, March/April 1999.
16. Johnson, James W., *Double No-Hit: Johnny Vander Meer's Historic Night Under the Lights,* Lincoln: University of Nebraska Press, 2012, p. 107.

## Chapter 9

1. Johnson, James W., *Double No-Hit: Johnny Vander Meer's Historic Night Under the Lights*, Lincoln: University of Nebraska Press, 2012, p. 99.
2. Richman, Milt, "Lombardi's Epitaph: Baseball Painful," United Press International, September 28, 1977.
3. Richman, *ibid*.
4. Richman, *ibid*.
5. "Lombardi Planning Trip 'Home,'" *Cincinnati Post*, July 11, 1958.
6. Lombardi, *ibid*.
7. Williams, Joe, "Deacon Bill McKechnie," *The Saturday Evening Post*, September 14, 1940.
8. Swope, Tom, "Hit First Good One! That's McCormick's Batting Formula," *Cincinnati Post*, April 26, 1939.
9. Swope, *ibid*.
10. Zerby, Jack, "Wally Berger," Society for American Baseball Research, no date.
11. "Wally Berger, 83, Dies; Baseball Star In '30s," *New York Times*, December 3, 1988.

## Chapter 10

1. Kirksey, George, "Derringer, Whose Career Resembles His Own Curves, Credits 'McKechnie Influence,' For Rise To Real Stardom," *The Sporting News*, September 26, 1940.
2. Coutros, Pete, "Paul Derringer: A Thirst To Win," *New York Post*, April 7, 1986.
3. Coutros, *ibid*.
4. Coutros, *ibid*.
5. Coutros, *ibid*.
6. Kirksey, *ibid*.
7. Kirksey, *ibid*.
8. Kirksey, *ibid*.
9. "Bite Of Insect Made Pitcher Out Of Walters," *Brooklyn Eagle*, July 28, 1935.
10. Williams, Joe, "A Conspiracy With Wine Made Walters Take Up Pitching," *New York World-Telegram*, September 30, 1939.
11. Williams, *ibid*.
12. Williams, *ibid*.
13. Williams, *ibid*.
14. "Bite..." *ibid*.

## Chapter 11

1. Johnson, James W., *Double No-Hit: Johnny Vander Meer's Historic Night Under the Lights*, Lincoln: University of Nebraska Press, 2012, p. 120.
2. Johnson, *ibid.*, pp. 120–121.
3. Johnson, *ibid.*, p. 121.
4. Schumacher, Gerry, "Gehrig Incentive And Hard Work Marked McCormick's Ball Success," *New York Journal and American*, July 30, 1938.
5. "The Time Hershie Laughed," no newspaper, National Baseball Hall of Fame Library Archives, no date.
6. Stalwick, Howie, "Spotlight: Lonny Frey," August 23, 2005.
7. "Went Home For Cake, Now Takes It At Short," no newspaper, National Baseball Hall of Fame Library Archives, only date 1935.
8. "Went Home... *ibid*.
9. Siglin, Burton W., "Young Myers New Redlegs' Hope: 'He'll Make It,' Famous Dad Says," United Press International, February 11, 1954.
10. Kelley, Brent, "Bill Werber—The Reds' Winning Edge," *Sports Collectors Digest*, June 17, 1994.
11. Kelley, *ibid*.
12. Kelley, *ibid*.
13. Kelley, *ibid*.
14. Harber, Paul, "Wally Berger, Set Rookie HR Mark That Stood for 57 Years, At 83," *Boston Globe*, December 1, 1988.
15. Murray, Jim, "He Got More Hits Than Recognition," *Los Angeles Times*, July 24, 1988.
16. Murray, *ibid*.
17. Murray, *ibid*.
18. Graham, Frank, "Setting The Pace: The Consensus Was Ival Goodman," *New York Sun*, August 29, 1939.
19. Graham, *ibid*.
20. Graham, *ibid*.
21. Paul, Gabe, Cincinnati Reds Press Release, 1940.
22. Van Blair, Rick, "Harry Craft: Speedy Outfielder Played For Two N.L. Champs," *Sports Collectors Digest*, April 30, 1993.
23. Van Blair, *ibid*.
24. "Roman Colony At First Base Has Newcomer In Scarsella," no newspaper, National Baseball Hall of Fame Library Archives, July 8, 1936.
25. "Roman Colony...

## Chapter 12

1. Johnson, James W., *Double No-Hit: Johnny Vander Meer's Historic Night Under

*the Lights,* Lincoln: University of Nebraska Press, 2012, p. 122.

2. "Why Walters Was Shifted," no newspaper, National Baseball Hall of Fame Library Archives, October 17, 1940.

3. Walters, Bucky, "How I Pitch: My 'Sinker Ball,'" Associated Press, July 18, 1941.

4. Brumby, Bob, "Derringer To Hurl Here; Suit Settled," *New York Daily News,* July 7, 1939.

5. "Junior Newest Comet in Senior Circuit Sky," National League Service Bureau, July 1939.

6. Meany, Tom, "Thompson Eases Reds' Mound Worries," *New York World-Telegram,* September 14, 1939.

7. Van Blair, Rick, "Junior Thompson And The 1939, 1940 Reds," *Sports Collectors Digest,* July 9, 1993.

8. Van Blair, *ibid.*

## Chapter 13

1. Evans, Andrew, "The Black Sox Baseball Scandal," history.com, October 9, 2014.

2. Schoor, Gene, *The History of the World Series,* New York: William Morrow, 1990, p. 174.

3. Schoor, *ibid.,* p. 174.

4. Staff, "Full Text Of Lou Gehrig's Farewell Speech," *Sports Illustrated,* July 4, 2009.

5. Feder, Sid, "Series Odds Hold Steady, Still Favoring Yankees At 1–3," *Cincinnati Enquirer,* October 4, 1939.

6. Saxton, Bob, "Red Rooters At New York Are Hoping, But Not Bragging," *Cincinnati Enquirer,* October 4, 1939.

7. Smith, Lou, "Twenty-six Reds Are To Get Full Shares; Grissom To Be Deacon's No. 1 Relief Hurler," *Cincinnati Enquirer,* October 4, 1939.

8. Feder, Sid, "Dahlgren, 'Weak Sister,' Of Yank Hitters, Stars Again, *Cincinnati Enquirer,* October 6, 1939.

9. Smith, Lou, "Pearson Blanks Redlegs With Two Blows," *Cincinnati Enquirer,* October 6, 1939.

10. Smith, Lou, "Reds Confident They Will Get Going In Series Play Here," *Cincinnati Enquirer,* October 6, 1939.

11. Rogers, C. Paul III, "Lefty Gomez," Society for American Baseball Research, no date.

12. Van Blair, Rick, "Junior Thompson And The 1939, 1940 Reds," *Sports Collectors Digest,* July 9, 1993.

13. Kindred, David, "Ernie Lombardi A Bitter Recluse Because Of 'Snooze,'" *Louisville Courier-Journal,* February 8, 1977.

14. Rosenbaum, Art, "One Out From Hall Of Fame," *San Francisco Chronicle,* September 28, 1977.

15. Rosenbaum, *ibid.*

16. Van Blair, *ibid.*

17. Kindred, *ibid.*

18. Kindred, *ibid.*

19. Kindred, *ibid.*

20. Kindred, *ibid.*

21. Oechsner C. Frederick, "Nazis Hope F.R. Will Intervene In Peace Effort," United Press International/*Cincinnati Enquirer,* October 7, 1939.

## Chapter 14

1. Johnson, James W., *Double No-Hit: Johnny Vander Meer's Historic Night Under the Lights,* Lincoln: University of Nebraska Press, 2012, p. 123.

2. Johnson, *ibid.,* p. 123.

3. Biddle, Joe, "Antioch Native Whose Baseball Career Spans 51 Years Dies," *Nashville Tennessean,* November 30, 1998.

4. Shannon, Paul, "Jim Turner, 20-Game Winner For The Bees, Credits Success To 'Cutting Corners' And Expects To Repeat," *Boston Post,* March 10, 1938.

5. Rogers, C. Paul, III, "Mike McCormick," Society for American Baseball Research, no date.

6. Swope, Tom, "Mike McCormick, Born Where Gold Rush Started In '49, Looks Like 'Pay Dirt' As Leftfielder for Cincinnati," *Cincinnati Post,* April 25, 1940.

7. Swope, *ibid.*

8. Wedge, Will, "Thompson Valuable To Reds," *New York Sun,* August 24, 1940.

9. (No byline), National League Service Bureau, January 1940.

10. Nack, William, assisted by David Fischer, "The Razor's Edge," *Sports Illustrated,* May 6, 1991.

11. Nack Fischer, *ibid.*

12. Swope, Tom, "Hershberger Suicide No Unpremeditated Act," *The Sporting News,* August 8, 1940.

13. Faber, Charles F., "Willard Hershberger," Society for American Baseball Research, no date.

14. Faber, *ibid.*
15. Nack Fischer, *ibid.*
16. Faber, *ibid.*
17. Nack (Fischer), *ibid.*
18. Nack (Fischer), *ibid.*
19. Nack (Fischer), *ibid.*
20. Nack (Fischer), *ibid.*
21. Nack (Fischer), *ibid.*
22. The Old Scout (syndicated sports column), "Hershberger Worried Much," August 5, 1940.
23. Sampson, Arthur, "Cincinnati Ball Player Suicide As Team Plays Bees," *Boston Herald*, August 4, 1940.
24. Sampson, *ibid.*
25. Sampson, *ibid.*
26. Faber, *ibid.*
27. (No byline), "Frank McCormick Takes The Stand," no newspaper, National Baseball Hall of Fame Library Archives, January 30, 1941.
28. Johnson, *ibid.*, p. 127.
29. Johnson, *ibid.*, p. 127.
30. Johnson, *ibid.*, p. 129.

## Chapter 15

1. Ferkovich, Scott, "Hank Greenberg," Society for American Baseball Research," no date.
2. Sloope, Terry, "Rudy York," Society for American Baseball Research," no date.
3. Bak, Richard, *Cobb Would Have Caught It: The Golden Age of Baseball In Detroit*, Detroit: Wayne State University Press, 1993, p. 285.
4. Berger, Ralph, "Bobo Newsom," Society for American Baseball Research, no date.
5. Dow, Bill, "Schoolboy Rowe Was On Top Of The World As The Tigers' Ace In 1935, vintagedetroit.com, June 11, 2011.
6. Smith, Lou, "Reds 25 Percent Stronger Than Last Year, Says Deacon," *Cincinnati Enquirer*, October 2, 1940.
7. Smith, *ibid.*
8. Greene, Sam, "Greenberg Takes Blame For Loss Of 2nd," *Detroit News*, October 4, 1940.
9. Greene, Sam, "Baker Defends His Choice Of Trout—'Had To Gamble,'" *Detroit News*, October 6, 1940.
10. Lieb, Frederick G., "Death Takes Newsom's Dad After First Victory; Then Buck Goes Out To Win Another 'For Him,'" *The Sporting News*, October 10, 1940.
11. Meany, Tom, "Derringer's One Pitch Decided Series," *New York World-Telegram*, October 9, 1940.
12. Garretson, Joseph Jr., "Derringer Toast Of Town As Reds Come Back With Fighting Hearts To Become World Champions," *Cincinnati Enquirer*, October 9, 1940.
13. Garretson, *ibid.*
14. "Reds are world champions, Paper Blizzard Blankets City After Game," *Cincinnati Enquirer*, October 9, 1940.
15. "Reds win world baseball championship, Cincinnati's Downtown District Becomes Bedlam," *Cincinnati Times-Star*, October 8, 1940.
16. Garretson, *ibid.*
17. Garretson, *ibid.*
18. Swope, Tom, "Ol' Bobo Big Hero In Series," *Cincinnati Post*, date missing.
19. (No byline), "The Champions," *Cincinnati Times-Star*, October 9, 1940.

## Chapter 16

1. Johnson, James W., *Double No-Hit: Johnny Vander Meer's Historic Night Under the Lights*, Lincoln: University of Nebraska Press, 2012, p. 131.
2. Griffith, Nancy Snell, "Elmer Riddle," Society for American Baseball Research, no date.
3. Talbot, Gayle, "Elmer Riddle Arrives Year Late For Redlegs," Associated Press, July 19, 1941.
4. Lardner, John, "The Sports Parade: A Riddle That's Hard To Solve," *New York Herald-Tribune*, July 19, 1941.
5. Lardner, *ibid.*
6. Trimble, Joe, "Riddle Tells You How He Wins—The Reds Score More Runs," *New York Daily News*, July 11, 1941.
7. Trimble, *ibid.*
8. Johnson, James, "Johnny Vander Meer," Society for American Baseball Research, no date.
9. (No byline) "7 Dead In Georgia In Bus-Auto Crash," Associated Press/*New York Times*, December 6, 1941.

## Chapter 17

1. Feller, Bob, "Gun Captain To Legendary Pitcher," military.com (Answering The Call), no date.

2. Feller, *ibid.*
3. Muder, Craig, "President Roosevelt Gives 'Green Light' To Baseball," baseballhall.org (no date).
4. Muder, *ibid.*
5. Cohane, Tim, "Lew's Double Wrecks Thompson's No-Hitter," *New York World-Telegram,* May 13, 1942.
6. Bohn, Terry, "Ray Starr," Society for American Baseball Research," no date.
7. Bohn, *ibid.*

## Chapter 18

1. Johnson, James W., *Double No-Hit: Johnny Vander Meer's Historic Night Under the Lights,* Lincoln: University of Nebraska Press, 2012, p. 135.
2. Turkin, Hy, "Tip-Top Tipton," *New York Daily News,* May 19, 1943.
3. Turkin, *ibid.*
4. Johnson, *ibid.*, p. 137.
5. (No byline), "Woodrow Williams, Baseball Player, 82," *The New York Times,* February 27, 1995.
6. The Old Scout (syndicated sports column), "Miller Peerless Double-Play Maker," May 23, 1944.
7. (No byline), "Just Work, No Pressure, Shoun Says Of No-Hitter," *Cincinnati Post,* May 16, 1944.
8. (No byline), *ibid.*, "Just Work…
9. Swope, Tom, "Reds Wonder Where They'd Be Without Wonder-Man Walters," *Cincinnati Post,* July 20, 1944.
10. (No headline), Cincinnati Reds team press release, February 1946.
11. "Libke Regular In Left" (no newspaper, National Baseball Hall of Fame Library Archives), June 1945.
12. Stinson, Mitchell Conrad, *Deacon Bill McKechnie: A Baseball Biography,* Jefferson, N.C.: McFarland, 2012, p. 193.
13. Walters, Bucky, Letter to Special Services Division, Armed Forces of the United States, undated, 1945.
14. Walters, *ibid.*
15. Walters, *ibid.*
16. Walters, *ibid.*

## Chapter 19

1. Paul, Gabriel, Cincinnati Reds Press Release, November 1946.

2. Paul, *ibid.*
3. Stinson, Mitchell Conrad, *Deacon Bill McKechnie: A Baseball Biography,* Jefferson, N.C.: McFarland, 2012, p. 194.
4. Johnson, James W., *Double No-Hit: Johnny Vander Meer's Historic Night Under the Lights,* Lincoln: University of Nebraska Press, 2012, p. 138.
5. Johnson, *ibid.*, p. 138–139.
6. Siler, Tom, "Baseball Has Never Seen The Like," *The Saturday Evening Post,* April 1948.
7. Siler, *ibid.*
8. Goldstein, Richard, "Ewell Blackwell, 74, Pitcher Noted For His Whip-Like Style," *New York Times,* October 31, 1996.
9. Siler, *ibid.*
10. Siler, *ibid.*
11. Murray, Jack, "Ewell Blackwell— Invincible Until His Arm Lost Its 'Whip,'" *Cincinnati Enquirer,* July 11, 1976.
12. Murray, *ibid.*
13. "He Was Wicked 'Whip,' *New York Daily News,* November 13, 1996.
14. Goldstein, *ibid.*
15. "Summit Mourns Death of 'Sleeveless Slugger' of '59 White Sox," *Desplaines (Illinois) Valley News,* April 1, 1988.
16. Harmon, Pat, "Gabe Uncovers 'Sally Rand Rule'—Change Bars Klu's Bare Arms," *Cincinnati Post,* November 5, 1956.
17. Lawson, Earl, "'Doctor Klu' Has Quick Cureall When Reds Feel Down At Dish," *The Sporting News,* March 1, 1975.
18. Johns, Walter L., "Sauer's Got Power," *Sportfolio,* September 1948.
19. Yeuter, Frank, "Bucky Walters Recuperating From Duodenal Ulcer Operation," *The Philadelphia Bulletin,* March 16, 1962.
20. Lowitt, Bruce, "Have Gun, Will Travel Into Baseball History," *St. Petersburg Times,* July 1997 (exact date missing).
21. Lowitt, *ibid.*
22. Pavolich, Lou, Jr., "Master Of Inventions," *Collegiate Baseball,* April 16, 2004.
23. Johnson, *ibid.*, p. 139.

## Chapter 20

1. Staff Special, "Vander Meer Joins Tribe On Trial Basis," *Cleveland Press,* April 1952. Exact date missing.
2. Ballew, Bill, "Johnny Vander Meer Discusses His Baseball Career," *Sports Collectors Digest,* May 25, 1990.

3. Corbett, Warren, "Bill McKechnie," Society for American Baseball Research, no date.
4. (No byline), "Lombardi, Ex-Dodger Catcher, Cuts Throat In Suicide Attempt," *Brooklyn Eagle*/United Press International, April 9, 1953.
5. Twombly, Wells, "Lombardi's Bitterness Overflows," *The Sporting News*, July 6, 1974.
6. Durso, Joe, "Doerr, Lombardi Voted To Hall Of Fame," *New York Times*, March 11, 1986.
7. Rosenbaum, Art, "The Knockout Delayed 'Fame' For Lombardi," *San Francisco Chronicle*, March 11, 1986.
8. Biddle, Joe, "Antioch Native Whose Baseball Career Spanned 51 Years Dies," *Nashville Tennessean*, November 30, 1998.
9. Geracie, Bud, "Babe Vs. Bonds: Former Teammate, 97, Sticks Up For Babe," *San Jose Mercury News*, May 30, 2006.
10. Kelley, Brent, "Bill Werber—The Reds' Winning Edge," *Sports Collectors Digest*, June 17, 1994.
11. Vascellaro, Charlie, "Werber Glove Found In Trash Is A Treasure," *Sports Collectors Digest*, March 1, 1996.
12. Dressman, Denny, "A List Of Lasts For Crosley Field," *Cincinnati Enquirer*, June 25, 1970.
13. (No byline) "Vander Meer's Feat Remembered," Associated Press/*Albany Times-Union*, June 13, 1988.
14. Anderson, Dave, "Vander Meer Holds His Breath," *New York Times*, July 10, 1983.
15. Sandomir, Richard, "On Old Cassette, Barber's Voice Brings To Life Game He Missed," *New York Times*, December 22, 2008.
16. "Johnny Vander Meer May Be Facing Heart Surgery," United Press International, December 11, 1974.
17. Chick, Bob, "The Long Road To Recovery," *St. Petersburg Independent*, March 1, 1975.
18. Trust, Dick, "The Way They Are: Johnny Vander Meer," *Quincy (Massachusetts) Patriot-Ledger*, January 8, 1977.
19. Trust, *ibid*.
20. Ballew, *ibid*.
21. Ballew, *ibid*.
22. Marcus, Steven, "80 Years Later, Johnny Vander Meer's Consecutive No-Hit Feat Still Stands," *Newsday*, April 28, 2018.
23. Goldstein. Richard, "Johnny Vander Meer, 82, No-Hit Master, Dies," *New York Times*, October 7, 1997.

# Bibliography

## Books

Bak, Richard. *Cobb Would Have Caught It: The Golden Age of Baseball in Detroit.* Detroit: Wayne State University Press, 1993.

Cook, William A. *Big Klu: The Baseball Life of Ted Kluzewski.* Jefferson, N.C.: McFarland, 2012.

Johnson, James W. *Double No-Hit: Johnny Vander Meer's Historic Night Under the Lights.* Lincoln: University of Nebraska Press, 2012.

Schoor, Gene. *The History of the World Series.* New York: William Morrow, 1990.

Shannon, Mike. *The Good, the Bad and the Ugly: Cincinnati Reds.* Chicago: Triumph Books, 2008.

Stinson, Mitchell Conrad. *Deacon Bill McKechnie: A Baseball Biography.* Jefferson, N.C.: McFarland, 2012.

Weintraub, Robert. *The Victory Season: The End of World War II and the Birth of Baseball's Golden Age.* New York: Back Bay Books, Little, Brown, 2013.

Zanger, Jack. *Great Catchers of the Major Leagues,* New York: Random House, 1970.

## Magazines

Baseball Magazine
Collegiate Baseball
Saturday Evening Post
Sportfolio
The Sporting News
Sports Collectors Digest
Sports Illustrated
Timeline

## Newspapers

Boston Globe
Boston Herald
Boston Post
Brooklyn Eagle
Cincinnati Enquirer
Cincinnati Post
Cincinnati Times
Cincinnati Times-Star
Cleveland Press
Des Plaines (Illinois) Valley News
Detroit News
Los Angeles Times
Louisville Courier-Journal
Nashville Tennessean
New York Daily News
New York Herald-Tribune
New York Journal and American
New York Sun
New York Times
New York World-Telegram
New York World-Telegram & Sun
Philadelphia Bulletin
Quincy (Massachusetts) Patriot-Ledger
St. Petersburg Independent
San Francisco Chronicle
San Jose Mercury News

## Press Releases

Cincinnati Reds
National League Service Bureau

## Websites

baseballhall.org
Bleacherreport.com
History.com

Miltary.com
Society For American Baseball Research
vintagedetroit.com

## *Wire Services*

Associated Press
United Press International

## *National Baseball Hall of Fame Library Archives*

J. Edgar Hoover Letter
Bucky Walters Letter

# Index

Adams, Bobby 163
USS *Alabama* 145
Albany, New York (minor league) 81
Aleno, Chuck 158
Alexander, Dale 83
Alfonso, Pete 66
American Association 108, 110
American League 16, 28, 81, 90, 94, 96, 106, 121, 123, 124, 145, 147, 155, 167, 169
Americus, Georgia 144
Amytrophic lateral sclerosis (Lou Gehrig's Disease) 96
Angels Camp, California 110
Arnovich, Morrie 110, 139
Averill, Earl 123, 124, 134
Avon Park, Florida 80

Baker, Bill 115, 118, 125, 129
Baker, Del 121, 124, 126, 130, 131, 132, 133, 135
Baker Bowl 161
Baltimore Orioles 66, 96, 171
Barber, Red 82, 178
Barrett, Red 90
Barrow, Ed 96
Bartell, Dick 126, 127, 128, 129, 132
Baseball Hall of Fame 1, 2, 6, 8, 10, 12, 14, 19, 21, 30, 38, 40, 41, 56, 64, 66, 71, 77, 85, 95, 96, 97, 105, 121, 124, 146, 147, 150, 171, 174, 175, 176
Baseball Writers Association of America 28, 63
Battle of the Bulge 146, 159, 164
Baumholtz, Frank 166, 167
Beck, Walter (Boom-Boom) 161
Beckley (minors) 26
Beckley, West Virginia 24
Beggs, Joe 109, 111, 112, 113, 117, 119, 129, 139, 146, 155, 164
Belgium 161
Bellinger, Cory 66
Bench, Johnny 169, 176
Benjamin, Stan 143
Berger, Wally 20, 22, 37, 38, 39, 40, 46, 47, 48, 49, 66, 67, 83, 85, 98, 99, 109

Berra, Yogi 146
Bible 42
Black Sox Scandal 2, 95, 169
Blackwell, Ewell 150, 166, 167, 168
Bloomington, Indiana 169
Bongiovanni, Nino 85
Bordagary, Frenchy 85
Bosnia 43
Boston Bees (Braves) 8, 12, 13, 16, 17, 20, 36, 37, 38, 39, 40, 41, 42, 53, 59, 60, 61, 62, 63, 66, 72, 73, 77, 78, 83, 88, 92, 108, 112, 114, 115, 116, 118, 148, 158, 166, 167, 170, 171, 179
Boston Red Sox 19, 33, 64, 72, 81, 85, 88, 94, 142, 144, 147, 161, 165, 175
Boston University 83
Boudreau, Lou 167
Bowman, Joe 161
Brack, Gibby 48
Braves Field 83, 115, 116
Breitenstein, A.E. 100
Bridges, Tommy 124, 125, 129, 130
Briggs Stadium 129, 130
Brooklyn (Los Angeles) Dodgers 2, 10, 11, 16, 21, 26, 29, 30, 32, 36, 40, 43, 44, 46, 47, 48, 49, 50, 51, 52, 53, 55, 58, 63, 66, 77, 80, 82, 83, 92, 111, 112, 125, 138, 139, 142, 146, 149, 157, 158, 160, 161, 165, 167, 173, 178
*The Brooklyn Eagle* 5
Buffalo (minor league) 110
Bunning, Jim 41, 51
Busch Stadium 176
Butcher, Max 46, 47, 48

California 5, 114, 174
California Gold Rush 110
Camilli, Dolph 46, 47, 48, 50
Campbell, Bruce 123, 126, 127, 129, 130, 132, 134
Candlestick Park 174
Cantor, Eddie 124
Carey, Max 16
Carter, Arnold 158
Chance, Frank 14,
Charles River 83

191

Charlotte, North Carolina 175
Chattanooga, Tennessee 119
Chicago 101, 145, 169
Chicago Bears 22, 69
Chicago Cubs 8, 12, 14, 20, 30, 36, 44, 49, 57, 63, 64, 65, 75, 78, 80, 81, 86, 88, 89, 90, 94, 110, 111, 118, 121, 122, 138, 142, 147, 155, 161, 164, 170, 172, 173, 179
Chicago White Sox 2, 94, 95, 169
Cicotte, Eddie 95
Cincinnati (Queen City) 2, 6, 94, 97, 100, 106, 126, 135, 136, 137, 160, 164, 177, 178
*Cincinnati Enquirer* 100, 106, 115, 135
Cincinnati Reds (Cincinnati Red Stockings), 1, 2, 3, 5, 8, 10, 11, 12, 13, 14, 16, 17, 18, 19, 20, 21, 22, 23, 24, 25, 26, 27, 28, 29, 30, 33, 34, 35, 36, 39, 40, 41, 42, 43, 44, 46, 47, 49, 51, 52, 53, 55, 56, 57, 58, 59, 60, 61, 62, 63, 65, 66, 67, 68, 69, 71, 72, 74, 75, 77, 78, 79, 80, 81, 82, 83, 84, 85, 86, 87, 88, 89, 90, 91, 92, 93, 94, 95, 98, 99, 100, 101, 102, 103, 104, 106, 107, 108, 109, 110, 111, 112, 113, 114, 115, 116, 117, 118, 120, 121, 122, 124, 125, 126, 127, 128, 129, 130, 131, 132, 133, 134, 135, 136, 137, 138, 139, 141, 142, 143, 144, 146, 148, 149, 150, 151, 153, 154, 155, 156, 157, 158, 159, 160, 161, 163, 165, 166, 167, 168, 169, 170, 171, 172, 173, 174, 175, 176, 177, 180
*Cincinnati Times-Star* 135
Clark, Watson 58
Clay, Dain 164
Cleveland 146
Cleveland Indians 71, 94, 95, 110, 121, 123, 124, 145, 164, 166, 173
Cobb, Ty 30, 58, 121, 133
Cochrane, Mickey 121
Cohen, Dan 116, 117
College World Series 171
Columbia Pictures 8
Columbia, South Carolina (minors) 23
Columbus, Georgia 140, 144
Columbus, Ohio (minor league) 9, 80
Congress 147, 152
Constitution of United States 152
Cooke, Dusty 36
Coolidge, Calvin (President) 16
Cooney, Johnny 37, 39, 40, 61
Cooperstown, New York 56, 97, 171
Copley Plaza Hotel (Boston) 114, 116
Corbitt, Claude 165
Corcoran, Larry 2
Coscarart, Pete 46, 48, 82
Craft, Harry 38, 39, 46, 47, 48, 49, 50, 60, 64, 84, 85, 98, 99, 109, 110, 139, 149, 178
Crosetti, Frankie 98, 102, 103, 105
Crosley, Powel, Jr. 10, 19, 166
Crosley Field (Redland Field) 5, 6, 20, 35, 36, 77, 84, 100, 101, 102, 103, 106, 110, 111, 118, 125, 126, 127, 129, 132, 133, 142, 153, 159, 166, 176

Crowder, General Enoch 147
Cuba 158
Cuccinello, Tony 38, 39, 40
Cuyler, Kiki 16, 21, 22, 46, 47, 48, 49, 85
Cy Young Award 143, 159
Czechoslovakia 106

Dahlgren, Babe 97, 99, 100
Davis, Peaches 77, 90, 91
Davis, Spud 21
Day, Leon 147
Dayton (minor league team) 8
D-Day 146, 159
Dean, Daffy 125, 179
Dean, Dizzy 6, 57, 83, 125, 179
Debs, Eugene V. 61
Declaration of Independence 152
De la Cruz, Tommy 158
Derringer, Paul 3, 5, 51, 67, 68, 69, 70, 71, 72, 75, 76, 78, 89, 90, 91, 92, 98, 99, 102, 103, 107, 108, 110, 111, 112, 116, 119, 126, 127, 130, 131, 133, 134, 139, 149, 155, 179
Des Moines (minor league) 10
Detroit 123, 129
Detroit Tigers 41, 83, 121, 122, 123, 124, 125, 127, 128, 129, 130, 131, 132, 133, 166
Dickey, Bill 84, 97, 99, 100, 102, 103
DiMaggio, Joe 84, 97, 99, 100, 102, 103, 104, 146, 152, 167
DiMaggio, Vince 37, 39, 40, 85, 125
Doby, Larry 147
Doehring, John 22, 23
Doerr, Bobby 175
Dressen, Chuck 5, 6, 11, 18, 19, 21, 22, 25
Dreyfuss, Barney 14, 16,
Duke Athletic Hall of Fame 156
Duke University 81, 156
Durante, Jimmy 29, 30
Durham (minor league) 8, 19, 26, 56, 65
Durocher, Leo 46, 50, 69, 71, 125

Eastern League 81
Ebbets Field 42, 43, 49, 52, 53, 55, 57, 82, 149, 165, 178
Edison, Thomas 171
*Eight Men Out* (movie and book) 95
Ellisville, Mississippi 85
English, Gil 38
English, Woody 49
Enola, Pennsylvania 80
Errickson, Dick 60
Europe (European war theatre) 106, 144, 152, 159, 161

Federal Bureau of Investigation (FBI) 59, 60
Federal League 13
Feller, Bob 2, 52, 145, 146, 148, 152, 167
Felsch, Oscar (Happy) 95
Fletcher, Elbie 39, 41, 60
Florida 77, 82, 107, 108, 139, 169

## Index

Florida State University 171
Forbes Field 14
Fort Benning, Georgia 142, 144
Fort Worth (minor league) 90
Fox, Howie 170
Fox, Pete 123, 125
France 161
Frey, Lonny 37, 38, 39, 40, 46, 47, 48, 49, 79, 80, 82, 85, 98, 99, 109, 134, 146, 149, 155, 163, 175
Frisch, Frank 125, 161
Furillo, Carl 167, 168

Galan, Augie 166
Gamble, Lee 85
Gandil, Arnold (Chick) 95
Garfield, James (president) 58
Garms, Debs 61
Gedeon, Elmer 146
Gehrig, Lou 27, 58, 59, 79, 84, 96, 97, 98, 100, 101, 104, 105, 122
Gehringer, Charlie 121, 122, 125, 126, 127, 128, 129, 132, 134
Geoffrion, Bernie "Boom-Boom" 161
Georgia State League 80
Germany 106, 144, 152, 159, 161
Gettysburg College 147
Gibson, George 14
Giles, Warren 10, 11, 12, 13, 16, 19, 20, 21, 25, 26, 32, 35, 36, 38, 43, 57, 58, 59, 63, 72, 76, 119, 164, 166, 176
Gionfriddo, Al 167
Gleeson, Jim 139
Gomez, Lefty 6, 7, 97, 101, 122
Gooch, Johnny 8
Goodman, Ival 37, 38, 39, 40, 46, 47, 48, 49, 60, 79, 83, 84, 85, 98, 99, 102, 103, 104, 109, 110, 111, 127, 128, 130, 132, 138, 142, 149
Gordon, Joe 97, 99
Gorsica, Johnny 128, 133
Gowdy, Hank 19, 23, 115, 117, 146, 164
Grange, Red 58, 59
Granger, Wayne 176
Great American Ball Park 176
Great Britain 106
Great Ohio River Flood 6
Greenberg, Hank 121, 122, 125, 126, 127, 128, 129, 130, 132, 134, 146, 148
Gregg, Hal 165
Grimes, Burleigh 47, 48, 50
Grissom, Lee 5, 6, 7, 8, 22, 77, 91 102, 109, 112
Grissom, Marv 7
Groh, Heinie 95
Grove, Lefty 18, 19, 23, 150
Gumbert, Harry 158, 164, 165

Haas, Bert 146, 149, 163
Hadley, Bump 101, 102
Hafey, Bud 90
Hafey, Chick 21, 22, 85

Halladay, Roy 2
Hamlin, Luke 48, 49, 82
Harris, Bucky 124
Hartnett, Gabby 12, 30
Hartsville, South Carolina 131
Hassett, Buddy 46, 47, 48, 49
Hatton, Grady 163
Hawaii 147
Henrich, Tommy 97
Herman, Babe 30, 32
Hermanski, Gene 167
Hershberger, Claude (father) 114
Hershberger, Maude (mother) 135
Hershberger, Willard 79, 85, 103, 109, 113, 114, 115, 116, 117, 118, 119, 121, 125, 134, 135, 137
Heusser, Ed 158, 160, 164
Higgins, Mike (Pinky) 123, 127, 129, 130, 134
Hilldebrand, Oral 101, 102
Hiroshima 159
Hitler, Adolf 106, 152
Holland 7, 161
Hollingsworth, Al 21
Holmes, Ducky 52, 53
Hoover, J. Edgar 59
Hornsby, Rogers 58
Houston (Colt .45s/Astros) 38, 90, 163
Hoyt, Waite 150, 157
Hubbell, Carl 83, 179
Hudson, Johnny 49
Hutchings, Johnny 131
Hutchinson, Fred 124, 133
Hutchinson, Ira 60

Indiana University 169
Indianapolis (Federal League) 13
Indianapolis (minor league) 108, 109, 110, 119
International Association of Amateur Baseball 171
International League 79
Irvin, Monte 147
Iwo Jima 147

J. Louis Comiskey Memorial Award 28
Jackson, Joe (Shoeless) 95
Jacobs, Art 90
Japan 106, 144, 159
Johnson, Ban 147
Johnson, Hank 90
Johnson, Walter 58
Joost, Eddie 109, 128, 134, 139, 149
Jordan, Jimmy 26
Jordan, Tim 83
JUGS gun 171

Kahle, Bob 40, 41
Kampouris, Alex 20, 22
Kansas 130
Kansas City Monarchs 147
Keeler, Willie 29
Keller, Charlie 97, 98, 99, 100, 102, 103, 104, 105

# 194 Index

Kelley, Mike 40
Kelly, George 40
Kentucky 41, 166
Kluzewski, Ted 166, 169, 170
Korean War 146
Koufax, Sandy 2, 52, 178
Koy, Ernie 46, 47, 50
Koy, Ernie, Jr. 50
Koy, Ted 50
Krichell, Paul 81

Lakeman, Al (Moose) 160
Lamanno, Ray 146, 148
Landis, Kenesaw Mountain 2, 95, 110, 147, 161
Lane, Frank 36
Lavagetto, Cookie 46, 47, 48, 49, 53, 165
Lee, Bill 64, 110, 142, 179
Leonard, Emil (Dutch) 26, 161
Lewiston, Pennsylvania (minor leagues) 80
Libke, Al 160, 163
Litwhiler, Danny 143, 171
Livengood, Wes 90
Lobert, Hans 73
Lombardi, Bernice (wife) 174
Lombardi, Ernie 3, 22, 29, 30, 31, 32, 33, 34, 36, 37, 39, 42, 46, 47, 48, 49, 50, 51, 57, 63, 64, 66, 78, 79, 85, 98, 102, 103, 104, 105, 106, 109, 111, 113, 127, 128, 134, 137, 139, 143, 148, 163, 174, 175
Lopez, Al 8, 173
Lou Gehrig Day 97
Louisville Colonels 14,
Lukon, Eddie 163, 164
Lumley, Harry 83
Luxembourg 161

MacFayden, Danny 37, 38, 39, 40, 41
Mack, Connie 81, 147
MacPhail, Larry 5, 9, 10, 11, 25, 42, 44, 46, 52, 53, 63, 65, 166
Maggert, Hal 41
Major League Baseball 1, 8, 9, 11, 13, 14, 25, 29, 33, 39, 41, 43, 46, 49, 61, 80, 82, 83, 91, 94, 95, 120, 123, 124, 130, 143, 146, 147, 152, 156, 157, 160, 164, 169, 180
Maloney, Jim 2
Maranville, Rabbit 14, 38
Marion, Marty 157
Maris, Roger 2
Marshall, Max 149, 156
Marshall Islands 145
Martin, Pepper 125
Martinez, Edgar 33
Mathewson, Christy 13
May, Lee 176
Mayo Clinic 96
McCarthy, Joe 84, 96, 98, 99, 101, 102
McCormick, Frank 3, 22, 24, 25, 26, 27, 28, 36, 37, 38, 39, 40, 41, 47, 48, 49, 60, 65, 66, 79, 82, 85, 86, 98, 99, 103, 104, 109, 111, 118, 119, 127, 128, 130, 133, 134, 139, 148, 149, 155, 157, 158, 159, 160, 163
McCormick, Mike (Myron) 109, 110, 120, 126, 129, 130, 132, 139, 146, 149
McCosky, Barney 123, 126, 127, 128, 129, 130, 132, 134
McCovey, Willie 32, 175
McGraw, John J. 13, 14, 94
McGwire, Mark 66
McKain, Archie 130
McKechnie, Bill 3, 11, 12, 13, 14, 15, 16, 18, 19, 20, 21, 22, 23, 26, 27, 30, 32, 35, 36, 40, 44, 50, 51, 53, 57, 58, 62, 63, 64, 66, 71, 74, 75, 76, 78, 79, 82, 84, 85, 87, 91, 92, 98, 99, 100, 102, 105, 107, 108, 109, 110, 112, 113, 114, 115, 116, 117, 118, 119, 125, 126, 127, 128, 129, 130, 131, 132, 134, 135, 136, 137, 139, 141, 149, 150, 153, 156, 159, 160, 164, 165, 167, 174
McKechnie, Mary (mother) 13
McMullin, Fred 95
Medwick, Joe 125
Michaels, Al 52
Michigan State University 171
Midland Park, New Jersey 7, 43, 55, 56, 57, 59
Miller, Eddie 157, 158, 160, 163, 167
Milwaukee Brewers (minors) 170
Mississippi College 85
Missouri 76, 84
Mize, Johnny 63, 71, 119
Moline (minor league) 10
Montreal Expos 64
Moore, Gene 37, 39
Moore, Lloyd (Whitey) 91, 93, 102, 109, 115, 127, 128, 129, 131, 149, 155
Moran, Pat 95
Morgan, Joe 169
Mountain City, Tennessee 155
Mueller, Ray 41, 155, 157, 163
Musial, Stan 33, 146, 155, 159
Myers, Bill 22, 36, 38, 39, 40, 46, 47, 48, 49, 80, 81, 82, 85, 99, 103, 109, 127, 128, 129, 134
Myers, Eddie 80

Nagasaki 159
Nagurski, Bronko 69
Naktenis, Pete 90
Nashville (minor league) 8
National Basketball Association 148
National Commission 147
National Football League 11, 50, 148
National Hockey League 148
National League 1, 3, 5, 6, 7, 9, 12, 19, 20, 27, 28, 30, 36, 39, 46, 61, 62, 65, 66, 69, 71, 74, 75, 76, 78, 79, 81, 83, 87, 88, 93, 94, 106, 107, 110, 111, 113, 119, 125, 134, 137, 139, 141, 142, 148, 150, 153, 155, 157, 159, 165, 166, 168, 169, 170, 172, 173, 174
National League Service Bureau 112
Nazis 106, 144, 152
NCAA baseball tournament 171

# Index

Neale, Greasy 13
Negro Leagues 147
Netherland Plaza Hotel (Cincinnati) 131
Neun, Johnny 165, 166, 169, 172
New York (Manhattan, Bronx, Yorkville) 7, 24, 25, 27, 90, 92, 98, 115
New York Giants (San Francisco Giants) 13, 16, 20, 24, 27, 28, 36, 38, 51, 60, 63, 65, 66, 78, 88, 89, 92, 94, 96, 111, 112, 114, 135, 139, 163, 170, 174, 176, 178
New York Mets 40, 66, 179
New York Supreme Court 89
New York Yankees (Murderers Row, Highlanders) 2, 6, 7, 10, 13, 40, 49, 50, 81, 85, 90, 94, 95, 96, 97, 98, 99, 100, 101, 102, 103, 104, 105, 107, 109, 113, 121, 124, 125, 127, 146, 155, 165, 175, 178
Newark (Federal League) 13
Newark (minor league) 79, 117
Newhauser, Hal 124, 167
Newsom, Bobo 123, 124, 126, 127, 131, 132, 133
Newsom, Skeeter 144
Niggeling, Johnny 90
North Carolina 39
Nuxhall, Joe 159

Oakland, California 29, 86, 148, 175
Oakland Athletics 66
Oakland Oaks 29, 33
Ohio 77
Ohio River 94
Oklahoma 84
Omaha Beach 146
O'Neil, Buck 147
O'Neill, Harry 146, 147
Orlando, Florida 73
Ortiz, David 32
Ott, Mel 161
Owen, Mickey 32
Owens, Jesse 44

Pacific Coast League 29, 160
Pacific Front 152
Pacific Ocean 145
Parrot, Harold 52
*Paterson* (New Jersey) *Morning Call* 43
Paul, Gabe 113, 116
Pearl Harbor, Hawaii 106, 144, 145, 147, 152, 159
Pearson, Monte 99, 100
Pennsylvania 76
Perez, Tony 169
Phelps, Babe 46, 47, 48, 49, 50
Philadelphia 147
Philadelphia Athletics 19, 24, 81, 147, 158
Philadelphia Phillies 9, 12, 20, 21, 36, 41, 46, 48, 63, 72, 73, 74, 78, 87, 88, 89, 92, 109, 119, 125, 143, 161, 163, 170, 171
Philadelphia Sports Writers 123
Philippines 145

Piedmont League 26
Pittsburgh Pirates 12, 13, 14, 16, 36, 46, 61, 63, 64, 65, 77, 78, 80, 89, 92, 119, 121, 125, 135, 142, 157
Pittsburgh Steelers 22
Poland 106
Polo Grounds 27, 28
Pressnell, Tot 47, 48
Prospect Park, New Jersey 7
Pyle, C.C. 58, 59

Quillen, Henry 131

Reese, Pee Wee 32, 167
Reis, Bobby 38, 39
Reuther, Dutch 95
Reynolds, Allie 2
Rice, Grantland 103
Rickey, Branch 10, 69
Riddle, Elmer 90, 140, 141, 142, 143, 144, 149, 155, 157
Riddle, Johnny 38, 39, 142
Riggs, Lew 22, 37, 38, 39, 41, 46, 47, 48, 50, 58, 81, 85, 109, 115, 117, 138, 149
Ripken, Cal 96
Ripple, Jimmy 109, 125, 127, 128, 129, 130, 133, 134, 138
Risberg, Charles (Swede) 95
Riverfront Stadium 176
Rizzo, Johnny 109, 122, 134
Robinson, Frank 66
Robinson, Jackie 82, 146, 147, 167, 168
Robinson, Wilbert 30
Rochester (minor league) 10, 11, 12, 13, 39
Rolfe, Red 97, 98, 99, 100, 102
Roosevelt, Franklin D. (president) 9, 58, 106, 144, 147, 148
Rose, Pete 169
Rosen, Goody 50
Roush, Edd 6, 13, 95
Rowe, Edna 124
Rowe, Lynwood (Schoolboy) 124, 125, 128, 129, 131, 132, 133
Ruffing, Red 97, 98, 99
Ruppert, Jacob 96
Ruth, Babe 2, 6, 42, 49, 58, 73, 81, 83, 94, 96, 121, 122, 123, 150, 168, 175, 177
Ryan, Nolan 2, 52, 1787

St. Louis 80, 111, 161
St. Louis Browns 49, 96, 101, 123, 159
St. Louis Cardinals 8, 9, 10, 12, 16, 26, 33, 36, 57, 63, 68, 69, 71, 77, 78, 80, 90, 94, 112, 119, 125, 142, 150, 154, 155, 157, 158, 159, 165
Sallee, Slim 95
Sarasota, Florida 19
Sauer, Hank 146, 170
Scarsella, Anna (wife) 86
Scarsella, Les 85, 86, 87, 108
Scherzer, Max 2

Schlitz Brewery 174, 179
Schott, Gene 6, 36
Schumacher, Hal 179
Schwab, Marty 6
Scranton (minor league) 8,
Seattle (minor league) 160
Selective Service Act 147
Selkirk, George 97, 99
Sheehan, Tom 6
Sherman, Texas 5
Shibe Park 92, 143
Shotton, Burt 26
Shoun, Clyde 155, 158, 164
Simmons, Al 85, 103
Smith, Clay 130
Smith, Lou 115, 125
Snider, Duke 167
South Carolina 131
Southworth, Billy 146
Soviet Union 52
Spahn, Warren 146, 152
Spalding, Dick 73
Spears, Clarence 69
*The Sporting News* 5, 56
Sportsman's Park 111
Springfield, Kentucky 68
Springfield High (Kentucky) 69
Stanky Eddie 167, 168
Starr, Ray 150, 155
Stengel, Casey 40, 41, 42
Stevens, Chuck 180
Stewart, Bill 51
Stockton, Roy 161
Sullivan, Billy 127, 132, 134
Summer Olympics (Berlin) 113
Sundra, Steve 98, 102, 103
Syracuse (minor league) 8, 160, 170, 174

Tampa, Florida 5, 51, 107, 178
Tampa (minor league) 174
Tamulis, Vito 49
Tarawa 145
Tebbetts, Birdie 122
Tennessee 108
Terry, Bill 6, 27
Texas Christian University 85
Third Reich 159
Thome, Jim 32
Thompson, Gene (Junior) 91, 92, 93, 101, 102, 104, 105, 108, 111, 112, 113, 119, 129, 131, 137, 139, 146, 149, 175
Thorn, John 180
Thorpe, Jim 13
Three-I League 174
Three Rivers, California 118
Three Rivers Stadium 176
Timbuktu 43
Tinker, Joe 157
Tipton, Eric 149, 156, 157
Tiskilwa, Illinois 10

Tobin, Jim 158
Toney, Fred 13,
Topeka (minor league) 174
Traynor, Pie 16, 18
Trout, Dizzy 124, 130, 131
Trucks, Virgil 2
Tulsa (minor league) 173
Turner, Jim 108, 109, 118, 129, 139, 149, 175

Uncle Sam 153
United States 7, 106, 144, 145, 147, 152, 159
U.S. Armed Forces 106, 146
U.S. Army 19, 145, 150, 153, 156, 166
United States Baseball Federation 171
U.S. Coast Guard 145
U.S. Marines 145, 153
U.S. Navy 3, 145, 149, 153, 156, 163, 165
University of Illinois 58
University of Michigan 146
University of Minnesota 69
University of Texas 50

Vance, Dazzy 83
Vander Meer, Jacob (father) 7, 56
Vander Meer, Johnny 1, 2, 3, 5, 8, 9, 11, 18, 19, 22, 35, 36, 37, 38, 39, 40, 41, 42, 43, 44, 45, 46, 47, 48, 49, 50, 51, 52, 53, 54, 55, 56, 59, 60, 61, 62, 63, 64, 66, 75, 76, 77, 78, 85, 86, 87, 89, 90, 91, 92, 101, 105, 107, 108, 109, 110, 112, 119, 120, 131, 135, 137, 138, 140, 141, 142, 143, 146, 150, 151, 153, 155, 156, 158, 163, 164, 165, 166, 167, 168, 170, 171, 172, 173, 176, 177, 178, 179, 180
Vander Meer, Kathy (mother) 56
Vander Meer, Lois (Stewart, girlfriend/wife) 56, 57, 179
Van Meter, Iowa 145
Vaughan, Arky 64, 77
Verlander, Justin 2

Wagner, Honus 15
Walker, Dixie 167
Walker, Gee 149, 156, 157, 158
Wallace, Bobby 19, 25
Walsh, Christy 58
Walters, Bucky 3, 20, 21, 22, 36, 67, 72, 73, 74, 75, 76, 78, 82, 87, 88, 89, 90, 91, 92, 98, 99, 100, 103, 105, 107, 108, 111, 112, 118, 119, 125, 126, 127, 128, 132, 133, 139, 144, 149, 154, 155, 158, 159, 160, 161, 162, 164, 166, 170, 171, 179
Waner, Lloyd 77
Waner, Paul 77
Wartsler, Rabbit 38, 39
Washington, D.C. 16, 59
Washington Nationals 90
Washington Senators 16, 24, 101, 110, 123, 124, 146
Weaver, Earl 171
Weaver, George (Buck) 95
Weaver, Jim 90

# Index

Werber, Bill  81, 82, 83, 85, 98, 99, 102, 103, 109, 111, 114, 118, 127, 129, 130, 132, 138, 149, 175, 176
West, Dick  109, 146
West, Max  115
West Virginia  25
Western League  10
White House  16
Wichita (minor league)  10
Wilkinsburg, Pennsylvania  13
Williams, Claude (Lefty)  95
Williams, Joe  6
Williams, Ted  64, 146, 152, 167, 175
Williams, Woody  157
Wilson, Hack  122, 161
Wilson, Jimmie  12, 72, 73, 74, 88, 125, 128, 133, 134, 135, 138, 141, 160
Winter Olympics (Lake Placid)  52
World Series  1, 2, 10, 12, 16, 90, 94, 95, 96, 98, 99, 100, 101, 102, 104, 105, 106, 107, 109, 112, 117, 121, 125, 126, 130, 132, 133, 134, 136, 137, 138, 147, 159, 165, 169, 171, 172, 174, 175, 176
World War I (Great War)  13, 14, 19, 106, 135, 147, 148, 152
World War II  3, 19, 81, 106, 121, 123, 144, 145, 146, 148, 152, 156, 157, 159, 161, 169, 170, 176
Wright, Clarence  60
Wrigley Field  86, 90, 101

Yankee Stadium  78, 88, 94, 97, 98, 99
Yastrzemski, Carl  33
Yellow Horse, Moses Y. "Chief"  14
Yonker, Orie  55
York, Rudy  122, 126, 127, 130, 134
Young, Babe  167
Young, Cy  2, 58, 143

Zanesville, Ohio  52

www.ingramcontent.com/pod-product-compliance
Ingram Content Group UK Ltd.
Pitfield, Milton Keynes, MK11 3LW, UK
UKHW042010140426
5217IPUK00015B/1081